MILITARY
MAVERICKS

D0714087

Also by David Rooney

Burma Victory
Kwame Nkrumah
Mad Mike
Wingate and the Chindits

Military
Mavericks
Extraordinary men of battle

DAVID ROONEY

CASSELL

Cassell Military Paperbacks

Cassell & Co
Wellington House, 125 Strand
London WC2R OBB

First published 1999
This Cassell Military Paperbacks edition 2000
Reprinted 2001

British Library Cataloguing-in-Publication Data
A catalogue record for this book is available from the
British Library

IEdited and designed by DAG Publications Ltd
Printed and bound in Great Britain by
Cox & Wyman, Reading, Berks

Contents

PREFACE

In this book I have not sought to present dramatically new interpretations of well-known wars or leaders, but rather, in describing the careers of some outstanding characters, to introduce readers to certain aspects of military history with which they may not be familiar. In addition to background information about their campaigns, I have attempted to provide sufficient details about the characters to make them come alive, and I hope that my approach has been sufficiently interesting to prompt further reading.

When I wrote *Burma Victory*, *Wingate and The Chindits* and *Mad Mike*, I tried to simplify the totally confusing and complex campaign in Burma by ensuring that every place-name in the texts also appeared in a relevant sketch-map. I have not quite achieved that standard here, but most chapters have sketch-maps of the campaigns.

In preparing the book, I have relied on very extensive use of the Cambridge University Library — a true wonderland of every book published in this country and many from abroad. Fortunately for me, Cambridge University has no department of Military History, and I have never had any difficulty in obtaining the books I require. I am grateful to the Library and its admirable staff.

I am deeply grateful to my wife for her support and for her labours in typing the text. Also, to Jean Watson for her help at a critical time.

David Rooney, Cambridge, 1999

INTRODUCTION

A study of characters spread across more than 2,000 years of blood-thirsty conflict, can hardly support a general theme, except that they were all mavericks and leaders. On a much narrower field, it is extremely difficult to provide any sensible definition of what makes an effective military leader. Omar Bradley, who in the Second World War had to cope with 'Blood and Guts' Patton, tried to give a definition. This included knowledge, energy, confidence, character, consideration for others, but then his theory falls down on several famous or notorious – and especially fascist – leaders.

Total dedication to a cause might come close to providing a link between the twelve characters assembled here. Orde Wingate, the most complete maverick, qualifies as an outstanding leader under almost any criteria, and certainly for his almost fanatical devotion to a cause. Yet, he was able to transfer his enthusiasms, for example from the Jewish Special Night Squads in Palestine in 1938, to the cause of Emperor Haile Selassie in Abyssinia – one of the earliest victims of fascism. After Wingate had assisted in the restoration of Haile Selassie to his kingdom in Addis Ababa, he transferred his enthusiasms to his own creation, the Chindits.

His distant relative, Lawrence of Arabia, had the same total dedication to a cause, almost to the exclusion of everything else. In leading the Arab Revolt with Feisal, Lawrence illustrated many of the qualities of military leadership.

Military upbringing and military traditions coupled with serious professional training could supply a possible theme, but this would be undermined by Lawrence, whose military training consisted of a few sporadic visits to the Oxford University OTC in 1908. It would also be undermined by Garibaldi, one of the really great unorthodox military leaders, who had no military training at all. Mussolini was later to quip that Garibaldi was fortunate not to have read Clausewitz, or he would have lost all his battles. Similarly, Giap, who had little formal military training, by his dedication and leadership defeated the most powerful military nation the world had ever seen. He achieved this by methods and tactics which gave the lie to at least some of the confident assumptions of Clausewitz, and brought defeat to his devotees.

John Keegan has argued that heroic leadership is now obsolete, yet, again, Giap showed heroic qualities in one of the last great conflicts of the 20th century. Heroic leadership is certainly a quality shared by all the characters in our study. They all proved their leadership in battle, and enhanced their reputation by personal bravery, and their demeanour in the firing line. Thus Stonewall Jackson received his nickname.

The invention of gunpowder brought the biggest single change in the conduct of war, but made little difference to the qualities needed for successful military leadership. Alexander the Great exemplified those qualities which stand out in most modern military leaders; his men would follow him to the ends of the earth. He was also essentially modern in the way he developed new weapons for new situations. He built new and bigger siege-towers for attacking fortresses, and his approach came close to that of men like Hobart, who developed new contraptions for D-Day and the Normandy landings. Alexander's military genius merely shows that little has changed in war. At the time of Alexander, Jerusalem was a Stronghold, referred to in the Old Testament exhortation 'Turn to the Stronghold ye prisoners of hope'. Wingate, who had a phenomenal knowledge of the Old Testament, used this very idea to establish 'The Stronghold', one of the brilliant and successful concepts used in the second Chindit campaign.

Wingate shares with Garibaldi, Patton and others, the quality of calmness under fire. This was suggested by Michael Howard, who served in the Coldstream Guards in the Italian campaign in 1943, as an absolute essential of military leadership, from company or battalion level up to the highest command.

The ability to study the tactics of war and to invent new weapons links Alexander with Shaka Zulu, who in the age of the African assegai, invented the short stabbing spear. The ruthless and skilful use of this weapon was the key to his military success, and led to the foundation of the Zulu nation, which has become a permanent factor in the uneasy racial balance in southeast Africa.

Today, detailed and serious study is directed to the question of command and control of troops in battle, and the subject has succumbed to high-tech. assessment and high-tech. jargon as well. One may wonder what Garibaldi or Stonewall Jackson would have made of the latest of these concepts: command; control; communication and intelligence; computers. All summed up in the acronym C4 (see *Leadership and Command*, ed. G. D. Sheffield, 1997).

Yet two other characters in our study owed some of their success to the early realisation of the significance of control and communication. Heinz Guderian, who was sent on a wireless signals communication course from the Berlin War Academy in 1913, was among the first to experiment and try out wireless communication in battle. Because of his determination, and his early interest in the tank, German tanks were superior in this respect to those of their rivals. Guderian – a contemporary of Patton's – but a more seriously professional tank expert, gained his greatest fame when his ideas resulted in the creation of the panzer division, and its use in the *Blitzkrieg*, with the support of dive-bombers as mobile artillery. This had a significant strategic result in terms of command and control, when the panzer advance in May 1940, led by Guderian, brought about the collapse of the French command system, and the collapse of the nation.

Lack of effective communications was one of the many problems faced by the generals on the Western Front in 1914–1918, because the power of weapons, guns and tanks had greatly outpaced the science of communication. Yet, at the same time, Von Lettow-Vorbeck in German East Africa (Tanganyika), despite acute communication problems, managed, with a couple of thousand men, to hold at bay for four years until 1918, Allied forces of more than 300,000 men led at different times by more than 100 generals.

The crucial issue of command and control was powerfully demonstrated by Giap in Vietnam. He had virtually undivided control over both the political and military factors in the struggle of the People's Liberation Army. His single-minded and completely ruthless control, and his use of the Ho Chi Minh trail as a supply line, in the end defeated the forces of the USA which suffered from divided command, from constant interference by outside commanders, and even by President Lyndon Johnson himself.

The Gulf War gave great prominence to logistics, yet this aspect of military command was hardly new. Alexander the Great excelled in this field perhaps even more than in his tactical and strategic genius. His logistical skill in taking a force of more than 70,000 men across the Syrian deserts to win great victories in the Euphrates valley was exceptional, and can compare with those of the Gulf War or D-Day.

One final factor, so crucial in battles from 300 BC onwards, and at which all the figures in this study excelled, was their determination to be close to the front, and to refrain from making decisions until detailed reconnaissance of the terrain had been achieved. Many commanders have lost their battles, their reputations, and the lives of thousands of their troops, because they ignored or overlooked this basic premise.

For centuries, European nations achieved total supremacy over other cultures, brutally illustrated by G. K. Chesterton's rhyme:

'Whatever happens we have got

The Maxim gun, and they have not.'

This brought domination of much of the modern world, but when turned on itself in two world wars very nearly destroyed civilisation. One is left wondering whether the necessary lessons from all this carnage have yet been learnt.

ALEXANDER THE GREAT

In 336 BC Alexander succeeded to the throne of his father Philip of Macedon. In the customary vicious squabbles of the time Philip had been plotting to reduce the influence of his divorced queen, Olympia, and it is suspected that to save the inheritance for their son Alexander, she had instigated Philip's murder. Suddenly elevated to the throne at the age of twenty, Alexander acted decisively. The succession of the eldest son was by no means widely accepted, and with the assistance of his mother Alexander had several possible rivals eliminated. Philip had established control over most of the lands around the Aegean Sea – Greece, Macedonia, Thrace and the western fringe of Turkey – and he had armies already probing into the lesser known wastes of Asia. By swift and decisive action Alexander ensured that these Asian armies did not become a threat to his succession.

Likenesses of Alexander have survived. He is known to have been a handsome man with a very white skin, unusually long hair cultivated in the image of the lion, but clean shaven, which was considered effeminate. Portraits or carvings could not depict his most significant feature – that he was only five feet tall. His short stature went with a powerful constitution which had already been proved since the age of sixteen in leading his father's armies in campaigns throughout the empire.

In Philip's reign the crude and pugnacious Macedonians had considered themselves to be superior to the Greeks, though Greek culture pervaded the court. Few youths can have had such educational advantages as Alexander. Nurtured under the influence of Euripedes and Socrates, he was personally tutored by Aristotle. As a boy he had been regaled with stories from the history of the Persian wars by Herodotus, the doyen of all military historians, and he modelled himself on Achilles, the hero of Homer's *Iliad*. A fanatical hunter, he was also a fine horseman and gave a lifetime's devotion to his horse Bucephalus. Another side of his character showed a lifelong interest in music and poetry, and an intense devotion to his homosexual lover Hephaestion who grew up with him and eventually commanded Alexander's cavalry in successful actions.

Alexander inherited the powerful military machine which his father Philip had created. Under him the tough Macedonians, more accustomed to horses than were the Greeks, had been settled in the spacious newly conquered eastern lands, and became a crucial element in the co-ordination of cavalry and infantry which Philip developed with outstanding skill. Philip had also trained companies of archers, and developed catapults for destroying city walls.

On the murder of his father, Alexander moved swiftly. He overcame resistance in Thessaly by a brilliant tactical move and then advanced southwards to Corinth and Athens to stifle any possible opposition. He did not anticipate serious difficulties since he knew the Athenians were aware that his armies in the east and his naval power in the Dardanelles could easily cut off their main grain supply from the Black Sea.

Like most monarchs and military leaders he chose his most reliable favourites to command and develop the Household Cavalry and regiments of Foot Guards as the nucleus of his personal power. Under his tuition they developed the wedge formation to make cavalry charges more effective, and used this in conjunction with a disciplined central mass of infantry armed with the *sarissa* (a long pike). Alexander insisted on all ranks, including senior officers, achieving peak physical fitness, capable of marching thirty miles a day carrying their own supplies and existing on a diet of bread and olives. The elimination of a heavy baggage train enabled him to defeat his more cumbersome enemies by speed and mobility. Alexander constantly developed new ideas for weapons and tactics, and as his armies advanced farther east into rougher terrain the long and heavy *sarissa* was abandoned for more flexible weapons. He established too an élite group of Shield Bearers which was used for commando-style assaults. All these military developments, which required massive manpower, were made possible by the large-scale use of slaves who had been taken during Philip's campaigns.

In the spring of 335, one year after his accession, in order to safeguard his lines of communication to the east, Alexander brought Thrace under effective control in a brief campaign during which he recruited 1,000 javelin-throwers into his already formidable army. He next advanced to the Danube where, confronted by a difficult crossing, he remembered his Herodotus and got his men across on rafts made from stuffed animal hides, after which they surprised and routed the enemy.

After this victory he had to hurry back to suppress difficulties at home. First, his disciplined troops overcame the warring tribes to the north of Macedonia and they sued for peace. In Greece, the potentially dangerous opposition had focused on some distant family members, but this was thwarted by his mother, Olympia, who had had several of them murdered. More serious was a major uprising based on the central city of Thebes, which posed a real threat to his supremacy. Alexander had to act swiftly before Thebes could gain support from Corinth, Athens or other disaffected cities. Within the space of a fortnight by forced marches he was at the gates of Thebes with 30,000 troops. A fierce and prolonged encounter took place, hand-to-hand fighting continuing over several days. At last an unguarded entry to the city was found and this turned the battle. Alexander exacted terrible retribution. Thebes was destroyed and 30,000 people were sold into slavery. After the lesson of Thebes, Athens would not risk overt opposition and a sullen peace prevailed.

Alexander proved himself a maverick by refusing to conform to any accepted traditions; he carved out a totally new concept of war, but one based on the foundations laid down by his father. His unique character shaped the expedition on which he set out in 334 and which lasted the rest of his life. Educated by Aristotle; nurtured in the art of war by his father Philip of Macedon; given command at the age of sixteen; when he became king, he felt himself driven by a divine mission both to conquer the world and to be a reconciler. He never aimed to crush or dismember his enemies, as Romans or Europeans did later, but after conquering a people he sought to rule 'like a kindly father' and to establish concord and peace.

As a warrior he had overweening ambition backed by a remorseless will, with a readiness to kill or massacre when necessary, but he respected his enemies, cared for their wounded as he did his own, and won the respect of the peoples he conquered from Greece and through the Middle East to India.

Inspired by such a philosophy, Alexander brought to his task the mind and character which made him the most successful military leader of all time. In every battle he led the foremost charge, frequently showing foolhardy bravery. This was based on his faith in the Olympian gods and having been brought up in the belief that he was descended from Zeus, which perhaps gave him at least a half-belief in immortality. But he was no reckless adventurer. He focused his brilliant mind on every aspect of war and battle. He enjoyed an extraordinary versatility of invention, with speed and precision of thought in the calculation of risk, and in anticipation of the enemy's reaction. All this brilliance would have come to nothing if he had not been equally able in the organisation of his logistics and the detailed planning of an expedition which crossed nearly all the known world from

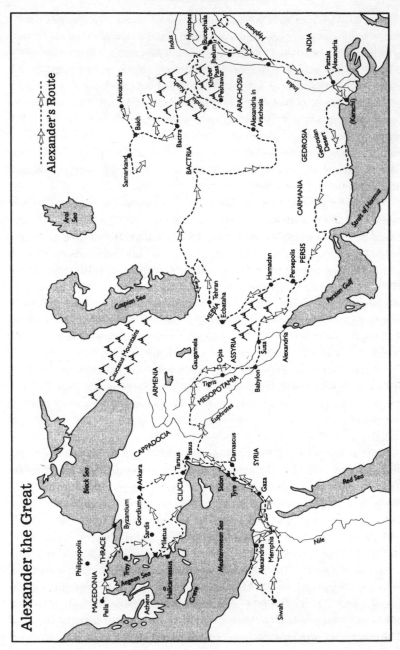

Alexander the Great

Alexander's Route

Greece to India, and lasted twelve years. Finally, to these formidable skills he added a real genius for the development of new weapons to overcome new threats. In India when his armies faced terrifying phalanxes of elephants, he armed his forward infantry with axes to slash the legs of the elephants. At the siege of Tyre he developed new contraptions to overcome the defences, just as centuries later Hobart developed 'unorthodox' weapons for the D-Day landings. Backed by this inspired leadership 48,000 soldiers, 16,000 camp-followers, 6,000 horses and 2,000 pack animals set off in May 334 to conquer the Persian empire. Alexander moved through Thrace and crossed the Dardanelles without opposition. When he landed in Asia Minor, observing the ancient customs hallowed by Homer, he paid tribute at the site of Troy – by that time a mere village. He was joined in certain naked tributes by his lover, Hephaestion.

Alexander's enterprise faced formidable problems. He had launched the expedition in terms of a crusade, suggesting – in order to gain the support of the Greeks – that its purpose was to avenge the destruction of Athens and the Acropolis by the Persian armies of Xerxes in 480. Even with Greek support, Alexander's forces and financial backing were puny compared to those of the Persians. King Darius had financial reserves of several hundred thousand talents and could raise 120,000 troops for a major battle. To this could be added an almost inexhaustible supply of horses and ponies from the wilder borders of the empire, as well as 30,000 javelin-throwers, archers and horsemen. Persian infantry were weak and not well disciplined, but even in this field, there were enough Greek exiles among them to bolster their resolve.

Alexander's commanders found it difficult to comprehend the vast extent of the Persian empire. It stretched from Egypt, through Arabia, past the Lebanon and through the valleys of the Tigris and Euphrates to the Punjab and Afghanistan. Far from being barbaric, much of the empire was highly civilised and stable with a plentiful supply of food from prosperous agricultural areas around the cities. This was in stark contrast to the food shortages and poverty of much of Greece which over the years had prompted so many Greeks to seek their fortunes in the service of Persia.

From Troy, Alexander marched roughly southwards hoping to gain support from the predominantly Greek cities in the coastal area, and to engage the enemy in battle. A Greek exile serving with the Persians proposed a scorched earth policy to weaken Alexander's forces, but the high command overruled him and ordered an attack. There is some dispute about the details of the battle which was distorted by later historians to emphasise Alexander's heroism and leadership. The truth appears to be that a fairly small and badly led Persian army of indifferent troops faced Alexander across the river Granicus. Alexander crossed before dawn, and after successfully engaging the Persian cavalry won a decisive victory. He had neither the facilities nor the supplies to take over the large number of expatriate Greeks serving in the Persian forces, so 15,000 were slaughtered and others sent to Macedonia as slaves. Shrewdly he thanked the Athenians for their support, pointing out that he had not received support from Sparta.

After the victory of the Granicus he advanced southwards through Asia Minor towards the Greek cities along the coast which generally had flourished under the light and beneficent rule of the Persians. Alexander strictly forbade plunder, and as his disciplined forces moved south they were well received. Accepting the surrender of the town of Sardis, east of Izmir, including its valuable treasure, he imposed generous terms, and left a Companion to ensure good government. Twenty miles further south, the garrison of Ephesus (Izmir) fled at his approach. Here he installed a democratic regime in place of the Persian-backed oligarchy which had previously dominated the city. This action established his reputation, and thereafter many welcomed him. He gained further support from the people by putting a stop to the annual Persian tribute, but he obtained financial support in less obvious ways.

In this favourable situation he was able to advance swiftly southwards, his heavy equipment being transported by sea. He suffered a slight hold-up at Miletus where a coastal fort expected help from the Persian naval forces, but Alexander seized the fortress and by holding firm was able to disperse the Persian ships. Then, for financial rather than military reasons, he decided to disband his naval forces. This proved unwise, and later he had to re-activate them when the Persian navy had gained a dominant position in the Aegean.

As he advanced beyond Miletus, he was welcomed by an elderly queen who was glad to obtain his support against the Persians, and she was able to give him valuable information about their forces now concentrating near Halicarnassus, another seaport south of Miletus. This was the most powerfully fortified city of its time, and military and naval forces put up determined opposition, but Alexander's skilled use of siege engines and catapults, and his personal direction of his forces in attacking the enemy gradually overcame the defences. In the end the Persians abandoned the greater part of the city, but retreated to two fortresses on the sea which, with the help of the Persian navy, held out for nearly a year. This victory sealed Alexander's reputation as a decisive commander both in open battle and in directing siege operations.

Next, aware of the problems of supply for an army during a winter campaign, and to reward his loyal Macedonians, he announced that those who had married before the campaign began could go home and spend the winter with their wives. This enabled him to trim down and streamline his forces for his winter campaign which was to drive slowly eastwards along the southern coast of Cappadocia (modern Turkey). At the same time he established his policy of granting land to his loyal supporters, but he insisted that they become citizens of the local towns, which enabled him to exercise some control of the towns, and prevent the development of a powerful landed class separate from them.

After a relatively stable winter campaign in the area of Phaselis on the southern coast of Turkey, he moved off in the spring northwards to Gordium which lay on the Persian Royal Road. Here he had planned to meet his reinforcements. At first Alexander won a series of victories, but the Persians still had substantial advantages. Darius had appointed the able Greek exile Memnon to command his forces. From his base on the island of Cos, Memnon, with approximately 300 ships, was able to dominate the Aegean and to cut Alexander's supply line across the Dardanelles. Memnon also overthrew several successful military leaders. Then Alexander had a stroke of luck. In June 333, in the middle of his campaign, Memnon suddenly died and there was no adequate Persian leader to replace him. Alexander thereupon left Gordium and, sweeping aside minor opposition, marched east and then southwards until he reached the area of Tarsus.

Here he was helped by his knowledge of military history including the earlier campaigns of Xenophon. Facing a dangerous defile, he personally led a night attack which drove off the enemy and brought his armies on to a lush and fertile plain. During the summer of 333, while operating in the area of Tarsus, Alexander became seriously ill and, lacking his personal leadership, his armies made no decisive moves. While he lay sick at Tarsus, the huge forces of Darius began slowly to move westwards from their bases near Baghdad. Alexander did send a section of his army eastwards, but made no major move himself until October 333. Then, as winter approached, the opposing armies drew close to one another near the small town of Issus.

Both sides lacked accurate intelligence of the other, and the movements of the armies became confused and chaotic. Alexander marched swiftly south along the coast, while Darius moved north a few miles inland. Thus Alexander found himself cut off by substantial Persian forces astride his line of communication back to Tarsus. He promptly turned his army about and prepared to attack the Persians before they could fully assemble their forces.

Darius had assembled his army near Issus where several small rivers crossed the plain between the mountains and the sea. To approach the plain, Alexander, having moved off before dawn, had led his forces through a difficult defile but reached the plain without opposition. Once on level ground they fanned out into their normal battle formations. As the two armies drew closer, Alexander detached a small force, including archers, into the foothills to prevent the Persians turning his right flank. At the same time he moved a cavalry unit supported by archers to the left flank near the sea, where he anticipated a cavalry charge. Before the army moved off, and again immediately before the battle commenced, Alexander personally addressed his different units and received their resounding acclamations.

Having posted units to secure both his flanks, Alexander hoped that the battle would be decided by a fierce cavalry charge in the centre to break the Persian line. Surrounded by the 'Companions' – the most formidable cavalry unit of its day – Alexander personally led this charge. This broke the Persian lines – one of the best examples in warfare of the Household Cavalry fulfilling its role. Alexander again exhibited his outstanding qualities of leadership. Many military commanders, from that day to this, have caused disasters because they were too far behind the action, and had not studied the ground. Alexander did not fall into that trap. Instead, in the fiercest fighting, as soon as the Persian line broke, he wheeled his infantry to the left and fell upon the main body of Persian infantry in the centre. Here the powerful forces of Darius – bolstered by large numbers of Greeks – had advanced against the Macedonian phalanxes, inflicted severe losses and had managed to split them. At this critical moment when the outcome of the battle was closely poised, Alexander's charging cavalry proved decisive. From the sea side flank, the cavalry unit which had been given a defensive role in fact swept the opposition aside and with well-disciplined tactics wheeled to the right and assaulted the Persian infantry just as Alexander's attack reached its climax. Here, according to legend, Alexander and Darius met in personal combat, and from the centre of the fight, as the November darkness fell, Darius fled the field, leaving his brother and other generals to cope with the aftermath of a decisive defeat.

Alexander and the Companions chased after him, hoping to catch such a rich prize, but he got away. Alexander returned at midnight sweaty, muddy and exhausted, to enjoy the luxury of Darius' tent, with its incense-scented bath, elegant sofas, and a dining-table laid out. Hearing women weeping, he was told it was the mother of Darius, and his queen. Accompanied by Hephaestion, Alexander went at once to console them and to ensure that they were treated well. Next day, as was his custom, he visited his own and the enemy wounded and honoured them for their bravery. He could afford to be generous for the real prize of the battle of Issus was the great city of Damascus. Here he took over thousands of talents and hundredweights of silver, vast military supplies and equipment, and numerous valuable prisoners. He also acquired a distinguished and beautiful mistress named Barsine.

After his victory at Issus, Alexander rejected overtures from Darius and moved towards the coastal cities of Tyre and Sidon to secure his base and reinforce his fleet before marching off to Egypt. The towns along the coast varied in their support for the Persians. Sidon surrendered and welcomed him. Its fleet transformed his naval strength, but Tyre taxed his ingenuity and his resources to the limit. It was a powerful fortress on an island just off the coast, and was supported by a major part of the Persian fleet.

Alexander's ingenuity was backed by teams of engineers and craftsmen, whose task was to develop new devices, new weapons and new techniques. A mole was built along the causeway which led to the fortress from the shore. Huge siege towers with accommodation for archers at different levels were pushed forward, as were recently developed stone-throwing catapults which could breach the stoutest walls. The defenders were equally ingenious, and sent fire-ships to burn the siege towers. While the siege progressed, Alexander went off to Sidon where he heard the encouraging news that a substantial fleet based on the city had now defected from Darius. At the same time he heard that the kings of Cyprus, who controlled a fleet of more than 1,000 ships, would support him. These included the newly developed quinqueremes which, lashed together in pairs, could be used as a battering-ram. The enemy again matched their ingenuity, sending divers down to cut the ships' cables, improvising flame-throwers, and pouring down red-hot sand on the attackers.

The siege dragged on throughout July 332 and the defenders, realising the danger posed by the quinqueremes, sent several warships to ram them. This prompted Alexander to launch an all-out assault with new siege towers, bigger and better catapults mounted in ships, new ships adapted as battering-rams, and assault craft crammed with infantry. The walls were breached and Alexander personally led his troops in. This was a classic example of siege warfare in which engineers played a crucial part. He had been held up for seven months and was in no mood to be lenient. Some 8,000 of the defenders had been killed, and after the town was taken 2,000 were crucified and 20,000 were sold as slaves.

After the capture of Tyre, Alexander hurried southwards towards Gaza, another stronghold which was too powerful to be left astride his lines of communication. Here a different approach was needed; his engineers threw up a high mound to raise the siege towers and catapults, and sappers dug tunnels until sections of the wall collapsed. After a few weeks Gaza fell. The victories at Tyre and Gaza show that Alexander was absolutely outstanding as a commander in terms of leadership, personal bravery, daring and inspiration. All the men in Gaza were killed and all the women and children enslaved.

In November 332 Alexander pressed on to Egypt, one of the most important kingdoms of the Persian empire. Persian rule had never been popular there, and he was welcomed with gifts of talents and gold crowns. Seen as the avenger of Persian misrule and sacrilege, he appears to have been crowned Pharaoh of Upper and Lower Egypt. In 331, on the western margin of the Nile delta, he chose a site for a new city to be called Alexandria and personally directed its layout.

He then embarked on one of his most remarkable journeys, which illustrates another significant aspect of his character. Travelling westwards into the Libyan desert, he arrived at Siwah, an isolated oasis where there was a shrine dedicated to the god Ammon; here he consulted the oracle. Featuring in both Greek and Egyptian mythology, Ammon and Zeus became intermingled, and after Alexander's visit he was known as 'Alexander the son of Zeus, or Ammon'. Stories began to circulate about a visit by Ammon or Zeus to Alexander's mother, Olympia, before he was born. It appears that to Alexander, this move was not so much to discredit Philip, as to emphasise his own direct links to the Father of the Gods. Whatever the truth of what happened at the oasis, the idea of a god fathering a son by a mortal woman was widespread, and the belief in

'Alexander son of Zeus or Ammon' lasted a long time, positively fostered by Alexander's flattering historian Callisthenes.

News of troubles in Greece and the Aegean caused Alexander to leave Memphis, his Egyptian capital on the Nile, where he had been occupied in the reorganisation of the government of Egypt, and return to Tyre where he stayed for several months. He had to deal with intrigues by Sparta, and many naval problems in the Aegean islands. He also had to consider his strategy against Darius who, he heard, was raising a major army. At the same time he had to deal with trouble in his own army where rival groups, bored by prolonged inactivity, had started serious fighting. Alexander intervened, stopped the fights and arranged for a public duel between the leaders. Thus he prevented serious mutiny by turning it into an entertainment.

Before embarking on a campaign which would take him into new and dangerous territory, Alexander had to solve major logistic problems. His advance would take his forces into an area of desert where they could not live off the land, so the supply of food and munitions had to be on a large scale. This involved months of work by engineers and armourers, and the collection of provisions from a wide area. Eventually, in July 331, he set off eastwards without waiting for his Macedonian reinforcements to arrive. There were two possible routes to Babylon, both of which necessitated crossing the Euphrates at Thapsacus, after which the army could follow the fertile and well-supplied Euphrates valley, or march farther east and cross the swift-flowing Tigris to approach Babylon from a more northerly direction. Darius, foreseeing the decision Alexander would have to make, sent a detachment to Thapsacus. To encourage Alexander to take the northerly route, they started to burn the crops and villages in the Euphrates valley.

Alexander's ever loyal friend Hephaestion had gone ahead of the army to prepare the river crossing at Thapsacus, and when Alexander and the main army arrived they duly took the northern route, aiming to cross the Tigris near Mosul. They made fairly leisurely progress, but then Darius made what appeared to be a major blunder, when he allowed the enemy army to cross the Tigris unopposed, at a point where a few determined troops could have held up an entire army. On the other hand it may be that he preferred to lure Alexander towards terrain where the Persian forces would have immense advantages. Darius could call on tens of thousands of troops, and on well-chosen ground could use his outstanding cavalry – drawn from as far away as the Punjab – and their renowned scythed chariots to gain the best advantage over what they considered the puny forces – about 45,000 men – of Alexander.

By the end of September 331 Alexander had advanced some sixty miles eastwards from where he crossed the Tigris, and near the village of Gaugamela his leading scouts reported the first sign of Darius' army. After a brief lull Alexander drew up his troops in battle formation, intending to make a surprise night attack, but then he paused to assess the intelligence coming from further reconnaissance.

Faced by overwhelming numbers of Persian infantry and a large preponderance of cavalry, supported by the dangerous scythed chariots and by fifteen elephants, Alexander drew up a battle plan which shows his true brilliance as a military commander. At the centre of his line stood his devoted Foot Companions, 10,000 strong, and armed with their formidable *sarissas*. On their right stood the shield-bearers, bolstered by javelin-throwers and archers, to join up with the Household Cavalry Companions, led by Alexander himself. On the left flank, a large force of Greek cavalry, interspersed and strengthened by infantry units, had specific orders to hold their position, but if they were in danger of being outflanked to wheel round and form a hollow square behind the main front line. Finally, a reserve infantry force, 20,000 strong, was drawn up behind the front line and they had been trained to face about if the army was encircled by the Persians.

On 1 October 331, Alexander launched his attack. As his combined forces moved forward, he changed their main thrust to the right and by doing this was able to destroy the Persian advance on that flank. This also helped his defenders to get the better of the scythed chariots, which proved ineffective against the accuracy of the javelin-throwers. Alexander, in the thick of the fighting, and able immediately to control or alter the momentum of the attack, saw a gap which had opened between the Persian cavalry and their central infantry force. Leading the way, he plunged the Cavalry Companions into this gap, which enabled them to avoid the elephants and brought them close to Darius himself. This decisive attack led by Alexander broke the Persian line and caused Darius to flee.

Elsewhere the Persian cavalry did break through, but instead of wheeling into the flank of Alexander's infantry, like Rupert of the Rhine 2000 years earlier, they charged off towards the reserve baggage – hoping perhaps to rescue the family of Darius. Here, however, they were immediately assaulted by Alexander's powerful reserve force and quickly despatched. At this stage the Persians were close to defeat. Alexander has been criticised for leaving the battlefield and, with a few close companions, engaging in a fierce mêlée in an attempt to capture Darius. In fact Darius escaped by chariot and horse, and fled eastwards to the mountains.

The Persian commanders, knowing that Darius had fled, quickly followed and soon all impetus was lost. The battle of Gaugamela has been studied by most military leaders, including Napoleon and Clausewitz, and most agree that the key to Alexander's great victory was his concentration of force at the crucial spot, and his ability personally to control and change the direction of attack at a critical moment.

After Gaugamela his army advanced through the prosperous and fertile Euphrates valley, past crops and fields which promised luxury and abundance. Babylon was a centre of inestimable wealth which now fell to Alexander. As he neared the city, Maseus, who had commanded the Persian cavalry in the battle, and who had also fled, now came forward and offered the city to Alexander. At the formidable city walls, the gates were thrown open and he was welcomed by the city's rulers with gifts and displays of wealth and opulence.

Alexander was well received because he respected the customs and the religious rites, and promised to reverse the less popular customs of the previous regime. He reinstated some of the Persian satraps (governors), but always installed a trusted Macedonian to oversee them. He took up residence in a 600-room palace built by Nebuchadnezzar, and inherited such wealth in the city that he never again faced financial problems.

Even with the capture of Babylon the fight was far from over, for Darius was still at large with his army. Alexander therefore left Babylon with a fairly small contingent in November 331 and made for Susa on the Tigris, more than 200 miles to the east. On the way he was joined by Macedonian reinforcements, making his numbers up to 15,000. At Susa the satrap welcomed him to the city and presented him with twelve elephants. Susa contained vast riches, including Athenian treasures captured 150 years before. These Alexander sent back to Athens. He had a slight problem in Babylon. He was so short that he had difficulty sitting on the magnificent throne of Darius. From Susa he plunged on in pursuit of Darius towards Persepolis, 150 miles east of the Persian Gulf. On the way his army fell into a dangerous ambush in a deep ravine which cost many lives, but he extricated his men, and exacted a merciless revenge on his assailants. Persepolis, the real capital of the Persian empire, fell without a fight and yielded up further wealth, including a cache of 120,000 talents. By January 330 he was firmly in control. To reward his soldiers after such prolonged and fierce campaigning he allowed them to sack the city, and soon afterwards he burnt down the palaces of Persepolis – a final revenge for the sacking of Athens and the Greek cities.

In May Alexander again set out after Darius. Arriving at Hamadan, he learned that his quarry had fled shortly ahead of him, so he rode off with a small detachment of cavalry in hot pursuit. Plagued by pathetic indecisiveness, Darius had virtually been kidnapped by marauders, and when Alexander overtook a small caravan of brigands, the body of Darius was found. Alexander brought it back to Persepolis and staged an elaborate royal funeral; later he tried to round up his murderers.

At Persepolis he took steps to establish control of the complex cosmopolitan bureaucracy, and during this time he began an affair with a handsome and attractive youth named Bagoas, but this did not appear to affect his relationship with Hephaestion who still played a major part in Alexander's life. His close relations with both these men continued until his death.

Leaving Persepolis, Alexander led his army through difficult country until he reached the shores of the Caspian Sea. Amazed at its extent, he wondered if it was the edge of the world. Here he had to make a major decision: return to Macedonia or seek further conquests in the east. He put this question to his assembled forces and they strongly voted to continue.

Before a new campaign could be started, Alexander faced a major crisis. He received evidence of a conspiracy against his life which seemed to point to Philotas, the son of his most senior and trusted general, Parmenion, who at that time had been left in command of 20,000 reserve troops near Persepolis. Alexander acted resolutely; both father and son were executed, an action generally approved by the army when the evidence was made public.

In September 330 Alexander set out with 40,000 men, travelling eastwards towards Kandahar and the mountains of the Hindu Kush. Then they travelled along a difficult mountain route over snow-bound passes where men and animals suffered appalling privations from cold and hunger. He led his army from Kandahar to Kabul – a route close to that which would be taken in reverse 2,000 years later by General Roberts. Pushing on through the mountains, the army reached the valley of the Oxus which flowed into the Aral Sea.

The main purpose of the campaign in the Oxus valley was to apprehend Bessus, one of the conspirators in the murder of Darius, who had then declared himself the new king of Asia. After a lengthy and dangerous campaign in wild border country, Bessus was taken, but Alexander was wounded in the leg during a skirmish with hostile tribesmen, and for some time had to be carried on a litter. In this way he reached Samarkand, which lay about 100 miles north of the present border of Afghanistan. Here he founded another city to be garrisoned by his own troops to maintain order along the border and check any threat from eastern barbarians.

His stay in this area witnessed the biggest threat to his authority. The Scythians – hardy independent semi-nomads – resented the plundering of occupying forces and the constant requisition of food and stores. Alexander sacked the seven nearest villages, but this did not quell the uprising which quickly spread across the whole area. Sending a detachment of more than 2,000 experienced troops to reinforce the garrison at Samarkand, he led his army against the enemy. He had to fight a serious battle using his well-tried tactics of a firm stand by the infantry in the centre of the line, linked to a powerful cavalry charge from the flanks. It was a costly clash with numerous casualties. He was still suffering from his wound and probably from dysentery too, so pursuit of the defeated foe was called off. This expensive victory was followed by dire news from Samarkand, which emphasised how much of the expedition's success depended on Alexander's military genius. The detachment sent to Samarkand had been commanded by experienced senior officers, but they disagreed about the tactics to be employed when confronted by a very large force of Scythians, including fast-moving mounted archers. The detachment was trapped and slaughtered almost to a man.

After these setbacks Alexander spent the winter in the relative security of Balkh, and his problems were eased by the arrival of reinforcements from home.

In the spring of 328, the seventh year of his campaign, he divided his army into six sections in order to hold down the area and to pursue the Scythians more actively. This proved to be a desultory campaign, although Alexander continued to show his ingenuity in the conduct of sieges against fortresses on daunting mountain peaks. After capturing one of them he found enough food and livestock to keep his army for two years. Alexander's entourage already included his mistress Barsine, who was expecting a child, and two male lovers – Hephaestion and Bagoas – and in the summer of 328 he fell in love with Roxane, the beautiful daughter of the local ruler, and married her in a sumptuous wedding ceremony. Hephaestion was best man.

Having married into a powerful local family, Alexander took action to establish his regime on a more permanent basis. He therefore ordered 30,000 local youths to learn Greek and to undergo military training using Macedonian methods and weapons.

In the more stable situation after his marriage to Roxane, he had once again to face problems arising from his troops' prolonged inactivity. Feuds developed between Macedonians and Persians, often over trivial customs like the exchange of kisses. He once again survived a plot against his life, and Callisthenes the historian came under suspicion and was executed.

In the lull before his next campaign he carried out a major military reorganisation. Many of his trusted Macedonians had been left to garrison and control his vast empire, so new blood had to be brought in. The number of archers was increased – particularly the mounted archers from the Oxus valley, and large numbers of Persian horsemen were brought in to strengthen the cavalry. By 327 much of the command structure of the old Companions had been changed, but the logistics still included the siege towers, the catapults and their attendant armourers. All of this was the prelude to his next great adventure, the invasion of India, but knowing the dangers posed by the climate, he kept his army in the relative cool of the Hindu Kush during the summer of 327 before venturing farther.

The invasion of India started with Hephaestion and a group of trusted Companions leading a large contingent to Peshawar to establish a crossing over the Indus. While they accomplished this, Alexander led his main force of more than 20,000 men through the Swat Highlands where he continued to capture mountain fortresses. After subduing an area, he usually made an ally of the ruler – rather like Lord Lugard and his system of indirect rule in West Africa in the early 20th century. After the capture of one large fortress Alexander found a herd of some 200,000 cattle which solved many of his food problems. After his great success at Tyre, he seemed to relish the challenge of a siege. In the Swat Highlands lay the natural fortress of Pir-Sar – considered to be impregnable – and therefore a challenge Alexander could not resist. A deep ravine protected the fortress but Alexander had this filled with thousands of felled fir trees, and then with his shield-bearers personally led the attack, climbing the rock face with ropes and metal spikes. The defenders were so amazed at this that they quickly surrendered. After this startling success he moved down, joined Hephaestion and crossed the Indus into the great plain around Rawalpindi, 100 miles east of Peshawar.

Here he was soon to have to fight another battle, this time with the added complication posed by his enemy's elephants. The capable enemy commander, Porus, had concentrated his powerful forces along the bank of the Jhelum, a tributary of the Indus. Alexander had to face the problems of a river crossing, similar to those of Slim's Fourteenth Army as they advanced through Burma after the victory at Imphal in 1944.

While constantly harassing the enemy forces with offensive patrols by night, he let it known that he would wait until after the monsoons before tackling the river. Meanwhile reconnaissance had revealed a possible crossing point in a ravine several miles upstream. In his swiftly formulated battle plan, the movement of his troops would depend entirely on how Porus deployed his elephants. Alexander would lead a strong group of élite cavalry and infantry across the river by night, leaving the main army under a trusted general with explicit instructions: after the alarm was raised in the enemy camp, if the elephants were brought up to attack Alexander's group, the main army would cross the river immediately; if not, the main army would not attack.

After meticulous planning, with effective diversions, Alexander had just begun the crossing when a violent monsoon storm struck. He was leading the way on his beloved horse Bucephalus, but instead of reaching the bank, he found himself on an island in the river. Alerted, the enemy sentries rode off to raise the alarm and Alexander and his troops were able to get ashore.

Porus immediately attacked with 2,000 cavalry and 100 chariots, but these were quickly defeated by showers of arrows and javelins from the Companions. Porus was undecided whether to keep his main force in reserve and his hesitation gave Alexander the initiative. Confronted by 100 elephants with massed infantry behind them, he led the Companions in a sudden cavalry charge on the left wing which drew off Porus' own cavalry, and at the same time sent a cavalry group to attack the enemy's weaker right wing, and his élite shield-bearers to advance on the centre. He had armed the latter with axes to slash the elephants' legs and scimitars to slash at their trunks. This deployment worked brilliantly - fifty of the elephants were quickly put out of action while the rest stampeded wildly among their own terrified infantry. The enemy host rapidly disintegrated, and Porus surrendered. Alexander had won a dramatic victory by meticulous planning, the shrewd use of unorthodox weapons, and by being at the front of the action where he could make immediate decisions to influence the outcome. For him personally the most grievous cost of the battle was the loss of his charger Bucephalus.

This brilliant victory proved to be the climax of his military achievement. After it he had to face very different problems. The monsoon created appalling conditions for his troops. Thousands died from fever. Floods brought pythons, cobras and scorpions into their bedraggled tents, and a desperate shortage of food could not be remedied by ravaging the local land. At last his loyal followers refused to venture farther, and Alexander had to face the difficulties of leading his huge force down the Indus valley to the sea. He had large barges built – bigger than the Indians had ever seen – but they were sucked into rapids and whirlpools which smashed them to pieces. Alexander himself had to swim for his life from the wrecked royal barge. Powerful and warlike tribes inhabited the valley of the Indus, and his forces had to fight their way forward. Their progress was barred by one powerfully defended city, and Alexander, as ever at the front of the action but showing foolish bravado, led his men up ladders to scale the wall. His ladder broke, and he fell, totally isolated among the enemy. Only the greatest luck and a frenzied attack by his Household troops saved his life, but he was carried away, seriously wounded. His dynamic personal leadership now curbed, his troops eventually reached the coast and prepared for the journey home.

At Pattala – near modern Karachi – they developed a harbour and built shipyards. From here Alexander planned to send part of his force by ship westwards into the Persian Gulf, and despite his wounds made the reckless decision to lead a large force overland through the Gedrosian desert. This force suffered very serious privations because of the intense heat and serious lack of water and food. Original sources give conflicting descriptions of this campaign. One suggests that Alexander only went through with it because he believed that Cyrus the Great, the founder of the Persian empire, had done it before him. This appears to have been another maverick decision, and it resulted in very heavy casualties, including the loss of many women and children in an unexpected flash flood. Ironically, Auchinleck, as Commander-in-Chief India in 1946, in assessing the threat of a possible Soviet attack, ordered a detailed reconnaissance of this route, and was assured that it was impassable even for a modern army.

Alexander, as he led the remnant of his armies back in 324, deteriorated both physically and mentally, becoming autocratic and unpredictable. He punished and even executed some of the Macedonians he had left in charge of districts and who had become corrupt. When his forces arrived in the valley of the Tigris, he joined in massive celebrations with his surviving veterans, and encouraged mass weddings between Macedonians and Persian women. He also enrolled thousands of Persians into the army and this provoked another revolt by his veterans. Later that year the celebrations were marred by the death of his lifelong friend Hephaestion. Fairly soon after this he moved his headquarters to Babylon and there in 323, after bouts of heavy drinking, he caught a fever and died soon afterwards.

Alexander, with his belief in his link with Zeus, the Father of the Gods, constantly attempted to match the achievements of antiquity. He is justly regarded as an outstanding and inspiring military leader in every aspect of war. As a tactician he was unrivalled – in direct leadership in battle, in the development of new weapons both for sieges and for battles, in the direct control of troops in battle, and in speed of movement. All these attributes would have come to nothing if he had not organised the most remarkable logistic system to support his armies across most of the then known world.

Throughout his life, despite his constant military campaigns, Alexander sought to reconcile the peoples he had conquered and to bring peace and concord. Yet his real legacy was one of disaster. Macedonia, led to greatness by his father Philip of Macedon, was depopulated and ruined by the loss of its ablest men to Alexander's armies. After his death the vast lands he conquered were soon engulfed in civil war and disaster, and the example of his career was emulated by ruthless military adventurers and tyrants down the ages.

SHAKA ZULU

Early in the 19th century the great Shaka had begun the process of transforming a tiny tribe into the greatest warrior nation in Africa, the Zulus, who were to confront the British as they advanced from the Cape northwards, into what is now Natal, and fought fierce battles against the power and might of the British Empire at its peak. The legend of Shaka is controversial, being often at odds with the reality. Was he a brilliant military leader who developed new weapons and tactics to ensure his supremacy, and who built up a sound, well-ordered and law-abiding society, or merely a bloodthirsty savage on a par with the worst tyrants in history? Contemporary accounts share both views, though the early favourable reports from shipwrecked sailors in the 18th century, who spoke of the Zulus as a cheerful, happy, prosperous and law-abiding people, were later overshadowed by Victorian sources which stressed the savagery of Shaka and his people.

The Zulus, living in what is roughly modern Natal, enjoyed a fertile, well-watered land which teemed with game and supported vast herds of cattle with ease. Cattle were central to the Zulu tribal and social system, and contributed to the male domination of society, where polygamy flourished. At the time of Shaka's birth in 1787, the Zulus were a small and fairly insignificant tribe, but one which held its own in the vicious internecine struggles over cattle or land. The white intrusion, which was to dominate the next century, had barely begun, except for a small Portuguese settlement at Delagoa Bay to the north of the Zulu homelands. The Portuguese, in a desultory manner, traded in ivory, and to some extent in slaves, though the main slave-trade flourished under the Arabs, much farther north. Shaka's brief rule of twelve years forged a nation which dominated the history of south-east Africa during the 19th century, and which still today sees itself as independent, even in post-apartheid South Africa.

Land was the key factor in the serious friction between black and white which was to dominate the new century. Even Shaka suffered from unscrupulous whites, who tricked him, by a meaningless thumb-print, into handing over land at Port Natal. This blatant dishonesty – most Africans had no concept of land-owning in the European sense – was perpetrated all

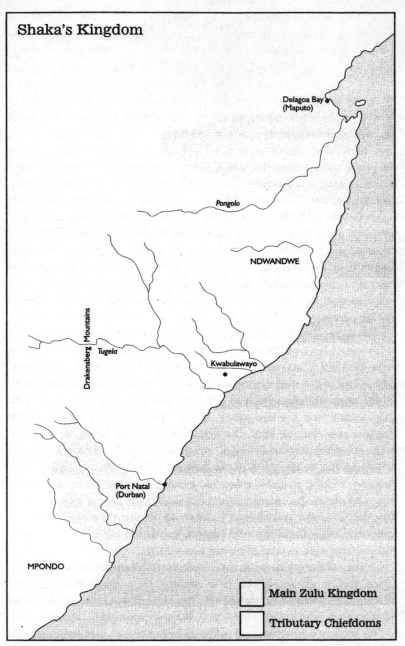

Shaka's Kingdom

Delagoa Bay
(Maputo)

Pongolo

NDWANDWE

Drakensberg | Mountains

Tugela

Kwabulawayo

Port Natal
(Durban)

MPONDO

Main Zulu Kingdom

Tributary Chiefdoms

over Africa, usually accompanied by those other powerful agents of colonialism – guns and gin. The tragic issue of land was summed up later in the century by an elderly chief speaking to a missionary: 'When you came to Africa you had the Bible and we had the land. Now we have the Bible and you have the land.' Shaka witnessed the early stages of this unprincipled land-grabbing by European predators.

Zulu society had strict rules and etiquette which imposed severe penalties on those who transgressed. Such customs applied particularly to sexual relations between young people and helped to prevent unwanted pregnancies. Shaka's mother, Nandi, an aggressive and headstrong woman, became pregnant and, although the father was a chief, she was disgraced and became an outcast. She and her baby – named Shaka, or beetle – in their exile suffered real hardship and ostracism. Shaka was badly bullied and was also teased about the size of his penis. This youthful suffering produced in Shaka a strong sense of grievance and resentment, which grew into a ruthless, determined and unforgiving ambition. His feckless father did become chief of the Zulus, but he ignored Shaka. Nandi wisely took Shaka away, because of the Zulu tradition of fathers eliminating their sons so as to prevent any future threat.

During his long and bitter exile, Shaka was enrolled in one of the youth training regiments of the Mthethwa tribe and spent some years on campaign. By now he had become a powerful and imposing figure with tempestuous energy which was soon remarked by the chief Dingiswayo. Shaka further enhanced his reputation when, so the tale goes, he confronted a madman who had been terrorising the neighbourhood. Soon after this, Shaka's father came to the court of Dingiswayo, but did not recognise his son. Dingiswayo introduced them and they were reconciled. A short time later the father and a half-brother died and Shaka became chief of the Zulus.

He acted quickly. Moving his headquarters to a strategically better place called kwaBulawayo, he immediately established the system of *amabutho*, which he had learnt as a youngster under Dingiswayo. It consisted of cadres formed from youths of the same age in each area. Shaka changed and developed this system, inculcating discipline, loyalty, determination and bravery, and giving the highest priority to martial skill. Some of his achievements may be legend, but it is generally believed that he drilled his troops on ground covered with thorn bushes so as to toughen the soles of their feet. This enabled them to dispense with clumsy sandals, and greatly increased their mobility in battle. These cadets were kept in their units for three years or more, and while their work tending livestock was important, the inculcation of loyalty to Shaka, and aggressive military attitudes, transcended all else. To increase the effectiveness of his regiments, he also changed the marriage laws of the Zulus, which enabled him to retain the young men for a longer period of training. As his military system was built up, women were given a more specific and positive role in carrying supplies and giving support to the army when on campaign. These reforms, rejecting many old customs, were the foundation of his future power, enabling him to become, as John Laband wrote: 'the black Napoleon, who deployed superlative military and organisational skill'. It is well known that Shaka was always talking about war, and would kill people with hardly a thought. A European who had been at his court as a boy described him as a man of great ability, but cruel, capricious, ruthless and aggressive. Others added that he was an inhuman and savage tyrant – a compound of vice and ferocity.

While the fearsome aspect of his character is best known, his genius in building up a nation from indifferent beginnings is equally important. He had suffered the bitterness of exile and rejection, and felt no obvious loyalty to the tribe or system which had rejected him, but his tribulations had inspired him to create a law-abiding community based on hard work, civic duty, respect for superiors, and self-discipline – albeit backed up by fierce penalties.

Initially, Shaka had to tread warily so as not to offend the powerful conservative elders, but he was able to effect one tactical change which brought almost immediate reward. During the campaigns under Dingiswayo, Shaka had studied the fighting methods of both the Zulus and their enemies. Most battles followed a stylised sequence, with the sacrifice of a bull, the treatment of the meat by witch-doctors, the drinking of a potion, the shouting of insults, and the throwing of spears. This is where Shaka made his most significant change. He abandoned the long assegai, which had to be thrown, in favour of a short stabbing spear, which he had personally developed. His troops went into action carrying a tough hide shield, which was an effective defence against even a shower of enemy spears. Then in close combat they used their stabbing spears to deadly effect. Within a unit, a few would retain the longer hunting spears, which were accurate up to about 30 yards, and others carried a battleaxe. Shaka's stabbing spear was as significant in his rise to power, as the siege train of Alexander, or the panzers of Guderian.

Shaka soon had the opportunity to test his new system. His fast-moving warriors – without their sandals, but clutching their stabbing spears – put to flight the Buthelezi clan, and then turned on his mother's people who had disgraced both her and him. Shaka destroyed the Buthelezi kraals, killing even women and children, and then he slaughtered the elders of the tribe. This was never forgotten. Soon afterwards, Shaka faced a more daunting challenge, when the aggressive chief, Zwide, defeated and killed Dingiswayo – Shaka's nominal suzerain.

Zwide was one of many ruthless and bloodthirsty leaders who, during what was known as the *mfecane* – a period of turbulence and chaos covering much of south-eastern Africa – used terror, violence and fear to subdue his enemies. Shaka's first reaction to the threat posed by Zwide was to appeal for help to a neighbouring tribe where he had spent part of his youthful exile. Their chief replied contemptuously, even making insulting references to Shaka's penis. Shaka immediately sent an impi (force of warriors) to attack. They won a quick victory, and the chief who had insulted Shaka was killed. His successor quickly made an alliance which helped Shaka to establish his hold over the entire area. His reputation for power and for magic spread rapidly. Then, in 1818 Shaka fought the first of two battles against Zwide. This is described in detail by Shaka's biographer, E. A. Ritter, who estimated that there were 8,000 casualties, though this figure is strongly disputed by recent scholars. The Zulus certainly sustained heavy casualties, and after the battle Shaka set about building up his now formidable regiments with the young men of his new allies, and he strengthened even further the awesome discipline. After a battle any man who had showed cowardice was usually executed in the presence of his regiment, and several were despatched on this occasion. Furthermore, the Zulu oral tradition was positively developed to nurture attitudes of bravery and leadership, so that pride in the regiment and the nation was encouraged.

In 1819 scouts brought word that the powerful armies of Zwide were preparing to attack. Shaka abandoned many settlements north of kwaBulawayo, and called on all available men to strengthen the six regiments, which were now distinguished by different coloured shields. Then Shaka carried out a skilled military tactic, gradually withdrawing his troops before the advancing enemy over a period of several days, until the enemy's water and rations were exhausted. Each night Zulu warriors infiltrated the enemy camp to increase their apprehension, and a clever decoy drew the enemy to the place where Shaka had decided to stand.

When the battle started, Zwide's warriors threw their showers of spears, but then the Zulus in their disciplined regiments, and trained in the use of the short stabbing assegai, moved forward and at close quarters exacted a lethal toll. Both sides suffered heavy casualties, but the Zulus won. Relentlessly pursuing Zwide's demoralised survivors and slaughtering them all, they then razed his capital and killed all the inhabitants. This signal victory established Shaka's dominion over the whole country between the Drakensberg Mountains and the sea, and from Port Natal up the coast to Delagoa Bay.

The establishment and consolidation of Zulu power under Shaka caused serious upheavals in all the surrounding territories. Some chiefs, who refused to accept his domination, led their people northwards – against the general direction of Bantu migration – and into the area of modern Mozambique and Zimbabwe. Others fled westwards over the Drakensberg Mountains. Those who remained were absorbed into the growing Zulu empire, their men recruited into the harshly disciplined regiments, their cattle taken as tribute, and their young women taken for marriage alliances. The sufferings of many of the lesser tribes were compounded by a prolonged drought, which caused battles for food and water, so that only the strong and aggressive survived. Whole areas south of Shaka's kingdom became a desolate wilderness, inhabited by cannibals. This devastating upheaval throughout much of what is now Natal went on for several years, but by 1824 Shaka was in control of most of the region.

In Zulu society, power lay in the wealth from cattle, and in the pre-eminence of the disciplined regiments, grouped by age, under the direct control of Shaka. His so-called kraal, where he lived with the hundreds of women of his entourage, was close by the great Tugela river. This, the literal and figurative apex of his power, was said to be two miles in circumference, and protected by a ten-foot-high stockade. This encompassed a vast cattle enclosure, and the thousands of kraals of those privileged to live within the complex, and everywhere the obvious presence of the military caste. Here the Zulu tradition of home-loving and cleanliness was brought to perfection.

To increase his power, Shaka curbed the rights and privileges of lesser chiefs, including their significant role of acting as intermediaries with the ancestral spirits. He also installed his own trusted nominees as regional chiefs. He imposed more and more severe rules on the regiments, and kept the warriors totally isolated from women. There are many conflicting legends about Shaka's sexuality, but although his entourage included hundreds of young women it appears he was not promiscuous. Zulu society seems to have accepted that adulterers and cowards should face instant death – usually administered by impaling or having the neck broken. Shaka seems to have been totally capricious in ordering people to be killed. The earliest white visitors to Shaka's people were horrified at this casual carnage, but it appears to have been accepted as normal by the Zulus – probably because the discipline and fear had brought order and prosperity to the nation.

At this juncture, a new factor appeared, which was to dominate the rest of Shaka's life and the history of the Zulu nation. The Dutch, and the British, whose highest priority was the route to India, had begun to settle in the area of the Cape of Good Hope. Then in the aftermath of the Napoleonic Wars, when the Vienna Settlement awarded the Cape to Britain, both Dutch and British began to push northwards into the interior of Africa.

They first clashed with the proud Xhosa people, and it was from a remarkable Xhosa man named Jakot that Shaka learned about the white people and their ways. For many years, mostly as a slave, Jakot had been employed by both British and Dutch. He was highly intelligent, had learned both languages, and become an interpreter. Jakot was with an expedition along the east coast by two small British naval vessels, when they were wrecked. He survived and made his way to the kraal of Shaka, who questioned him thoroughly. Jakot remained at Shaka's court for many years as a confidant and adviser.

A vivid and colourful description of Shaka's court was given by a group of three young men – British and Dutch – who reached kwaBulawayo in 1824. Shaka presented them with gifts of ivory, and arranged a display to impress the visitors who described how 12,000 warriors paraded in full regalia, and were commanded by Shaka. More than 10,000 young women, naked but for a few beads, danced and sang and stamped their feet. Then before a gathering of some 80,000 spectators, huge herds of cattle were driven past, to demonstrate the power and wealth of the Zulu people.

Fairly soon after this visit, while one of the men, Henry Fynn, was still at Shaka's court, Shaka was badly wounded in an attempted assassination. Fynn dressed his wounds and stayed with him as he hovered close to death. After some days he began to recover, which gave Fynn great prestige. Subsequently Shaka became obsessed with finding the secret of the white man's medicine. He appears to have realised the tremendous potential power of the foreign intruders from over the sea, and hoped, by doing business with them, to forge an alliance and even to gain their support against his rivals.

This aspect of Shaka's plans became clearer in 1826, when he set out towards his northern border with a very powerful army to attack his old enemy the Ndwandwe, whose chief Zwide had been defeated in 1818. Zwide had since died, and his people were now to feel the power of Shaka's military strength. Fynn, who had described his original reception at Shaka's court, accompanied the expedition as an ally – and a hostage.

The expedition saw Shaka's military organisation at its peak. The army advanced in a long column, with boys driving the accompanying cattle, and girls carrying food and drink. As soon as the warriors entered enemy territory, they foraged aggressively, often moving into extended line to drive out game to augment the food supply. Scouts and spies were sent several miles ahead, trained to act as decoys and to entice the enemy to disclose his whereabouts. As soon as these were known, the boys and girls were sent home for safety.

Although Shaka had made great changes in organisation and tactics, there remained a fairly stylised ritual to the start of a battle, with the exchange of challenges and insults, followed by a great yell as the leading regiments advanced for the first clash. As the opposing warriors approached each other, Shaka would signal his customary tactic and the army would separate into four formations: one, the strongest, in the centre to engage at close quarters with their short assegais; one formation on each wing, directed by Shaka himself; one group held in reserve to assist in the central battle or to pursue the beaten enemy.

After a week's march, when water was in short supply, and even Shaka's fierce discipline could hardly prevent serious scuffles at water holes, the Zulus approached the Ndwandwe position. Their army was drawn up on a hillside, with large numbers of cattle, women and children in the rear. Fynn gives a vivid description of the battle. The front ranks of the armies 'with a tumultuous yell' attacked each other, the central phalanx of the Zulus stabbing viciously with their assegais. This sudden clash lasted only a few minutes, then both sides briefly drew back – each having sustained casualties. Then they gave another yell, and charged in again. This mêlée lasted longer than the first, and the enemy lost many more men. Noticing this, Shaka urged his troops forward for a third charge, and the enemy lines gave way under the fury of the assault. Fynn described how immediately after the battle, the enemy were pursued and killed, as were all their wounded. Then the women and children were slaughtered too. The large herds of cattle were rounded up, the main reward for a great victory. Fynn estimated that the Ndwandwe must have lost about 40,000 people and 60,000 cattle.

The aftermath of the battle was almost as stylised as the start. Because of superstition, a Zulu warrior usually disembowelled his wounded enemy. Their own wounded were tended with poultices and splints, but medical attention was rudimentary. Shaka inspected his troops the following day, by which time the regimental commanders had had any cowardly men executed. Because of their intense belief in ancestral links, each warrior who had killed a man had to be ritually cleansed by a witch-doctor to prevent bad influences from the spirits. After this, each warrior took part in a ceremony and made a report on the battle, naming those who had acted bravely.

The decisive defeat of the Ndwandwe brought Shaka to the peak of his power. It secured his northern border, and caused some apprehensive tribes to flee farther northwards – some as far as Lake Tanganyika. His social and military system, based on military efficiency backed by terror, had been fashioned with the overall aim of military conquest, but in achieving this, a sound, prosperous, loyal and law-abiding society had been created.

This situation obtained throughout his reign, but later the Zulu people failed to adapt to the more sinister, destructive and deadly new challenge, which had begun to emerge even during Shaka's lifetime – white intruders with firearms. Years later, Chesterton was to observe, sadly, the carnage wrought by modern firearms against assegais:

'Whatever happens we have got
The Maxim gun and they have not.'

The signal victory over the Ndwandwe in the Dololwane Hills brought little satisfaction to Shaka. He decided to move his capital away from kwaBulawayo, but then changed his mind. His behaviour became more and more erratic, and his death sentences even more capricious. Then he appears to have been overwhelmed by the death of his mother Nandi.

Once again, Fynn gives a clear and most vivid description of her death and the dreadful events which followed. As the mother of Shaka, Nandi was held in great respect. She presided over her own kraal – in fact a large and impressive complex – and wielded considerable power. Fynn describes how he saw her a few hours before her death, apparently suffering from dysentery, but another version of the story, which is authenticated in Zulu oral tradition, suggests something else. Shaka had always been paranoid about the possibility of being usurped or challenged by his own son – a fairly common occurrence among the Zulus. Therefore if any of his young women became pregnant, she was forced to have an abortion, or the child was killed as soon as it was born. The other version of Nandi's death suggested that she was eager to have a grandson, and had deceived Shaka about the child of one of his young women. When he discovered the deception, in a rage, he stabbed Nandi, but then repented and tried in vain to save her. When she died, there was a huge gathering – estimated by Fynn at 60,000. He described how, after a night of mass lamentation, the next morning a massacre started. Fynn reckons that 7,000 people were killed because they did not show sufficient grief to prove their innocence of any complicity in Nandi's death. Shaka's grief (or sense of guilt) was such that for a year no milk was allowed to be drunk, no crops could be planted, and sexual intercourse was forbidden. During this terrible time any woman who became pregnant was executed with her husband.

Shaka was still dithering about leaving kwaBulawayo. One reason for moving was his growing interest in dealing with the British settlers at Port Natal. While welcoming the increase in trade, he was particularly anxious to gain access to the increasing supply of firearms which were beginning to come into the area; he also hoped to have British support in his future operations. In Port Natal were several characters including Fynn, and his rival King, who became deeply involved in Shaka's next move. In a volatile situation, these men reckoned that they could profit by fixing a deal whereby the British would support Shaka's rule in return for unrestricted trading rights. This proposal was made public in Cape Town, where it was reported that Europeans were living and trading amicably in the lands of Shaka. King proposed that Shaka should send a representative to Cape Town – ostensibly, as the Zulus understood it – to treat with King George. Shaka and the Zulus, uneasy about venturing to sea, chose a chief for the job who sailed for Cape Town in May 1828, bringing eighty ivory tusks as a suitable gift for a king. At about the same time, Shaka personally led a very large expedition to attack his southern neighbours the Mpondo, hoping to strengthen his southern border and take large numbers of cattle to reward his supporters. The Mpondo army was swiftly overcome, but the long-term results of the raid were disastrous for Shaka.

At Port Natal, King had purported to negotiate on behalf of Great Britain, but alas for Shaka, King had no status, even in Cape Town. In fact the Zulu envoys were not taken there, but were kept at Port Elizabeth, and virtually ignored for weeks. Shaka's affairs now came into the complicated arena of aggressive white domination, with little overall control, and with individuals pursuing conflicting aims. Some of the tribes – including the Mpondo – which Shaka had defeated, had fled southwards, and reports of his brutality had reached the Cape. At the same time a number of Shaka's enemies – including many Zulus – had fled to Port Natal in the hopes of finding a more liberal regime. Some of these welcomed the opportunity to profit from a situation in which the influence of white traders – and especially their guns – were seen to undermine Shaka's power. After weeks of delay at Port Elizabeth, a representative of the British Governor visited Shaka's envoy and told him bluntly that King had no status at all, that he was distrusted, and certainly had no authority to negotiate. The Zulus returned empty-handed to Shaka who, despite his disappointment, reacted patiently, but he became increasingly suspicious when King, the instigator of the proposition, became ill and died. Shaka was convinced that the British had poisoned him.

The Zulu tradition whereby sons challenged and usurped their fathers was the cause of Shaka's obsession against having a son, but rather surprisingly, considering his bloodthirsty misuse of power, he had not eliminated two of his half-brothers, Dingane and Mhlangana, who were children of his father by other wives. These two had become senior and trusted commanders in the army, but latterly were becoming alarmed at Shaka's increasingly capricious and mentally unbalanced behaviour. During his attempted negotiations with Cape Town, he had already sensed an atmosphere of conspiracy against him, and even suspected his half-brothers. By August 1828 he was facing a serious crisis. His overtures to the British had been rudely rejected. His expedition against the Mpondo had succeeded, but almost at once the British in Cape Town had despatched well-armed troops to impose their will on the frontier region. He was under intense psychological pressure, and his mental instability was exacerbated by his fears and forebodings. Before his army returned from the Mpondo campaign, Shaka executed the wives of 400 of his warriors for witchcraft. He then decided that as soon as the impi returned, he would send it off again towards Delagoa Bay. He deliberately included Dingane and Mhlangana in this order so as to keep them away from his court. The order to move north – given in mid-September – provoked strong resentment, because victorious

43

impis had traditionally been allowed a period of celebration and rest after a successful campaign.

Thus in an atmosphere of sullen anger and frustration, the impi moved off, but a few days later Dingane and Mhlangana, feigning illness, returned to their kraal. Together with Shaka's personal servant, they decided to kill him. On the evening of 23 September 1828, when Shaka was sitting outside his hut receiving a delegation, Dingane and Mhlangana, who had been hiding close by, rushed out and stabbed him. After his death they acted quickly, and there was surprisingly little upheaval among the Zulu people.

Shaka had ruled for twelve years and had only just turned forty when he died, yet to this day his image inspires pride among the Zulu people. He not only built up and led a powerful and successful army, but set standards and traditions for his people which lasted for decades. In the strong Zulu oral tradition, he is credited with warning his people that the white man would come and take over their lands. What he could not foresee was that the tradition he had established for the Zulu army would enable it to stand up to and even defeat the forces of Great Britain with their modern weapons. It was Shaka's hand which led the great challenges of Isandlwana and Rorke's Drift. The tragedy is that, while perhaps the British had to win in the end, they were not just winning battles but destroying a way of life. An outstanding modern scholar, Stephen Taylor, in his book *Shaka's Children*, summed up Shaka as follows: 'It is time analogies with such figures as Napoleon and Alexander were abandoned, although it is tempting to make a new one with Bismarck.'

STONEWALL JACKSON

The American Civil War highlighted the deep differences of attitudes and way of life between the people of Virginia and the southern states on the one hand, and the northern 'Yankees' on the other. While the election of Lincoln in 1860, with his views on the abolition of slavery, made war more likely, other issues, such as states' rights and secession from the Union accentuated the divide that separated the industrial north from the plantation-based south. The war, with its horrifying casualties and destruction, produced few characters more remarkable than the Confederate General Thomas 'Stonewall' Jackson, who proved to be one of the great military leaders of his day.

Born in 1824, and brought up by an uncle, he had had little formal schooling and was considered fortunate to get into West Point in 1842. There he responded well to a fiercely disciplined regime, and showed great determination backed by intense hard work. Having passed in at the bottom of the list, he graduated with high enough marks to entitle him to choose his arm of service – like Napoleon he chose the artillery. He soon had war experience in the Mexico campaign where, during an attack on Mexico City, he handled his detachment of guns so effectively that he was commended by General Scott, and promoted to major.

After the war he was posted to New York where several aspects of his character became prominent. Austere in manner and habits, and passionately religious, he became a hypochondriac and linked his health problems with divine intervention. He also became extremely cantankerous and aggressively litigious. Soon afterwards, in Florida, he had two serious legal disputes with fellow-officers. This unpleasant characteristic continued; during the Civil War he frequently court-martialled fellow-officers for, as he saw it, failing in their duties.

In March 1851 he resigned from the army to teach at the Virginia Military Institute at Lexington, a private academy, where he was an inadequate Professor of Artillery. Considered to be rather eccentric, he had serious disciplinary problems; for example, he was ragged by the students during his lectures on mechanics and optics. His life was far from happy, but he gained great solace from his activities at the local church, which also helped him

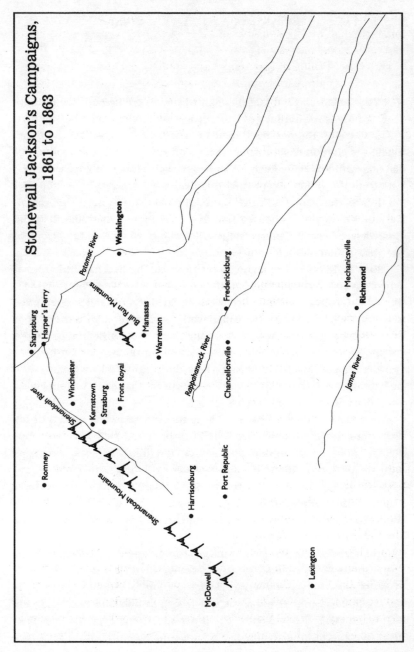

Stonewall Jackson's Campaigns,
1861 to 1863

Sharpsburg

Harper's Ferry

Potomac River

Washington

Bull Run Mountains

Manassas

Warrenton

Shenandoah River

Winchester

Kernstown

Strasburg

Front Royal

Romney

Rappahannock River

Fredericksburg

Chancellorsville

Mechanicsville

Richmond

James River

Shenandoah Mountains

Harrisonburg

Port Republic

Lexington

McDowell

through a period of deep unhappiness after the death of his first wife and infant child. As the divisions in the USA deepened, he strongly opposed the idea of secession and war.

After the shelling of Fort Sumpter in April 1861 – the real start of the Civil War – Virginia, following South Carolina, seceded from the Union. Jackson, as an experienced officer, was immediately posted to Richmond – capital of the Confederacy - to train recruits, but within days was promoted to colonel, and sent to the main Confederate arsenal at Harpers Ferry, at the junction of the rivers Shenandoah and Potomac. He was present at the hanging of John Brown, after the unsuccessful attempt to seize the arsenal. General Robert E. Lee ordered Jackson and colleagues from the Institute to take charge at Harpers Ferry, restore order among a mass of undisciplined recruits, and prepare its defences. Jackson was foolishly punctilious about orders and refused to hand over to a superior officer, Johnston, but then was given command of a brigade of Virginians, which became the Stonewall Brigade.

General Lee, anticipating a major advance by the Federal forces to capture Richmond, ordered the Confederate troops to defend Manassas Junction. Here on 18 July 1861 the first battle of the Civil War began when the defenders, drawn up along the Bull Run river, smartly repulsed the Federal advance. Then the slow-moving Federal forces gave Lee time to call up more troops and strengthen his defences. The main Federal attack on 21 July, led by Sherman, advanced across the Bull Run while a substantial formation moved around the northern flank in the hope of taking Lee's defenders by surprise. In this they were foiled because their advance was so slow, and impeded by a vast crowd of Washington society, which had come out to watch the Confederates being beaten. The attack on two fronts initially drove back the defenders, many units retiring in chaos and confusion, and fleeing south, over the Warrenton road, to where Jackson stood with his brigade. This was the moment when General Bee, trying to rally his panic-stricken men, shouted, 'There is Jackson standing like a stone wall.' The solidity of Jackson's brigade rallied many other Confederate units to form a firm line. Jackson, the skilled artillery specialist, quickly and effectively co-ordinated his fire on the Federal units. Throughout a long day of fierce fighting, the Federals were repeatedly driven back, only to regroup and recapture lost ground. Jackson, in the thick of the fighting, ordered his men to hold their fire till the enemy were within 50 yards, and then charge with the bayonet. After a final vigorous attack by his brigade, the Federal army withdrew towards Washington, again hampered by the disappointed sightseers.

Jackson's fame stemmed from his outstanding leadership, steady composure under fire, and calm determination in the midst of universal despair at this, the first battle of Bull Run. Afterwards, his personal care for the wounded and concern for food, supplies and comforts, made him the idol of his men.

In November 1861 Lee appointed Jackson – now a major general – to overall command at the northern end of the Shenandoah Valley. He was based at Winchester, west of the river, and from there organised raids on railways and canals to prevent supplies from reaching Washington. Staying with his second wife, Anna, with the local Presbyterian minister's family, this was a brief but intensely happy time for him. The idyll was ended by his own determination to drive the Federal forces out of north Virginia.

In January 1862 he set off with 9,000 men towards the River Potomac. Relentlessly, in bitter weather, he drove his troops on, severely repri- manding several commanders for lack of resolution. Capturing Bath, they continued their advance to the small town of Hancock where Jackson sent forward fighting patrols to destroy bridges and communications. Then in a blizzard of ice and snow he pushed his men on over the mountains to Romney. After very great privations and suffering, and much serious complaining from the troops, they reached Romney on 14 January, only to find that the Federals had left a few days before. Jackson's iron will and determination had forced his men forward, but it was not good leadership, and when he decided to move on again his men refused.

In the face of this opposition, Jackson had to deploy his forces to hold a line against possible attack. He withdrew the Stonewall Brigade to Winchester where he set up his HQ, but this infuriated the officers and men left in the inhospitable mountains. Complaints were made to the adminis- tration in Richmond, and Jackson was ordered to withdraw the troops of General Loring – one of the senior commanders he had already disciplined. Enraged at such interference, Jackson threatened to resign. This caused serious consternation, and after a wise approach from Johnson, overall commander in the Shenandoah Valley, and also from the Governor of Virginia, he withdrew his resignation, but pursued his charges against Loring nevertheless.

After the winter battles of January 1862, the defensive positions remained fairly static until the spring. Jackson withdrew most of his force southwards down the Shenandoah Valley to Woodstock, leaving a cavalry group under the excellent leader Ashby, a Virginian horseman, whose troops did invaluable work in harassing and reconnaissance. In April Ashby reported that Federal troops were withdrawing from the valley to reinforce their commander, General McClellan, for an attack on Richmond.

Ashby's intelligence was not accurate, and shortly afterwards at Kernstown, Jackson's troops were driven back by superior numbers of Federals. Furious at seeing the Stonewall Brigade actually retreating, Jackson grabbed hold of a drummer and forced him to beat the 'Rally!', but this did not stem the retreat, and the Confederates had to withdraw under cover of darkness to a position three miles south. Jackson had lost 600 killed or wounded, and 300 taken prisoner. His cantankerous and aggressive attitude towards commanders who failed in any measure again held sway. He court-martialled Brigadier Garnett, who had ordered the retreat after all ammunition had been expended. Jackson argued that he should not have retreated until he had used the bayonet. Kernstown was a tactical defeat, but the fierceness of Jackson's attack alarmed the Federal commanders, and they quickly recalled units which had been sent to reinforce the Federal attack on Richmond.

General Lee now encouraged Jackson to use his own initiative to cause diversions in the Shenandoah Valley. This he did enthusiastically. To deceive the enemy, he marched north up the east side of the river, then crossed through the Blue Ridge, and hurried his forces back by road and rail. With two brigades, including the Stonewall and the cadets from the Virginia Military Institute, he was ready to surprise a Federal force at M'Dowell. On 8 May 1862 he concentrated his troops at Sitlington Hill with the intention of mounting a flank attack on a strong Federal position, but the Federal commander instead made a direct assault on the hill. After four hours of hand-to-hand fighting, in which Jackson himself took part, the Federal troops withdrew, having inflicted nearly double the number of casualties on the Confederates. They ostentatiously left their fires burning during the night, but by the morning they had left. The Federals had withdrawn after the battle, but it was hardly the victory which Jackson claimed, though in this bleak period for the Confederates, it was hailed as a success. As the Federals withdrew, they burnt the thick forests, and greatly impeded their pursuers. During the pursuit, Jackson again exhibited his ruthless determination. Some men from his Stonewall Brigade, who were volunteers, now demanded their discharge. Their colonel passed the problem to Jackson, who regarded it as mutiny. He ordered the regiment to parade, with the mutineers unarmed. He then publicly ordered them to return to duty or be shot. They returned. Throughout the war Jackson was notorious for rarely ordering clemency when a man had been sentenced to death by a court-martial.

After Jackson's successful leadership during the bloody clash at M'Dowell, Lee again ordered him to the northern end of the Shenandoah Valley to bluff and threaten the Federals into withdrawing more units from the campaign against Richmond. This independent role suited Jackson perfectly. About 8,000 Federal troops were centred on Strasburg, with an outpost at Fort Royal, a short distance to the east. Jackson, with an effective cavalry screen under Ashby, moved rapidly north. Feinting towards Strasburg, he suddenly veered off, and after a swift march overwhelmed the garrison at Fort Royal. Jackson, in the vanguard of the Confederate cavalry, inflicted heavy losses on the retreating enemy, which gave rise to deep concern in Washington.

Determined to keep up the momentum, Jackson pushed his troops forward. Swiftly outmanoeuvring Banks, the Federal commander, he forced him to withdraw from Strasburg towards Winchester. Banks made some determined stands, but still Jackson came on. Close to Winchester, Banks was holding a powerful position on a range of hills overlooking the town. General Taylor, leading a tough and well-disciplined unit from Louisiana, made a dramatic attack, broke the Federal lines, and the Confederates charged into Winchester. This type of action saw Jackson at his best: brilliant leadership with swift effective movement personally controlled from the front. He was fiercely aggressive to any of his unit commanders who were tardy, and it was known by all that food might be lost, but ammunition must get through. In these actions Banks lost 1,500 killed or wounded, and 3,000 prisoners. Even more important for the Confederates was the capture of large supplies of weapons, ammunition and food. The threat from Jackson after the capture of Winchester meant that 20,000 troops were withdrawn from the armies advancing towards Richmond.

Jackson's brilliant drive to Winchester and beyond – indeed the Stonewall Brigade even reached Harpers Ferry – had achieved an outstanding strategic result, but his position was now vulnerable. The Federals launched a strong pincer movement from both west and east towards Strasburg. Facing this critical situation, Jackson again showed remarkable leadership in conducting a controlled retreat. He now used

Ashby's cavalry in a defensive role, in both recce and fighting patrols. By destroying bridges over swollen torrents, he was able to prevent the Federal advance guard from obstructing his retreat. In one of these actions the outstanding cavalry leader Ashby was killed.

As the swift retreat continued, Jackson made for Port Republic, at the junction of two arms of the Shenandoah. While deploying his troops defensively at Port Republic, he was surprised by an attacking Federal column. By quick thinking and brisk action in grabbing a gun and turning it on the enemy, the entire position was saved. While this was happening, a substantial Federal group advanced towards the village of Cross Keys, about two miles to the west, but was effectively repulsed.

At Port Republic, the Federal lines lay slightly to the north of the town, and on 9 June Jackson decided to attack. Throughout a day of heavy and close-quarter fighting, Jackson, always close to the front, directed his troops to crucial points. As the battle hung in the balance, he brought up a strong contingent from Cross Keys, and then called up his main reserve from Port Republic. In this way he was able to concentrate his force at key points, and in the end drove back the Federal army. This proved a decisive victory, and the following day he declared a day of thanksgiving and prayer, and personally attended a mass communion service.

This victory was virtually the end of the Valley Campaign. During it Jackson had completely dominated the Shenandoah Valley, causing acute apprehension in Washington. He had defeated four Federal armies, having cleverly prevented them taking joint action against him. For the loss of less than 1,000 men, he had inflicted thousands of casualties, taken 4,000 prisoners, and captured stores, ammunition and equipment vital to the hard-pressed Confederates. His outstanding strategic and tactical skills in the Valley Campaign placed Jackson high on the list of brilliant military commanders.

After the success at Port Republic, Jackson was all for an aggressive advance towards Washington, but, instead, Lee asked him to leave some troops in the valley to fool the enemy, and move his main force in great secrecy towards Richmond. Jackson, always obsessively secretive, to the frequent confusion of his own commanders, now carried it to absurd lengths.

By 24 June 1862 his troops were approaching Richmond from the north. The Federal commander there was McClellan, whose critics said he was so slow that he was nicknamed 'Virginia Creeper'. From 25 June a series of fierce struggles – known as the Seven Days' Battle – took place to the north and north-east of Richmond, as Lee and Jackson attempted to break the siege of Richmond, and defeat McClellan's army. Jackson approached from the west, and the first serious encounter took place at Mechanicsville, north-east of Richmond. In a fairly static fight both sides suffered very heavy casualties, and although the Federal troops really won the battle, they withdrew to a better defensive position afterwards. Jackson's leadership appeared to falter here, perhaps because his troops were worn out, and because he was unfamiliar with the swamp and forest terrain around Richmond.

A similar bloody fight took place next day as the Confederates advanced to Gaines' Mill. Here again Jackson's close control of his troops proved decisive but at a heavy cost. The Confederates lost 8,000 killed or wounded – nearly double the losses of the Federals, who had the advantage of an almost perfect defensive position.

After this the Confederates had to pause to ascertain which way the Federal forces would move. As soon as this became clear, Jackson's Corps advanced due east. After slow progress across swampy terrain they arrived at Frayser's Farm – too late to assist in the day's action there. Jackson was heavily criticised for this lapse. The Federal army then fell back to Malvern Hill, another good defensive position, surrounded by marshes and ravines.

Here the Federal armies, with well-placed artillery, linked to fresh and disciplined infantry, awaited the Confederate attack – which proved a disaster. Lee issued conflicting orders, and Jackson foolishly obeyed them to the letter. The consequence was a confused and ineffective attack in which the Confederate troops were slaughtered. They took more than 6,000 casualties and retreated in shocked disarray. Yet again, although the Federals had won a clear victory, they withdrew to Harrison's Landing on the James River, where their gunboats could bolster their defence. In this prolonged battle, Jackson did not excel as he had when in command in the Shenandoah Valley.

During June the Federal army was reorganised as the Army of Virginia, and put under an aggressive commander, General Pope – illustrating Lincoln's quip that if McClellan was not using the army he might borrow it. Pope threatened to hang any guerrillas or civilians who supported the Confederates, but Jackson was undaunted and retaliated in similar vein. Lee ordered Jackson to confront Pope, and, remembering the confusion at previous battles, suggested that Jackson keep his commanders better informed of his plans.

In August 1862, as the Federal army moved southwards, Jackson's troops were involved in a sharp clash at Cedar Run, on the vital route between Richmond and the Shenandoah Valley. In this exchange, despite Lee's advice, Jackson again caused problems by failing to brief his commanders fully. As the Confederates were preparing to attack, the Federal troops advanced aggressively in the centre of the line and drove back the Stonewall Brigade. At this crucial moment when his own brigade were retreating in disarray, Jackson plunged into the fight, rallied his men and gradually drove back the enemy. Once more, after a fairly even fight, the Federal forces withdrew and Jackson was able to claim another victory.

At Cedar Run there had again been horrendous carnage, and the morale of the troops had suffered at the loss of their comrades. The almost endemic dysentery – whether from tainted water, green apples and corn, or lack of salt for the raw uncooked beef – weakened the strongest. In the aftermath of the fighting, the cannibal stench of burning human remains further eroded morale. Jackson, a religious zealot who was compared to Cromwell, was driven by his absolutist faith, and his conviction for victory or death, but his ruthlessness hardly equated with Christian compassion. Many, even some of his staunchest supporters, were shocked at the customary execution of deserters, who were always shot in front of their own units – the executions usually accompanied by sanctimonious rantings by Presbyterian parsons. Further horror was added when units were paraded again to view the corpses, and it was noted that often the trousers and jackets of the victims had been stolen – leaving the bodies naked. Were such draconian measures really necessary to keep the army together?

By the end of August Lee had regrouped his armies. Initially he had intended to outflank Pope whose Federal army was drawn up fairly close to Manassas Junction, where the earlier great battle of Bull Run had taken place. Then, with Jackson, Lee concocted a more daring plan. Jackson, with three divisions, set off secretly and lightly armed, on a wide diversionary march, keeping well away from Pope's lines. After a march of more than twenty miles, he cut through the Thoroughfare Gap in the Bull Run Mountains, and moved towards Manassas Junction from the west. On the night of 26 August 1862, Jackson's advance guard took an outlying railway station, where there were massive stores. Substantial Federal forces were approaching, so Jackson's troops took everything they could before destroying the rest and hurrying north.

This move became totally confused, but it also confused the enemy, and Jackson had time to draw up his divisions in good order at Groveton Ridge, overlooking the road from Washington to Warrenton. This was the prelude to the great battle known as Second Bull Run. The Federal forces approached Groveton Ridge, apparently unaware of the Confederates drawn up on the ridge above the road. Jackson could not resist an attack on an unsuspecting prey, and ordered an immediate charge. In fact, the Federal units were tough and well disciplined, and Jackson's men suffered heavy casualties.

This costly clash was only the prelude to the major battle. Jackson's divisions were strongly entrenched on the ridge. Pope's forces made frequent and determined attacks, but after a long day's fighting, with savage losses on both sides, they were driven back. At the end of the day, another powerful contingent under General Longstreet reached the ridge to strengthen Jackson's right flank, and Lee arrived to take overall command.

The next day, 30 August, Pope launched a massive attack against the Confederates on the ridge, where close-quarter fighting caused grievous casualties. At one moment Jackson's right flank was sorely pressed, but Longstreet, a sound and shrewd tactician, instead of joining the defenders, moved his guns to the flank, and mowed down the attackers. This move finally broke the Federal troops who moved off to regroup along the road to Washington at Centreville. After this battle there were a few more rather indeterminate clashes, and the Federal side was helped by the arrival of 10,000 reinforcements.

After Second Bull Run, Lee ordered his troops to advance into Maryland where he hoped they would be welcomed. The physical and psychological reactions after so many hard-fought battles were creating serious problems. Both Lee and Jackson had been injured in accidents, and their soldiers looked like ragged ruffians. Jackson became even more cantankerous towards his commanders. He reprimanded General Hill, a brave and able leader, and arrested him for neglect of duty. Desertion and straggling became a major problem, and Jackson had yet more deserters shot in front of their units. In assessing the supply position, Jackson realised what a parlous position he was in. In terms of food, clothing, ammunition, weapons, equipment and supplies, he was almost entirely dependent on capturing stores from the enemy.

Next, in a famous incident, advantage was passed to McClellan – the 'Virginia Creeper' – who was once again commanding the Federal Forces in this theatre. Lee had given written orders to his three corps commanders for an attack on Harpers Ferry, and one copy of this order was found by some Federal soldiers and taken at once to McClellan. He was jubilant. The key to Lee's plan, and to McClellan's hopes of defeating it, lay at Harpers Ferry. This crucial point, where the Potomac joins the Shenandoah, was dominated by three isolated mountains. In planning his attack on Harpers Ferry, Jackson moved his troops very swiftly, and managed to get his artillery installed on each of these mountain features, where they were able to fire at will on the Federal positions. His bombardment started on 14 September, and by the following morning after a ceaseless barrage, the Federal garrison surrendered. This was a rare victory, won almost entirely by artillery. At a cost of fewer than 100 casualties, Jackson took more than 12,000 prisoners, but more important, more than 70 artillery pieces, thousands of small arms, hundreds of wagons, and vast quantities of supplies. This was a brilliant victory, at very slight cost.

Jackson's forces were now able to hurry off and support Lee, who was about to be attacked by McClellan with 90,000 troops. A battle took place on 16/17 September at Sharpsburg, where the Antietam Creek joins the Potomac. Here Lee and Jackson conducted a defensive battle against greatly superior forces. The Confederate lines, based on the Dunker church, faced eastwards. McClennan's army moved to attack from the north, and by skilful use of artillery caused very heavy casualties among the defenders. The attackers advanced after the bombardment, and prolonged hand-to-hand fighting took place. Jackson's men were driven back to the church. Then some Texan units made a gallant charge, but were repulsed by a pitiless artillery barrage. McClennan had reserve troops whom he did not use wisely. He ordered a fresh division forward into the battle, but because of confusion they moved in the wrong direction, and this gave Jackson another opportunity. He attacked them from the flank and destroyed them. Continuous fierce fighting took place in the centre and on the left flank of Lee's position. Towards the end of the battle, a Federal corps under General Burnside, which had been very slow to start, now advanced towards the village of Sharpsburg, on the southern flank of the battle. Burnside's leadership proved disastrous. His corps was attacked on both flanks, particular damage being inflicted by some of Jackson's units that had hurried over from Harpers Ferry. The Federals suffered a savage defeat.

In this terrible battle there were about 25,000 casualties. Jackson, with his imperturbable calm, had been Lee's staunchest supporter and, as usual, had been at the centre of the fighting directing units to the key points of the battle. Afterwards Lee wrote to President Davis, praising Jackson as a true, honest and brave man who spared no exertion.

After the savage victory of Sharpsburg, the Confederate forces spent some time regrouping in the Shenandoah Valley, and Jackson, based briefly again at Winchester, renewed his ties with his Presbyterian friends, and the minister, Dr Graham. During this lull, the Federal armies gradually moved off to support another campaign against Richmond. To prevent this, Lee, whose intelligence service was excellent, moved swiftly to establish a strong defensive position on the banks of the River Rappahannock. Here, starting on 13 December, an essentially modern battle took place. Under Lee's overall command, Longstreet held the left flank based on Fredericksburg, and Jackson the southern right flank along the river. These were strong positions, with good artillery placements. The Federal forces, now under Burnside, who had been so slow to advance at Sharpsburg, were divided into three. Two major attacks were planned, both depending on the construction of pontoon bridges – one against Longstreet in the town, the second about a mile further south against Jackson's position. The attempted crossing in the town was repulsed, but that against Jackson's position was not so hotly contested, and the Federal advance-guard achieved an effective bridgehead. Jackson was unperturbed, since he held a powerful position. Federal attacks, with artillery support, continued throughout the day, but at first made little progress. Then, after renewed assaults, the attackers turned the right flank of Jackson's lines, and now his situation had become very dangerous. Having assessed the situation in detail, he sent in such a powerful counter-attack that the Federal brigade was hurled back across the river under heavy artillery fire. Jackson's group inflicted 5,000 casualties on the enemy, but suffered heavy losses themselves.

The attack across the river at Fredericksburg continued all day. Some Federal troops managed to get across, but came under intense co-ordinated defensive fire, initially from artillery, and then from well-controlled infantry fire. Altogether fourteen major attacks were made, but Longstreet remained confident that they would all be repulsed. Disheartened by their lack of success, the Federal forces gradually withdrew, and Lee, having sustained 12,000 casualties, remained in his strong position. He realised that Federal artillery across the river would destroy any follow-up troops. Lee waited and eventually Burnside's army withdrew. The march on Richmond had been stopped.

After the great battle of Fredericksburg, Jackson established his HQ some way to the east of the town, and prepared for winter. During a relatively stable season, Jackson, by personal example of prayer and devotion, and a formal application for the provision of chaplains, did much to encourage religious devotion among his troops.

During the winter lull, 'Fighting Joe Hooker' had been given command of the Federal forces, and he improved their training and attitude. Towards the end of April 1863, he made preparations for what he called the 'Perfect Battle'. He sent a major part of his force on a wide flanking movement to Chancellorsville, a town on the main road a few miles west of Fredericksburg. When this movement started, Lee and Jackson planned their counter-attack. The thickly wooded area meant that artillery was ineffective and movement difficult. They therefore decided that Jackson would make a counter flank march with a substantial part of the Confederate army, and he set off early on 2 May. The Federals were drawn up with their defences and guns facing south, and Jackson planned to sweep round unobserved farther south and come at them from the west. He made good progress and remained unobserved. He now hurried forward to a position on the Turnpike road, on the Federals' west flank. Although it was late in the day after a long march, he launched a strong attack. Jackson, as always up with the forward troops, kept the momentum going and reached to within half a mile of Chancellor House at the centre of the village. Then in the muddle and mêlée of the fighting, Jackson was accidentally shot by his own troops. There followed another confused day's fighting, and then Hooker himself was injured, and from his sick bed he ordered his troops to withdraw. Jackson had been seriously wounded, and he was taken away for first-aid, and then further back away from danger of capture. His arm had to be amputated, and for some days he seemed to rally, but a few days later he died of pneumonia.

The northern industrial muscle of the Federal side may have made their victory inevitable, but many believe that if Jackson had lived the outcome of the war would have been very different. For the style of fighting in the Civil War, he was the character with flair, with leadership and panache, a sage strategist and fearless tactician – the perfect maverick commander.

GIUSEPPE GARIBALDI

How often has a guerrilla leader created a nation? Because of his military skill and passionately held convictions, Garibaldi played the most significant part in the *Risorgimento* – the struggle for the unification of Italy. With little education and even less formal military training, during the period 1848 to 1870 he upheld the cause of Italian unity, in the face of the dishonest and underhanded diplomacy of Cavour and King Victor Emmanuel of Piedmont, and of the other protagonists of unity. Decades later, when the Fascists tried to claim that they were heirs of the Garibaldi tradition, Mussolini – not renowned for light-hearted quips – said that it was as well that Garibaldi was virtually illiterate, because had he not been he would have read Clausewitz and so lost all his battles.

Against the reactionary arrogance of the monarchists of Piedmont and Naples, and the daunting power of the Catholic Church, Garibaldi kindled and kept alive the hopes of the Italian people. He created a situation in which the military power of Austria, which controlled most of northern Italy, the reactionary power of the Kingdom of Naples, which controlled southern Italy and Sicily, and France, the main support of the temporal power of the Papacy, were finally overcome. Garibaldi was the true maverick, who challenged and overcame the customs and traditions of decades of corrupt misrule in Italy. Napoleon by his reforms had given some hopes to patriotic Italians, but after his defeat, Metternich and the forces of reaction had strangled all aspirations to nationhood, and had restored reactionary priest-ridden regimes. It fell to Garibaldi to lead the campaign to overcome this and to establish Italian unity.

Born in 1807 at Nice, then a French possession, he was attracted, while still a boy, to the ideas of Mazzini and 'Young Italy'. For nearly ten years he worked aboard small trading vessels in the Black Sea and the Mediterranean, and then, after trying to cause a mutiny in the Piedmontese naval base at Genoa in 1834, he was exiled for sedition and fled first to North Africa and then to South America.

Here he soon plunged into the wars of liberation. On the open plains of Brazil and Argentina, he honed his skills in guerrilla warfare. A man of commanding presence, powerful physique, and with a stentorian voice, he fought for the republic of the Rio Grande, and quickly emerged as a successful guerrilla leader. He had a passionate sexual appetite, and his mistress Anita, whom he first spied through his telescope from his boat, shared his privations, fought in his campaigns and uncomplainingly bore his children. After several campaigns and the birth of two children they married in 1842.

Next he raised an Italian legion to fight for the independence of Uruguay, and his well-trained and fiercely disciplined legion had many successful clashes with the enemy. Here he established the red shirt – bought cheaply from the suppliers of the local slaughterhouses – as the uniform of his legion and, subsequently, of his Volunteers in Italy. He was

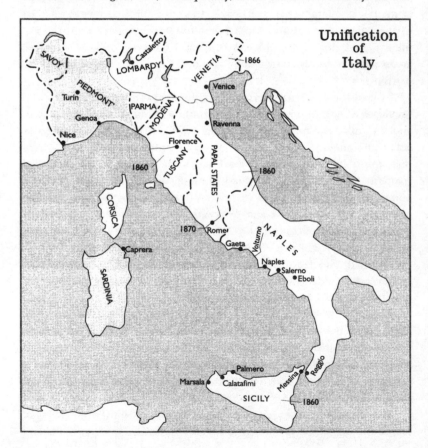

totally incorruptible, and as a general in the army of Uruguay he refused to draw his salary, even though Anita and his growing family lived in stark poverty during the years of the struggle for independence. Then he became sickened by the seedy corruption of the local politicians, and in April 1848 returned with his family and the coffin of their dead baby to Nice, which had been restored to Italy.

He returned not as an ignorant brigand, but as a charismatic leader with advanced and sophisticated views on the great issues of the day. Although he was spending his life fighting military campaigns, he realised the futility of war and nationalism, and looked forward to the unity of Europe. He supported women's rights and the rights of workers, and he opposed capital punishment. Although a guerrilla leader, he achieved world-wide respect and adulation. Later, Lincoln offered him a command during the American Civil War, and Gladstone and Palmerston supported him, while deploring the shady duplicity of Cavour. A century later Nehru looked to Garibaldi as an exemplar in the building of a new nation in India.

While Garibaldi was making his way home to Nice in the spring of 1848, revolutions were breaking out all over Europe. The people of Vienna drove out Metternich, the formidable Radetski was bundled out of Milan, Venice declared itself a republic, and the duchies of Parma and Modena drove out the Austrian garrisons. This was a situation Garibaldi had dreamt of, but when, after landing, he offered his services to Charles Albert, king of Piedmont, he was coldly received. Then when Charles Albert surrendered to Austria Garibaldi led guerrilla bands to attack Austrian troops in the foothills of the Alps. Eventually, with a few bedraggled followers, he reached Ravenna, about fifty miles south of Venice, but there was no uprising and no sign of support.

Garibaldi was rescued from this depressing situation by events in Rome. There the Pope's reactionary minister Rossi was shot, the people rose, drove out the Pope, and set up a republic. Soon afterwards, Garibaldi arrived in Rome with a large body of Volunteers to support Mazzini and the new republic. The Pope had immediately appealed for help to Roman Catholic countries, and France, in order to thwart Austria, rapidly responded. A strong French contingent landed in Italy and advanced on Rome. Their commanders foolishly expected to be welcomed as liberators, and were amazed when, as they approached the Vatican Hill, a cannon opened fire which brought them to a halt. Garibaldi saw his opportunity. Young student Volunteers facing companies of French regular troops had been swiftly dispersed, but Garibaldi called up more seasoned veterans and calmly rode out to lead a counter-attack. His presence inspired regulars and Volunteers alike, and they rushed at the startled French troops and forced them back up the road whence they had come. The French lost 500 killed or wounded, and 300 prisoners. Rome reacted wildly to this victory, and Garibaldi wanted to follow up his success, but he was not in overall command, and was prevented by Mazzini and the republican government. Experienced officers criticised the wild uncouth Volunteers, but soon saw how well Garibaldi installed effective discipline. They admired his 'patriarchal simplicity' as well as his brilliant guerrilla tactics. Another attack on Rome came from 5,000 Neapolitan troops, advancing from the south, and again Garibaldi led his men in a surprise assault on the marching columns. After several hours of hand-to-hand fighting the Neapolitans fled.

European politics then dictated events in Rome. The French, wishing to delay proceedings until more reinforcements arrived, sent de Lesseps – the builder of the Suez Canal – to negotiate. They offered to halt their troops, and also to prevent the Austrians and Neapolitans from attacking Rome. Mazzini's government were duped by this. They accepted the offer because reports were already reaching Rome of the barbarous behaviour of the advancing Austrian troops, who employed torture, rape and mutilation wherever they went. One Croat soldier marched through a village with a baby impaled on his bayonet.

The French duplicity was soon revealed: when their reinforcements including artillery arrived, they attacked. Mazzini then asked Garibaldi to command a section of the defences, but he, who had already witnessed one disaster caused by a timid elderly regular officer, refused to help unless he was put in overall command and given absolute powers. This was refused. The French announced that they would not attack before Monday 4 June 1849, but before dawn on the Sunday they attacked and overran the Villa Corsini – a key stronghold in the Roman defences. Garibaldi then offered to retake it. All approaches to the villa were difficult, and he decided that a frontal assault was the only possibility. Throughout a day of searing heat he sent wave after wave of young Volunteers to their death – mown down by the controlled fire of the disciplined French troops. Garibaldi was bitterly criticised by those who witnessed this hopeless carnage. He himself took part in one final disastrous attack which, almost miraculously, he survived. The people of Rome were furious at the French infamy, but the image of

Garibaldi sharing the dangers of that tragic day lived on and became the inspiration of the call throughout Italy – 'Rome or Death'.

Rome was virtually lost on 3 June, after which the French, having captured the Corsini Hill, could range their artillery on the rest of the city. Garibaldi commanded an area of defensive walls at the Janiculum, and he issued all his men with the red shirt which became their proud symbol. Under the almost constant barrage of French shells and bullets, he seemed almost to enjoy the danger, and his panache and leadership inspired devotion among the people. During the siege he clashed seriously with Mazzini and the high command. He did not believe that Rome could be defended against the professional forces of France and Austria, and he proposed that he and his Volunteers should fight their way out and continue guerrilla warfare on the enemy lines of communication. On 29 June the French launched a major assault, and Garibaldi, in the thick of hand-to-hand fighting, was finally beaten back. It was now agreed that Garibaldi and the Volunteers should break out. He addressed his men in challenging terms – effectively copied by Churchill in 1940: 'I offer hunger, cold, forced marches, battles and death. He who has the name of Italy in his heart follow me.'

In early July, the entry of the French caused an explosion of anger against the Pope and the priests, who were rightly blamed for the occupation. The American and British consuls, sympathetic to the cause of Italian unity, helped hundreds to escape the brutal suppression of the revolt by the French.

More than 3,000 ill-assorted Volunteers gathered at the Lateran Gate, and in total darkness Garibaldi led them out, accompanied by his beloved Anita who had come to join him in Rome. As they slunk away, Garibaldi had harsh words for the effeminate degenerates, who did not share his passion for a united Italy. His depleted band faced the ruthless opposition of French, Austrian and Spanish forces, which had rallied to the Pope's appeal. He used all his guerrilla skill to evade and confuse his pursuers. He used his horsemen to mislead, to spread rumours and false information, and to confuse the enemy about his line of march. He kept strict control of his group, but many marauding bands terrorised the area and exacerbated his problems. He raised forced loans from monasteries and towns without much prospect of ever repaying them, but he was briefly encouraged by the support of a rich and eccentric Englishman, Colonel Forbes – Oxford University and the Coldstream Guards – who had raised a regiment to support him. Nevertheless, his enemies were closing in, and his supporters were melting away. The Volunteers were frequently betrayed by priests, whom Garibaldi called 'pestilential scum'. With Forbes and Anita he reached the doubtful security of the independent state of San Marino.

Some of his followers accepted this refuge, for the Austrians shot every Volunteer they caught, but Garibaldi, with Forbes and Anita – now desperately ill – rode to the coast, hoping to find boats in which to reach Venice which was still holding out. They were exhausted and close to capture when a patriotic local landowner gave them shelter. Anita was now so ill that Garibaldi refused to leave her. She died in his arms. He wept uncontrollably.

The farmer promised to bury Anita, and Garibaldi left and fled into the forests of Ravenna. At a critical moment he was again helped by a patriot who refused the large reward the Austrians had offered. At last, exhausted and deeply distressed by the death of Anita, Garibaldi reached Genoa. Then, still feeling that he was a hunted fugitive, he refused sanctuary in Spain, in Gibraltar and in Tunis. Finally, he fled to Tangier, where he recuperated for a few months before leaving for New York.

His arrival there in 1850 was the start of a futile and frustrating period in his life. Crippled by rheumatism, he eked out a miserable existence doing various menial jobs. In Italy there were a number of ineffective republican uprisings, but Garibaldi slowly came to the view that the best hope for Italian unity would be based on the nucleus of the Kingdom of Piedmont under Victor Emmanuel.

During this depressing time he returned to Italy and went to Sardinia. Here he purchased part of an isolated and inhospitable island called Caprera. With a few close friends, he tried to establish a simple farm with vines, olives, corn, vegetables and goats. He took on a peasant girl, Ballistina, as his servant, and she became his mistress and bore him several children.

The fate of Italy now fell into the hands of three colourful characters: the able, ruthless, machiavellian Cavour, prime minister of Piedmont; the crude, powerful, lecherous Victor Emmanuel, king of Piedmont; and Louis Napoleon, nephew of the great Napoleon, and now himself emperor of France. They all intrigued in their different ways, but all three saw that Garibaldi with his popular appeal could be used to forward the cause. Cavour schemed to obtain French military support to drive the Austrians out of northern Italy, and hoped that this would lead to further moves towards unity. His ruthless and disreputable schemes roused anger across

Europe, but the Austrians played into his hands by issuing an impossible ultimatum (April 1859), and then declaring war.

Cavour had already contacted Garibaldi, who came to Turin in an excited mood, and set about raising Volunteers. The king appointed him a major-general in the Piedmontese army. He was to command two brigades – approximately 3,000 men – but he found, as Wingate and the Chindits were later to find, that the regular army were loath to give arms and equipment to guerrillas whose only role, they considered, was to blow up bridges and cut telegraph wires. Cavour, who needed the impetus given by Garibaldi's popular appeal, insisted that he be better treated, but also schemed to ensure that Garibaldi did not receive too much credit for any success.

On 29 April 1859, a large Austrian army invaded Piedmont. The incompetence and poor leadership of the Austrian invaders were matched by those of the regular Piedmontese army. In contrast, Garibaldi, ignoring Cavour's orders, and using the freedom offered him by Victor Emmanuel, marched his Volunteers through the night and won a brilliant minor victory by capturing the town of Castaletto at the southern tip of Lake Maggiore. He then advanced eastwards and won another encounter with the Austrians at Varese. The Volunteers, with Garibaldi at their head, then advanced towards Lake Como. They made a wild and reckless charge and drove the Austrians out of a key small town. When they advanced silently for a night attack on Como itself, the entire population rose in a storm of excitement and euphoria. The Austrians left without a fight, abandoning a large store of arms, equipment and food.

While the people rose ecstatically to Garibaldi, and his victories near the lakes were significant, the real issue was decided elsewhere. The French and Piedmontese armies fought two major battles against the Austrians at Magenta and Solferino, and the appalling carnage at these battles prompted Henry Dunant to found the Red Cross organisation. All the participants now agreed to the peace treaty of Villafranca, but other European factors obtruded. Austria gave up Lombardy, but the Italian patriots were bitterly disappointed that no further steps to unity were achieved, and Cavour in fury resigned. In the turbulent and confusing weeks after Villafranca, the terms of which were rejected by most Italians, Garibaldi was invited to command troops in central Italy, but no further risings took place. Next, after falling in love with an eighteen-year-old girl, and making a fool of himself at a sham wedding, he returned to Caprera.

Some years before, Gladstone had visited Naples and focused attention on the brutal, corrupt, reactionary rule of King Ferdinand of Naples who ruled over southern Italy and Sicily. Italy seethed with frustration and intrigue, and a few abortive attempts were made to overthrow Ferdinand, but all failed. Garibaldi gave some impetus to the patriots by appealing for the 'Million Rifle Fund', but although many people asked him to strike, he remembered his suffering and humiliation at Ravenna in the spring of 1848, and refused to act until the people did something for themselves.

This stalemate was suddenly and unexpectedly resolved. In a secret treaty, Cavour, in return for French help in the battles against Austria, had promised to cede Nice and Savoy to France. This deal now became public, and Garibaldi, who had been born in Nice, claimed that he was 'made a stranger in the land of my birth'. He was so furious that he sent an insubordinate telegram to King Victor Emmanuel, and left at once for Genoa. He intended to raid Nice and destroy all ballot boxes in which the people had to vote, but was finally persuaded to stay his hand.

He went instead with a few trusted companions to a little seaport near Genoa, where he had strong support. It was believed that he might lead an expedition to Sicily. The situation was complex and difficult. Victor Emmanuel remained equivocal, and Cavour - now prime minister of Piedmont again - was forced officially to disapprove of any action Garibaldi might take. Cavour realised that if Garibaldi and his Volunteers did raise a revolt in Sicily and southern Italy, it could pose a direct threat to the Pope – still protected in Rome by French military force. This could ruin Cavour's political schemes.

'Garibaldi and the Thousand', one of the most successful guerrilla operations of the 19th century, started with near farce and disaster. Two small steamers were due to pick up Garibaldi and his 1,000 Volunteers at midnight on 5 May 1860. One ship's engine broke down, the loading of arms and supplies went wrong. The steamers eventually left in broad daylight next day in a strong swell which made most of the Volunteers violently sick. Few expeditions can have had such an inauspicious start.

It was generally expected that the expedition would make for Sicily, where there had already been some unsuccessful uprisings against the rule of Ferdinand of Naples, but Garibaldi intended to call in at various small ports in Tuscany to pick up supplies and more supporters. He and his second-in-command, Nino Bixio, used these occasions to impose a fearsome discipline on their ill-assorted troops, and to organise them into companies and battalions. Garibaldi also sent a small diversionary force to the Papal States, but this was a complete disaster. He had the charisma and the prestige to carry men with him, although when he announced the watchword 'Italy and Victor Emmanuel', some of his more staunchly republican supporters deserted the cause.

At last, on 9 May 1860, the two steamers left the coast of Tuscany and headed for Sicily. The expedition had not only to find a secure landing place, but also to elude Neapolitan warships, which were actively seeking them. As the Volunteers approached Marsala, at the western tip of Sicily, they were alarmed to see two cruisers, but the experienced Garibaldi realised that they were British. There followed a series of almost Gilbertian incidents. A Neapolitan frigate approached Marsala and, spotting two British warships, assumed that the Volunteers disembarking were British redcoats. Then the Neapolitan captain was asked by the British not to fire any shots near the Marsala wine warehouse. With these and other diversions the Thousand managed to scramble ashore without loss.

In the little town of Marsala the people remained coldly indifferent, but once the Thousand started marching towards the capital, Palermo, they were joined by armed groups of Sicilians, who had already risen against the hated Neapolitan government. When Garibaldi entered a small hill town, Salemi, it was publicly proclaimed that he was the dictator – the new ruler of Sicily.

Facing the Thousand in Sicily were 25,000 Neapolitan troops, but they were led by officers who were old, incompetent and afraid. On 15 May the Neapolitans mustered about 3,000 men supported by artillery at Calatafimi, about thirty miles from Palermo, but their commander was pathetically indecisive, and merely marched about the countryside.

As Garibaldi and the Volunteers approached Calatafimi, a small well-led Neapolitan unit attacked them. After an exchange of fire, the Volunteers rushed down the hill into the enemy line, and then continued their charge up a steep hill covered in olive trees, cactus and vines. The struggle on this hillside continued for several hours, and the Volunteers, ill-prepared for prolonged action, were gradually losing ground. Even the ferocious Bixio told Garibaldi that they would have to retreat. Garibaldi rebuked him furiously, saying: 'Here we shall make Italy or die.'

He gathered about 300 weary and dispirited men and, believing wrongly that the enemy were out of ammunition, climbed a bank and led a charge up the hill. At the top there was more fierce hand-to-hand fighting with

Garibaldi and Bixio in the lead. The enemy gradually gave way. The Volunteers lost 30 men killed and more than 100 wounded, but they had won a decisive and significant victory, news of which spread all over Sicily and beyond. The defeated Neapolitans withdrew towards Palermo.

As the Volunteers advanced they saw evidence of the brutality of the Neapolitan troops, who had gone through the villages burning and raping in an orgy of destruction. They saw, too, the equally brutal reprisals of the people against the troops. The euphoria after the victory of Calatafimi did not last. As the Thousand advanced they faced some strongly held positions, and after three days of torrential rain and more casualties, the fire of their enthusiasm burned low. When the Neapolitans repulsed their attacks and drove them back, deep divisions emerged between the Sicilians and the northerners.

The campaign of Garibaldi and the Thousand is remarkably well documented, and there are vivid eye-witness descriptions of his battles, notably by Royal Naval officers, who were present at Marsala, Palermo and elsewhere. In Palermo the British consul and Admiral Mundy, RN, visited the governor, seeking assurance for the safety of British subjects, only to be told the town would be bombarded if the people rose in support of Garibaldi. As the Thousand drew closer to Palermo, most villages gave their positive support. Some British Naval officers and the correspondent of *The Times* were able to stroll up the hill and wander into Garibaldi's headquarters which, they said, resembled a gypsy encampment. While they were there he learned that although there were powerful units of the Neapolitan army some miles away, there were very few reliable troops in Palermo where a weakly defended gate could be approached by a narrow path. Having checked that the Sicilian groups would support him, he decided to lead an attack that night.

The original Thousand had been reduced to 700, and many of these had been wounded, but when the attack began the Sicilian partisans numbered nearly 3,000. Many of these were an ill-disciplined rabble who nearly caused disaster by firing their flintlocks and alerting the garrison. When the defenders opened fire, many of them ran away. At this critical moment Garibaldi called for an advance to the centre of the city. Following his lead, their momentum carried them forward over a small river where, disciplined fire from behind a barrier caused casualties and again the advance wavered. Once again Garibaldi came to the fore and led another charge which overcame the barricade. Then Volunteers and Sicilians together poured into the city and spread through all the streets. Gradually the cowed population ventured out and began to lend support, but the governor ordered Neapolitan ships in the harbour to open fire and large areas of the city were flattened. The fighting continued for days, with Garibaldi directing operations from the front. He remained amazingly calm although the excitable Bixio had been wounded. His calm presence was sorely needed, for although the people were giving some support, the Neapolitan troops were strongly entrenched near the cathedral, and his dubious allies had used up much precious ammunition firing in the air. On the third day of fighting the Neapolitan troops launched a serious counter-attack and pushed the Volunteers back some considerable distance. Seeing his entire position endangered, Garibaldi led a furious charge against the regular troops and forced them back to the cathedral. This gave a brief respite, but his situation was now desperate, because large Neapolitan units were advancing into Palermo. The Neapolitan commander, who had lost some 1,000 killed or wounded, had never heard the admirable military precept – repeated by Mad Mike Calvert during the Second World War at the battle of Mogaung in Burma – that however bad your situation, the enemy's is probably worse. Just when Garibaldi faced almost certain disaster, the Neapolitan commander asked for a truce, and it was agreed that they should meet aboard Admiral Mundy's ship.

Mundy was to play a significant role in the conference which included representatives of the navies of France and the USA. The Neapolitan military commander Letizia first demanded that the French and Americans should leave, and then refused to speak to Garibaldi. Gradually Garibaldi's calm and imposing presence, and the firm determination of Admiral Mundy, put an end to Letizia's antics, and a truce was agreed. Despite the truce, Garibaldi was still in a very weak position, and if fighting had broken out again he would certainly have been defeated. As the truce held, more and more of the population came out in open support, and Garibaldi was hailed as a hero and a deliverer. He is believed to have solved one major problem by discreetly obtaining a large supply of gunpowder from the American ship. Even then the danger was not over, and he addressed vast crowds, exhorting them to help by putting up barricades against the Neapolitan troops, who had treacherously taken over some areas of the town under cover of the truce. Then, when another attack could easily have overrun Garibaldi's position, the feeble governor asked for an extension of the truce. Garibaldi agreed, provided that the contents Sicilian treasury be handed over. The extension of the truce, insisted on by the pathetic Neapolitan commanders, brought about their final defeat in Sicily, and on 7 June they started to withdraw from Palermo. During the next ten days the troops were pulled out and evacuated to Naples. At the same time another large contingent of Volunteers arrived – 2,500 strong and well armed.

With Palermo safely in his hands Garibaldi enjoyed a period of euphoria and adulation – the people flocked to him, and the bishops and even the nuns blessed him. There were still pockets of resistance elsewhere in the island and three columns were despatched to eliminate opposition, to establish the authority of Garibaldi the new dictator, and to gain material support. The most significant column operated eastwards along the north coast towards Messina. It eventually reached Milazzo, a very small port, about twelve miles west of Messina. In the meantime Cavour and Victor Emmanuel had been handling the volatile political situation created by Garibaldi's victories. While keen on the possibility of Piedmont taking over Naples and Sicily from the reactionary and unpopular King Ferdinand, they were afraid that if Garibaldi succeeded on the mainland there could be another uprising against the Pope – still protected in Rome by French bayonets.

At Milazzo the Neapolitans had an efficient unit of 2,500 men supported by artillery and even a cavalry squadron. The Volunteers attacking them included young men from many European countries and a so-called English regiment commanded by a Colonel Dunne, though it contained only a handful of British youths. Garibaldi's remarkable bravery in the heat of battle could easily have been a legend created after his great victories, but many English eye-witnesses testified at the time to the amazing impact his bravery and leadership had on all his men. When he led a charge, no one hesitated to follow him. This was certainly the case at the battle of Milazzo.

Milazzo lay across a narrow neck of land facing north. Garibaldi planned an attack with three columns, one in the centre, and one along the beach on each side. As they advanced, all three columns came under heavy fire and suffered casualties. Garibaldi took over the right-hand column, but although he was able to lead them forward, his group were effectively held up near a fish factory on the beach. He accepted that further progress was impossible at this point, and to the surprise of his companions sat down, washed his sweaty shirt in a stream and ate his lunch of bread and fruit. After smoking a cigar, he went to assess the situation on the left flank where the column had also been held up. There he found a small ship, the *Tukory*, anchored off the beach. It had ten guns and had recently deserted the Neapolitan navy to come to the support of the Volunteers. Garibaldi rowed out to the ship and was greeted enthusiastically. The captain readily agreed to approach the town and bombard the enemy positions.

The bombardment soon started, and in the late afternoon Garibaldi ordered all three columns to advance, and the troops were surprised to encounter very little enemy fire. Later it was found that when the off-shore bombardment started, the timorous colonel in charge had withdrawn all his men to a castle on the cliff edge. By evening the entire town was in the hands of the Volunteers, and barricades had been put up to fend off any counter-attack from the castle.

The brief bombardment of the little ship *Tukory* had amazing repercussions. The Neapolitan commanders became convinced that they could no longer hold out against Garibaldi's forces, even though they had 15,000 regular troops in Messina. Their débâcle was compounded by dithering feebleness from the king's government in Naples, which could not decide whether to withdraw the troops or order them to fight on. On 28 July they agreed to a truce and the withdrawal of all their forces from Sicily.

The weak vacillation of the Neapolitan army and government may give the erroneous impression that the campaign in Sicily had been a walkover. This was not the case. British visitors to Milazzo on the day after the battle, which had cost the Volunteers 800 killed or seriously wounded, described the sufferings of the young Volunteers – some as young as twelve – who lay in hospital, some with arms or legs amputated, and screaming in agony because there were no proper surgical instruments and no pain-killers.

A brief lull followed the truce, while the British, French and Austrian governments reviewed the situation. Louis Napoleon suggested an Anglo-French naval blockade to prevent Garibaldi crossing to the mainland. Great Britain was generally sympathetic to the campaign for Italian unity, and objected to this proposal. Victor Emmanuel wrote personally to Garibaldi forbidding him to cross to the mainland, but then wrote again to say that it would be all right if he did. Garibaldi, in a dignified reply, said that he felt he had to disobey the king on this one occasion, but if he succeeded in overthrowing the Kingdom of Naples, he would lay the territory and his sword at the feet of Victor Emmanuel. In Naples Cavour was actively stirring up trouble in an attempt to prevent a situation whereby a strongly republican force was seen to bestow such a gift on the king.

During the weeks after the truce in July 1860, Garibaldi, facing political rather than military problems, seemed to lose his calm, cheerful confidence. He even went off briefly to Caprera to see his mistress and their baby and look after his cattle. Then, as a result of strong republican support from all over Italy, he received several thousand reinforcements of a higher quality, and soon was able to plan an expedition of 3,500 men with two steamers from a small port just south of Messina.

The two ships, *Torino* and *Franklin*, sailed on 18 August, crammed with men and supplies. On a moonless night, they crossed to the mainland without incident, reaching the Calabrian coast before dawn and anchoring ten miles south of Reggio, the administrative capital – in almost the exact spot where part of Montgomery's Eighth Army landed in September 1943. In command of the troops facing Garibaldi was another elderly and windy general. He confined most of his troops to the castle with a small field force in the town square. The castle itself was in a precarious position overlooked from the main part of the town.

On 20 August at midnight, the Volunteers made a sudden and violent attack on the square. The Neapolitan commanding officer and his son were both killed, and Bixio was wounded twice. The Volunteers lost more than 100 men but the town was taken. Neapolitan reinforcements from the north, tardily approaching, were driven off and the remaining enemy forces were besieged in the castle. Garibaldi used snipers to pick off the gunners firing from the ramparts, and soon the whole garrison surrendered. News of the success at Reggio spread rapidly across the country and a wave of excitement brought more positive support. Another large group of Volunteers from Sicily then crossed the Strait of Messina – the Scylla and Charybdis of Odysseus – in a flotilla of rowing boats, safely eluding the Neapolitan patrols. After this, on both land and sea, operations by the Volunteers were helped immeasurably by information about the enemy, eagerly provided by the people.

Garibaldi, after worrying and frustrating weeks at Messina, was now elated by his success, and led his men forward with quiet determination. As he approached each town there was occasionally some desultory firing, but usually the white flag would be hoisted. After the Neapolitan troops had surrendered their weapons, Garibaldi would address them and offer them the chance of joining the Volunteers or starting their long walk home. He himself, having been vilified by the Pope as the anti-Christ, or the devil himself, was now approached by the downtrodden and superstitious people of Calabria as if he were divine. He was openly called the second Jesus Christ. As his forces advanced rapidly northwards some influential landowners joined the cause, and ambushed the retreating Neapolitan troops, who usually surrendered without a fight. Few wanted to give their lives for such a discredited regime.

For most of the advance Garibaldi and a very small group of close supporters, including two English colonels, Forbes and Peard, charged ahead of his main forces. He was spurred on by his determination to reach Naples before the wily Cavour, who still did not trust Garibaldi, could organise some obstruction to this progress and, instead, claim the victory for Victor Emmanuel. The most remarkable aspect of this advance, when most of the Volunteers were hungry and exhausted, was the level of discipline, imposed by Garibaldi himself. There was no looting, and an English observer saw a man shot for stealing a bunch of grapes. Garibaldi said, 'We cannot steal from our own people.'

The Volunteers had advanced through the central part of the country, but then veered over to the west coast for a short distance, and back inland for the final headlong rush for Naples. Garibaldi was leading their approach to one town where there was a large concentration of Neapolitan troops. The Volunteers advanced in tense silence, but the enemy troops were sitting or lolling about in the town centre and made no attempt to fight, but weakly handed over weapons, ammunition, horses, cannon, food and money.

Some English Volunteers who had joined the expedition as a bit of a lark, did not take kindly to the severe privations, and when they eventually reached Naples became a drunken rabble. In contrast, Colonel Peard commanded a disciplined and effective unit. He was a tall bearded man, and was frequently mistaken for Garibaldi. He too was called the second Jesus Christ. At Eboli, about forty miles south of Naples, because of his likeness to Garibaldi, he was able to play a decisive role in the advance. The officials assumed he was Garibaldi, and he went to the town centre and seized the telegraph office. He reckoned that the substantial Neapolitan forces would take a stand at Salerno – about halfway between Eboli and Naples. So he telegraphed to the Minister of War in Naples saying that 10,000 Volunteers were in the area and advising Neapolitan forces to withdraw. He took an incoming inquiry about a Neapolitan division and replied that they had all gone over to Garibaldi. Peard's friend Forbes was with him and told him not to waste his time, because no one would be fool enough to believe such rubbish. Forbes was wrong, for within hours Salerno was evacuated. Peard entered Salerno, and, with a great laugh, appeared with Garibaldi on a dais in the city centre. Eighty-three years later Salerno was not to be taken so easily.

In Naples, King Ferdinand presided over a mess of corruption and disloyalty. As the Volunteers approached, he could not decide whether to send his troops to oppose them, or to withdraw northwards to the defensive area of the River Volturno. Still vacillating, on 4 September he and his wife left by ship for Gaeta, a port halfway between Naples and Rome, and close to the line of the Volturno. His prime minister, having encouraged the king to fight, as soon as he left sent an effusive telegram to Garibaldi inviting him to enter Naples.

Garibaldi then showed the most remarkable qualities of bravery and leadership. Obsessed by the need to reach Naples swiftly, he ordered a special train, and with a handful of Volunteers, and almost overwhelmed by cheering and ecstatic supporters, directed it to the centre of Naples. He knew that the station lay well within the range of cannon from the fortress, but he did not hesitate. From the station, still surrounded by cheering, screaming crowds, he went in an open carriage towards the fortress. The guns remained silent. From the fortress he went to the main square, and in his magnificent voice spoke movingly of 'a day of glory when a people passes from servitude to the rank of a free nation'. After his speech, which brought tears to the eyes of some English visitors, he went to the cathedral to attend mass – to show that he opposed the Pope as an obstacle to the unification of Italy, but that he did not oppose the Church. There followed several days of fiesta with crowds, day and night, cheering exultantly.

The mood of euphoria did not last, and serious problems arose. In Naples it was difficult to discipline the Volunteers, and ruffians and criminals from all over the country soon arrived there to exploit the general chaos. Garibaldi was at his worst when facing complex civil problems, and very soon, because of his impetuous and arrogant dictates and the unwise actions of his senior staff, the delirious delight with which he had been greeted rapidly turned to sour disillusionment.

He was soon weighed down by the great political issues of the day. The staunch republican Mazzini arrived to advocate a march on Rome. Victor Emmanuel, equivocal as ever, hoped Garibaldi would advance north from Naples and stop short of Rome. Admiral Mundy, who had chaired the conference at Messina, now appeared again. Prompted by the British government, he conferred with Garibaldi, who in spite of all advice, remained obdurate that he would march on Rome. The European powers all feared that if he did attack Rome, the French would easily defeat him and this could lead to a European war. With the fresh and gruesome memories of the Crimean War only four years before, no one wanted this. Garibaldi realistically admitted that he would face an extremely formidable test at the Volturno, where 40,000 loyal Neapolitan troops held an ideal defensive line, including a fortress built by the great French military engineer Vauban. The Volunteers had been joined by a great rabble of dubious supporters, but Garibaldi thought he could muster about 20,000 reasonably effective fighters. While he pondered these problems, Cavour seized the initiative. Worried that Garibaldi might attack the French and lose every advance that had been made for Italian unity, on 11 September Cavour ordered the Piedmontese army to invade the Papal States. He had previously assured Louis Napoleon that he was taking this action only to prevent Garibaldi reaching Rome and attacking the French garrison. In a brief campaign the Piedmontese army drove back the papal forces which were commanded by a French general.

The line of the Volturno, which ran through the small town of Capua, was the scene of Garibaldi's final battle with the Neapolitan forces. On 1 October 1860 the Neapolitans advanced from the north over the river, and in a controlled night march moved out of Capua towards the Volunteers' positions around the small towns of Santa Maria and Caserta. Garibaldi, who had enjoyed great success as an attacking guerrilla leader, now had to conduct a defensive battle against a large and powerful enemy. Soon after dawn, the Neapolitan troops advanced against Santa Maria and were driving back the Volunteers, when Garibaldi arrived. He immediately led a charge against the Neapolitans and routed their forward units. As soon as the line was stable, he rushed off to another part of the line, which was also under pressure, and to the amazement of his own side and the enemy, he led one charge after another – a classic example of attack being the best means of defence. Both French and English observers described the effect Garibaldi had on his troops and how, frequently, he turned defeat into victory.

Close-quarter fighting continued throughout much of the day around Santa Maria and Caserta, with heavy casualties on both sides. Bixio, who was commanding the right flank of the Volunteers, had a close and hard-fought struggle against the ablest of the Neapolitan commanders, Von Mechel. He had created a situation where the Volunteers, could easily have been defeated, but his second-in-command, who was in reserve with 5,000 uncommitted troops, failed to move forward. At the same time Garibaldi, leading the battle from the left flank at Santa Maria, prepared a final bayonet charge.

At that moment an intrepid English lady tourist appeared and offered Garibaldi a glass of water. She had come to the scene of the battle with a group of English sailors, who had a day's leave from Admiral Mundy's ship, HMS *Hannibal*. They just wanted to witness the excitement, and asked if someone could give them some muskets. Garibaldi's campaign excited terrific interest in England, and many English visitors witnessed the battles. This, with some of the battles of the American Civil War, were the last times such observation was possible, before it was ended by the more serious carnage of the Franco-Prussian War in 1870.

For his final charge Garibaldi was able to bring together some effective troops, including a squad of English Volunteers led by Colonel Eber, and nearly 200 Hungarian cavalry, who rode horses which had been handed over by the Neapolitans after a previous battle. This charge against tired, hungry and dispirited Neapolitan soldiers finally broke their resistance, and they fled back to Capua.

Having driven the enemy from the field, Garibaldi remained in a very exposed position, with powerful enemy forces still holding Capua and the Volturno line. As had happened at Calatafimi and many times afterwards, it was lack of determination, feebleness and cowardice among the Neapolitan commanders which made possible Garibaldi's striking victories. His victory at Volturno had been won at a grievous cost. The Neapolitans lost more than 1,000 killed and wounded, and 2,000 prisoners, but the Volunteers had lost 2,000 killed and wounded. The latter were the least fortunate, there being no medical or hospital facilities. Several English women who had witnessed some of the battle now tried to do something to alleviate the pitiable condition of the wounded. These ladies were appalled that the people in Caserta, and also in Naples, who professed to being supporters of the Volunteers, did nothing whatsoever to help – not even bringing water to wounded men lying in the streets.

Garibaldi had won a clear victory at the Volturno battle, but it achieved little. Large contingents of the Neapolitan army still held Capua and Gaeta, and there was no possibility of the Volunteers marching on Rome.

Cavour again seized the initiative. Recognising the fierce welter of conflicting opinions surrounding Garibaldi in Naples, and realising that the idea of Italian unity under Victor Emmanuel and Piedmont was not universally popular in southern Italy, he quickly organised a referendum. On 21 October, the people had to answer 'yes' or 'no' to the simple question: 'Do you want a united Italy under Victor Emmanuel?' This clever ruse was strongly opposed by the diehard republican Mazzini, by many veteran Volunteers, and initially by Garibaldi himself, but the idea of a united Italy carried all before it. There were very few noes.

Garibaldi came to realise that, despite all his successes, it would be impossible for him to seize Rome and Venetia, and he reluctantly went along with Cavour's idea that he should meet Victor Emmanuel, and virtually hand over all he had achieved. Thus on 26 October 1860, less than a month after the Volturno battle, Garibaldi and his senior commanders rode north over the Volturno and met Victor Emmanuel and his generals on a modest country road. The king was courteous – his generals less so. The king and Garibaldi rode some way together, but it became too embarrassing because all the local people who saw the procession kept shouting 'Viva Garibaldi'. Soon afterwards, to avoid any more embarrassment, Garibaldi rode off back to his base near Naples.

In the confusing days which followed, violent tensions erupted between the Volunteers and the Piedmontese military leaders. General Fanti, who was in command of the Piedmontese army, was openly contemptuous of Garibaldi and the Volunteers. Garibaldi was infuriated at the cavalier way his veterans were treated, though a considerable number did join the Piedmontese army and later rose to high rank.

After a short time, Garibaldi, hating the tension and ill-feeling, decided to return to Caprera. Before he left he went to visit Admiral Mundy aboard the *Hannibal*. He expressed his deep gratitude for the admiral's help and support, but then, in an impassioned outburst, vilified Cavour and the Piedmontese, swearing he could never rest until Rome and Venetia were part of a united Italy. He left the ship and was rowed over to the *Washington* which was going to take him back to Caprera. In a venal age Garibaldi remained incorruptible. He had been offered riches, possessions and honours. He refused them all, and went off to Caprera with two horses, a few groceries and a box of macaroni.

On Caprera, with a few close friends who helped him extend the farmhouse and tend his farm and garden, he lived a modest simple life. After working in his garden he would go to the harbour and catch fish for supper. He received letters from all over the world. Queen Victoria and Lord John

Russell wrote. From the USA Abraham Lincoln offered him a senior command in the army. Garibaldi, still bedevilled by his own arrogance, refused the offer unless Lincoln made him commander-in-chief and immediately freed the slaves. Garibaldi's isolation on Caprera did not curb his popularity. Tourists came to obtain souvenirs, and romantic young women requested locks of his hair – requests that were rarely refused.

This idyllic interlude did not last. He soon gave in to demands that he should go to Turin as a delegate, to protest at the way the people of the south were being treated by the northern government. In his first speech in the Turin parliament, in the presence of Cavour and senior ministers, he made a violent attack on the government which resulted in uproar and turmoil. He demanded a huge corps of Volunteers to march on Rome and Venetia. This outburst caused violent antagonism involving the king, Cavour, and a senior general who challenged Garibaldi to a duel. In government circles Garibaldi was detested – the more so when Cavour, who had been the main target of his wrath, had a breakdown and died shortly afterwards.

After Cavour's death in 1861 the political situation remained turbulent and volatile. Without Cavour's cunning and ruthless control, the government became increasingly unstable and unpredictable. On more than one occasion, it encouraged Garibaldi to rouse the people, and even supported the idea of a campaign against the Austrians in Venetia, only to disown him at a critical moment. Then Garibaldi visited Sicily and Naples for a tour of the Thousand's battlefields and this stirred up dangerous enthusiasms – always on the theme 'Rome or Death'.

Then came the most poignant moment of his life. With the probable collusion of the authorities, he led another expedition from Sicily to Calabria, intending to march on Rome. With a sudden change of policy the government sent a military force of seven regular battalions to stop him. Garibaldi continued his advance – unable to believe that an Italian unit would ever oppose him. Then, at Aspromonte, in a miserable skirmish, in which he was trying to stop the firing, he was hit in the foot and collapsed. His captors treated him with respect, and he was carried to hospital, although some of his followers were rounded up and shot. A wave of sympathy and indignation swept across the country and the world. Gifts of books and cigars arrived every day in his hospital room. In England public subscriptions paid for eminent doctors to attend to his foot. After his wound had slowly healed he was able to return to Caprera in December 1861.

In England there had always been great enthusiasm for Garibaldi, and in 1864 he came on a private visit, although, as *The Times* pointed out, no official visitor had ever had such a rapturous reception. Wherever he went thousands flocked to cheer him. The aristocracy and members of the government lionised him, and the working people greeted him as their greatest hero. Gladstone, Palmerston, Florence Nightingale, Tennyson and the Prince of Wales all visited him, and spoke of his serene and noble dignity. Women of all classes were infatuated by him, and one swooned when she found a handkerchief he had dropped. He was the guest of honour at countless banquets and he was elected a Freeman of the City of London.

Garibaldi had always been the champion of downtrodden people – notably those of Poland, Hungary and Denmark – and he publicly expressed his support for their cause. This and his rapturous reception by the establishment caused a suspicious reaction from Prussia, Russia, Austria and France. Queen Victoria, under pressure from her royal cousins scattered across Europe, strongly disapproved of the adulation given to Garibaldi, and reprimanded the Prince of Wales for becoming a part of it. Fairly soon Garibaldi, bored by the interminable speeches, and concerned at the apparent cooling of the government's attitude, decided to leave. He visited Cornwall to see Colonel Peard, who had fought valiantly with the Thousand, and then sailed back to Caprera in the Duke of Sutherland's yacht.

By 1865, when he was back in Caprera, Garibaldi was still obsessed by the thought that although most of Italy was united Venetia and Rome still lay in foreign hands. In 1866 Victor Emanuel had made an alliance with Prussia against Austria, and Garibaldi was invited to lead a campaign in the Trentino. He achieved some minor success, but the main Italian armies were easily defeated by the Austrians at Custozza. In contrast, the Prussians annihilated the Austrian forces at the battle of Königgrätz in 1866, and at the Peace of Prague, which followed, forced Austria to hand over Venetia. By this time Garibaldi was sick and racked by rheumatism so badly that he could only move with the help of a crutch. Despite these disabilities and the strong discouragement of all his friends, he embarked on a hare-brained scheme to march on Rome. Believing he had the tacit support of Victor Emmanuel, who as always let him down, he crossed the frontier of the Papal States. The entire project was ill-considered and his pathetic forces were slaughtered by the modern weapons of the French garrison in

Rome. His followers suffered severely, but Garibaldi was taken back to Caprera yet again.

The end of the struggle for Italian unity came suddenly and unexpectedly. Bismarck engineered a war with France in 1870, and quickly defeated Louis Napoleon at the battle of Sedan. France faced a major defeat, and with Prussia investing Paris, had to call on every available soldier. Thus the French garrison was withdrawn from Rome. On 3 November 1870 Bixio, now a general in the Italian army, shared the glory of marching into Rome. Garibaldi remained in Caprera, but now that Louis Napoleon had been overthrown and a French republic established, he offered his services to the new French government. His offer was accepted and he commanded a force operating in the area of the Vosges mountains, fairly far away from the main battles around Paris. He achieved a few minor successes - remembered by a plaque in Dijon – and gained the respect of his Prussian opponents. He returned to Caprera at the end of 1870.

In his final years, though disabled and in poor health, he kept up an active correspondence on many major issues – trade unions, the International Court of Justice, education, capital punishment and many others. From time to time he sent rather arrogant messages to the new parliament. At times he became bitter and misanthropic because the united Italy had not achieved the things he had hoped for. He led a sad life beset by family problems and by the deaths of his old companions. As he approached death, he asked to be quickly burned on a fire of acacia and his ashes kept near his family vault. He was denied this wish. His funeral in May 1882 was attended by senior representatives of the Italian royal family, the government, the army and diplomats from all over the world, illustrating the continuing admiration for him as a man, as the inspirer and catalyst of a united Italy, and as their bravest military hero.

LAWRENCE OF ARABIA

The fame and the legend of T. E. Lawrence rests largely on his exploits in Arabia during the First World War, when he supported the Arab Revolt against the Turks. He described the revolt in his book *The Seven Pillars of Wisdom*. In the first edition he wrote: 'This does not pretend to be impartial'. In fact it was a romanticised description, heavily slanted in favour of Faisal and the cause of the Hashemite dynasty. After the war he gained further brief fame by his appearance with Faisal at the Versailles Conference. After this he sought anonymity and oblivion by enlisting as an aircraftsman in the Royal Air Force under the assumed names of J. H. Ross and later T. E. Shaw – perhaps to hide his embarrassment over the repercussions of his sado-masochistic activities with young men.

His over-sensitive nature had always been burdened in the snobbish society of Edwardian England with the knowledge that he was illegitimate. His father had abandoned his shrewish wife in Ireland and set up home with Sarah, a strong and devout Scottish girl who had been the family nanny. To safeguard their secret, they took the name of 'Lawrence'. They moved several times in England and briefly in France before settling at Oxford. Sarah, Lawrence's mother, conscious of her humble status, was socially withdrawn, but was strongly evangelical and established a sternly puritanical regime in the home. Lawrence, known to the family as Ned, rather resented his mother's domination, but her ascetic standards stayed with him.

Born in 1888, he went to Oxford High School in 1896, and in 1907 was awarded an exhibition in history to Jesus College Oxford. Here he developed a strong interest in the medieval world and undertook many expeditions in Britain and France, studying churches and medieval warfare. A brilliant tutor, Hogarth, encouraged his interest in the Middle East and helped him to arrange a visit to Syria. Lawrence's report helped him to gain a first in history in 1910. After he left Oxford, with Hogarth's help, he spent most of the next four years in the Middle East. He learned Arabic and became an outstanding but eccentric leader of many archaeological digs. He took part in several foolhardy expeditions in a generally lawless area. At Oxford he had had fairly close links with a homosexual group known as the

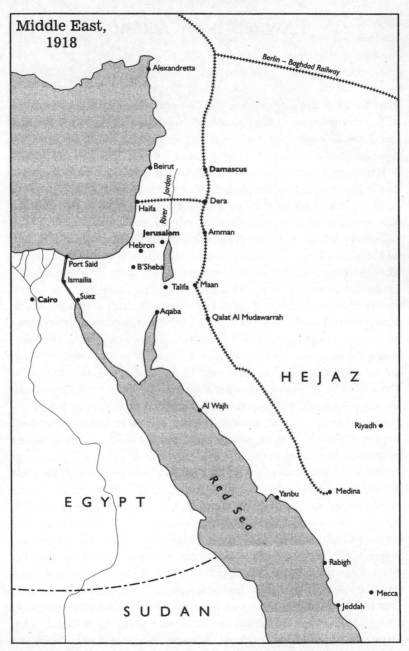

Middle East,
1918

Alexandretta

Berlin – Baghdad Railway

Beirut

Damascus

River Jordan

Haifa   Dera

Jerusalem   Amman

Hebron

B'Sheba

Port Said   Talifa   Maan

Ismailia

Cairo   Suez

Aqaba   Qalat Al Mudawarrah

HEJAZ

Al Wajh

Riyadh ●

Red Sea

Yanbu   ● Medina

EGYPT

Rabigh

● Mecca

Jeddah

SUDAN

Uranians, and during this period in Syria he enjoyed an intimate relationship with an Arab boy, to whom later he dedicated *The Seven Pillars of Wisdom*. The dedication began – 'I loved you.'

During these years Lawrence became fascinated by the aspirations of the Arabs and he conceived a fanatical hatred of the Turks. In 1914 he was invited by a Captain Newcombe to join what was nominally an archaeological expedition to Sinai, including Aqaba, but was in fact a valuable military reconnaissance. On the outbreak of war, although his military experience was limited to the Oxford University OTC, he secured a commission as an army staff officer which gave him the chance to contribute to the downfall of the Ottoman Empire.

By December 1914 Lawrence had been posted to GHQ Cairo, together with a number of other eccentric Britons, who had experience of the Middle East, and who were drawn into the growing band of Intelligence officers. Initially he worked for Colonel Clayton, a regular officer with an open mind who soon appreciated Lawrence's potential despite his eccentricities. Although amateurish in approach, the intelligence team soon broke the Turkish and German military codes. Lawrence, with his excellent knowledge of Arabic and local dialects, was employed to interview Turkish prisoners of war and to assess local feelings. The military command in Cairo feared that if the Germans and Turks were able to pose a threat to the Suez Canal, the Egyptians would rise against the British. Consequently great efforts were directed to its defence in order to safeguard the flow of troops to the Western Front from India, Australia and New Zealand. Turkish forces made a minor advance towards the Suez Canal in January 1915 but were quickly defeated.

Lawrence's knowledge of Arabic and his experience in the area was widely respected, and although he was a rather scruffy junior officer, he was welcomed into discussions with such senior figures as Sir Ronald Storrs, Sir Reginald Wingate (uncle of Orde Wingate) and Sir Henry McMahon, the High Commissioner. Lawrence shunned the crude and boisterous Cairo society, often dominated by unruly Australians, preferring a more serious intellectual circle who discussed the future of the Middle East after the Ottoman Empire had been overthrown. He had developed a strong antipathy to the Turks and a sympathy for the Arabs, and this influenced his views when, during 1915, both France and Russia began to plug their claims to the spoils of the Ottoman Empire. Lawrence was horrified when he first got wind of the secret treaty between Britain and France, the Sykes–Picot Agreement of 1915, which proposed that after the war France should have a sphere of influence or protectorate over the Lebanon and Syria, and Britain over Palestine and Jordan.

During 1915 the Allies considered many strategic proposals. The failure at Gallipoli concentrated attention back to the Western Front, and the War Office were loth to support anything they considered a side-show. Thus a plan to land a force at Alexandretta in south-eastern Turkey in order to advance and cut the Berlin–Baghdad railway was rejected. To the anti-French element in Cairo, of which Lawrence was a prominent member, the project would have had the added advantage of thwarting the French claim to Syria. Some of this group even feared that after the war France might attack the Suez Canal. The Turks and Germans caused more immediate problems when, in a bid to encourage Arab support for the Turkish cause, the Caliph declared Jihad, or holy war, against the Allies. It was broadcast throughout the Middle East that the Kaiser had converted to Islam. The Jihad gained little support among the Arabs, who generally detested the Turks, but it caused serious unrest on the North West Frontier of India, and further trouble in Ethiopia and Libya, where effective German agents tried to foment a Muslim uprising. A few mutinies broke out in some Muslim units of the Indian Army, but in general the Jihad failed.

The war was not going well for the Allies in 1915, and slowly the War Office – reluctant to release troops from the Western Front – came round to the idea of persuading the Arabs to revolt against the Turks. This idea received a very mixed reception: the Indian government strongly opposed it, the French saw it as a threat to their hopes of claiming Syria, and many Arab leaders thought that Germany and Turkey might win the war. Lawrence, almost alone, was delighted at the proposal and quickly saw its possibilities. He was further encouraged when in January 1916 the authorities set up the Arab Bureau in Cairo to oversee the project, and details began to circulate of a proposed agreement between Britain and the Arabs. It emerged in the form of letters between High Commissioner McMahon, and Hussein, the head of the Hashemites. In this Great Britain offered to support an Arab revolt and guarantee Arab independence in all areas taken from the Turks, with the exception of certain specified places.

In March 1916 Lawrence at last had the opportunity to be involved in some action. He was sent to Iraq in a bid to persuade the Iraqis to revolt and come to the aid of the British and Indian forces who were under siege from the Turks at Kut. The British and Indian commanders were aghast at the proposals Lawrence brought. He found most Indian Army officers positively hostile to the Arabs. The campaign at Kut was disgracefully incompetent and Lawrence could do nothing to alter the outcome. The entire episode merely reinforced his contempt for the regular army and the military establishment. During his brief visit to Iraq, Lawrence had continued his intelligence gathering, and was dangerously misled into thinking that large numbers of Iraqi soldiers were ready to rebel against the Turks. They were disgruntled at their brutal treatment by Turkish officers, but they were not in fact eager to fight for the British.

After this unsuccessful interlude, Lawrence returned to staff duties in Cairo. Here he found that Sir Reginald Wingate, whose nephew Orde during the Second World War was to gain fame when leading guerrilla Chindit attacks on Japanese railways in Burma, was more positively in favour of an Arab revolt and a proposed attack on the Hejaz railway line. Soon after Lawrence's return, news came in of uprisings against the Turks in Jeddah and Mecca, led by Hussein and his sons Abdullah and Faisal. Hussein was facing a dilemma. His forces in that part of Arabia were being hard-pressed by the Turks, who had a powerful garrison at Medina, at the southern end of the Hejaz railway.

He needed British help, but feared that his supporters would react adversely if a large infidel force were deployed close to the holy city of Mecca. Many Arabs, too, thought that any British force would come as an occupying power. On the British side, although there were fears that without help an Arab revolt would founder, the military establishment – after the disasters of Gallipoli and Kut – were not keen to detach British units away from the Sinai theatre. In Sinai there was to be a major build-up of forces to attack the main Turko–German armies and drive them out of Jerusalem and Damascus.

In this complex situation, where much information came from dubious spies and informers, Cairo HQ ordered Lawrence, whose views were widely respected, to go to Jeddah and assess the military situation. A strong Turkish attack was expected against Hussein's forces which were besieging Jeddah. Throughout the Arab Revolt, the followers of Hussein and Faisal were reluctant to attack disciplined Turkish troops, but at Jeddah, and on several occasions later, they received unexpected help which soon brought them victory. A British naval vessel, HMS *Fox*, anchored off Jeddah and bombarded the Turkish lines, and a naval seaplane dropped bombs and brought back information about Turkish troop movements. Shortly after the bombardment the Turks withdrew and Hussein was able to occupy Jeddah on 10 June 1916. This success encouraged Hussein, and in July he captured Mecca. The Turkish commander appeared unperturbed at this setback because he had a garrison of 12,000 men at Medina and could obtain supplies and reinforcements along the Hejaz railway.

In cosmopolitan Cairo, where the HQ included a large share of extrovert and eccentric characters, Lawrence had been accepted. When he arrived at an active service HQ with a more regimental outlook, things changed. In Jeddah he immediately clashed with the CO, Colonel Wilson, who referred to Lawrence's long hair and scruffiness, and called him 'a bumptious young ass who put everyone's back up'. Orde Wingate was often compared to Lawrence, to whom he was distantly related, and there is an interesting parallel. In 1944, General Pownall (Chief of Staff to Mountbatten), who was notorious for his acerbic comments, said of Wingate that 'he got people's goat and was a thoroughly nasty bit of work'. Other regulars added that he was a young puppy who would come to a bad end. So much for the establishment's view of the mavericks among them!

Soon after he arrived in Jeddah, Lawrence attended a conference with Storrs, Wilson and Hussein's son Abdullah. This meeting illustrated much of the future development of the Arab Revolt. The British refused a request for a brigade of troops, but offered the Hashemite Arabs £10,000 per month to support their campaign. Lawrence was already looking for a promising leader from the Hashemites to rouse the Arab tribes, and he quickly realised that ' 'Abdullah was not an Arabian Garibaldi'.

Although with considerable British help, Abdullah had taken Jeddah and Mecca, he was now facing formidable Turkish forces. Overcoming his religious scruples, he permitted Lawrence to visit Faisal; the meeting took place at the small Red Sea port of Rabigh, between Jeddah and Yanbu. The two men quickly established a rapport, and from now on Lawrence became completely immersed in the revolt on the Arabs' side. Lawrence appreciated the possibilities of striking at the Hejaz railway, and also agreed that the revolt would fail if the local tribes found British troops occupying the Hejaz. 'The Arabs', Lawrence wrote, 'are our good friends while we respect their independence, but they want guns, armoured cars and aeroplanes.' With his knowledge of Bedouin ways and tribal fighting, he saw the potential of Arab irregulars if led by someone like Faisal, but to the regular soldier they always appeared as anarchic and unreliable tribesmen, interested only in plunder, and who would always be defeated by disciplined troops.

After his discussions with Hussein and Faisal and his valuable reconnaissance, Lawrence returned to Jeddah on 4 November, and on the 8th he attended a conference at Khartoum with Sir Reginald Wingate. Lawrence strongly opposed sending British units to the Hejaz, but stressed that the Arab Revolt needed technical support. His report went to the War Cabinet – which was delighted not to have to send troops – and very soon guns, armoured cars and even aircraft were sent to Rabigh, together with some Egyptian troops and British specialists.

To his surprise Lawrence was chosen to liaise with and support Faisal, and he left Cairo in November to join him. Their good relationship continued. Lawrence anguished over his clash of loyalties between the British and the Arabs, and he became increasingly angry when he thought the Arabs were being duped by politicians. At the same time his passion for their cause often warped his judgement and led him to duplicity, deception and even blatant dishonesty. His rosy view of the Arabs was not shared by the British officers and soldiers involved with the Arab Revolt. Most were appalled by the Arabs' insolence, cowardice, ill-discipline and passion for looting. Many critics believed with justification that Lawrence's success depended largely on the vast supply of gold sovereigns which he was able to distribute. The Turks and Germans also made generous hand outs, and this additional income helped the Bedouin who were close to starvation as a consequence of the war. The British distributed colossal sums – for example nearly £300,000 per month to Hussein and Faisal – and there was truth in the criticism that they would not fight unless they were paid in advance. There was little concept of loyalty to a cause, and in one well-publicised incident a sheikh seized a shipload of weapons and used them for his own purposes.

Lawrence gave unstinting and uncritical support to Hussein and Faisal, but their ambitions were firmly opposed by other leaders, both in Arabia and Syria. The strongest rival was the powerful desert Sheikh Ibn Saud. Later he was to challenge the Hashemite forces, and at Khurma in 1918 he defeated Hussein's British-trained units, inflicting more than 200 casualties. In view of the remarkable achievements of Ibn Saud and the creation of Saudi Arabia, some have argued that Lawrence backed the wrong horse. Lawrence saw Ibn Saud as the enemy, and just before the end of the war believed that if he had had a squadron of tanks he could have defeated him.

By early 1917 the Turks were again advancing towards Yanbu and Rabigh, but British naval ships and aircraft once more kept them at bay. Various strategic plans were considered and then put aside. Support gradually built up for an active campaign against the railway as a part of Allenby's assault on Jerusalem and Damascus. Lawrence argued strongly in favour of guerrilla attacks on the railway to destroy Turkish flexibility and isolate the substantial garrison at Medina. There, the Turkish commander appeared relatively indifferent to the attacks because he had a huge supply of rails, sleepers and equipment for a proposed extension of the line to Mecca, and he received food and supplies from sheikhs hostile to the Hashemites.

The first action in 1917 took place when Faisal's forces advanced towards Al Wajh, a small port on the Red Sea north of Yanbu. Here again the Royal Navy played a decisive role. The threat of a bombardment forced the Turks to retire, and the town was taken by a detachment of 200 British marines. Faisal's force of 3,000 arrived later and appeared only to be interested in loot. Lawrence again made excuses for their serious shortcomings.

In May Lawrence set off with a small group, made a successful attack on the railway and then moved into the Jebel Druze north-east of the Dead Sea. Carrying £20,000 in gold sovereigns, he aimed to assess the level of support from the Syrian leaders. Most of them proved reluctant to commit themselves because they feared brutal Turkish reprisals, and their uncertainty about who would win the war. There are doubts about the authenticity of the reports of this episode, but there is no doubt about his next exploit – the attack on Aqaba.

Lawrence led a force of about 700 Arab irregulars which attacked and destroyed the railway line near Maan. They next advanced nearly twenty miles south-west and clashed with another Turkish unit. Displaying outstanding tactical leadership and bravery, Lawrence moved his main force to a reverse slope position safe from the Turkish guns. The Turkish unit had formed up in the valley below the ridge, and Lawrence led a wild charge of his Arabs mounted on horses and camels down the hill and into the Turkish position. His camel was shot from beneath him and in his fall he was knocked unconscious, but even the loss of his leadership could not halt the charge. The Turks were overwhelmed, with more than 300 killed and many more taken prisoner. The Turks had made brutal attacks on local women and children, and the Arabs vented their rage on many of their prisoners.

After this heartening success Lawrence led his force to Aqaba. Here, the threat of another naval bombardment, the approach of Lawrence, and his assurance that their lives would be spared, encouraged the Turkish garrison to surrender. Although Aqaba had been taken, the Turks had several battalions available for a counter-attack. Lawrence therefore rushed off to obtain food and reinforcements. He covered 150 miles in three days and on 13 July 1917, HMS *Dufferin* arrived at Aqaba bringing supplies and reinforcements, and taking off Turkish prisoners. In fact, Faisal had once again missed the action, but the capture of Aqaba was a great coup for the Arab Revolt, and Hussein in Jeddah ordered victory celebrations. Sir Reginald Wingate recommended Lawrence for the VC, but instead he received the CB. When the news of Aqaba reached Cairo, Lawrence became an instant hero and even Allenby joined in the praise, though later he was to change his opinion. At the time he was eager to support Lawrence and his plans for guerrilla attacks on the railway as part of his overall plan to advance on Jerusalem.

From a secure base at Aqaba, Faisal developed ambitious plans to advance north and destroy the railway between Maan and Dera, and then possibly to venture farther north and cut the railway north of Damascus. If this succeeded it would jeopardise all the Turkish forces in Palestine. Lawrence had a complex role to play. He felt that he alone could keep up the momentum of the revolt, and he had to deal with both Hussein and Faisal, who were worried at the speed with which events were moving. Hussein seriously doubted whether Faisal's ambitions in Syria could possibly succeed. Lawrence, in addition to leading sabotage raids, had to handle all the problems of co-operation between the Arab irregulars and the increasingly large force of regular troops from Britain, Australia, New Zealand, India and France with armoured cars, artillery and aircraft.

There are continuing arguments about the usefulness of these guerrilla attacks on the railway. While Lawrence and Faisal made substantial claims, H. Saint John Philby, the British adviser to Ibn Saud (father of Kim Philby who years later was to defect to Russia from Beirut) disputed these claims and pointed out that both supplies and reinforcements got through to Medina, and anyway the city was supplied by local sheikhs hostile to the Hashemites. Some thirty years later, establishment critics of Wingate and the Chindits were to dismiss their achievements as merely 'blowing up a few railways and bridges which were soon repaired'.

Lawrence's main campaign against the Hejaz Railway started in September 1917. One of his early attacks illustrates many of the problems and difficulties he faced. He set off with a mixed group of more than 100 Bedouin and two specialists on the mortar and Lewis gun. Most of his time and energy was spent settling quarrels and feuds between the Bedouin over booty, thefts of camels, blood feuds and tribal disputes. The group reached Qalat El Mudawarrah on 16 September, but the garrison there was too strong to attack. Instead, Lawrence placed an electrically operated mine below a bridge on the railway. His force, carefully drawn up ready for the attack, watched excitedly as a train of twelve carriages drawn by two loco-motives approached the bridge. At that moment a Turkish patrol fanned out, and Lawrence sent a decoy group to draw them away from the bridge. This succeeded. As the train started to cross the bridge Lawrence detonated the mine under the second locomotive. Then, under covering fire from the Lewis gun, the Arabs rushed the train. More than 70 Turks were killed and some 90 were taken prisoner. Most of the effective fire came from the mortar and Lewis gun, because some of the Arab groups allocated to give covering fire rushed to join in the looting. The Arab propensity for looting and murder was notorious, and Lawrence faced hysterical appeals from the German prisoners on the train. Then an Arab was shot, and in the pande-monium which followed, most of the prisoners were massacred.

After another attack north towards Maan, Lawrence was called away to report to Allenby and to receive orders on the role of the irregulars in the main advance. In Aqaba he found Faisal desperately afraid that the Turks would attack and retake the port, and depressed because of the poor and sometimes hostile response of the Syrian sheikhs. After a miserable meeting with Faisal, Lawrence flew to see Allenby at Ismailia.

Allenby ordered two operations for the Arab irregulars to coincide with the start of the main campaign. Colonel Newcombe took a small party to ambush the road from Beersheba to Hebron. He did this, but was captured soon afterwards. Lawrence set off on his own part of the operation on 24 October, intending to blow up the railway line between Dera and Haifa. His group got lost several times and were beset by problems, on one occasion exchanging fire with a group of friendly Arabs. They reached the target area on 4 November, but here a Turkish agent, who had successfully infiltrated Lawrence's group at Aqaba, ran off and alerted the Turkish defenders. Lawrence had to retreat rapidly, and failed in his objective, but he did manage to sabotage the line and derail a train between Dera and Amman. After this relatively unsuccessful expedition, most of his group returned to Aqaba, though Lawrence did not return with them..

The sequel to the failed expedition of November 1917 has aroused as much interest in succeeding years as Lawrence's military exploits. Although he did not report the matter at the time, he later claimed – for example in *The Seven Pillars of Wisdom* – that after the failed raid, he had gone in disguise to Dera to reconnoitre a way into the town. He alleged that in Dera he was captured and taken to the local Bey, who was a notorious pederast. This man made sexual advances to him which he rejected. He was then taken away by the Bey's military staff and repeatedly buggered. After further humiliations, he managed to escape and eventually got back to Aqaba.

For many years afterwards he gave conflicting descriptions of this event to several distinguished friends. Robert Graves, Bernard Shaw and E. M. Forster all recorded versions of the event, as told to them by Lawrence, which differ substantially in significant detail. His many critics maintain that the Dera rape was a figment of the inflamed imagination of Lawrence, who from his undergraduate days had indulged in homosexual fantasies. He had frequently shown his homosexual leanings towards his intimate entourage of attractive Arab youths. This general image was reinforced by his colleague Meinertzhagen, who, when he first saw Lawrence in his Arab robes, thought he was someone's pleasure boy. His critics' view seems to be backed up by events in his career later when it was clearly proved that for the rest of his life he indulged in sado-masochistic activities. Subsequent books and biographies and David Lean's film *Lawrence of Arabia* have dwelt at length on this aspect of his life and character, and have contributed to the controversial legend of Lawrence.

None of this was known when he returned to Aqaba at the end of November 1917 to become involved in the big military build-up at the port. Large numbers of British, French, Indian and Egyptian troops arrived, and Lawrence was widely respected for the colourful leadership he gave to this cosmopolitan group. British other ranks were amazed at his casual attitude and friendly approach – in severe contrast to most officers – and he dominated the entire operation. He cut a dramatic and impressive figure when he appeared in dazzling white Arab robes, and, occasionally, with his bodyguard similarly attired.

While the November raids from Aqaba proceeded, Allenby's armies had won important victories, and in December 1917 they captured Jerusalem. This presaged the final advance to Damascus and highlighted the continued importance of cutting the Hejaz Railway so as to isolate the Turkish garrison at Medina once and for all. Because the Syrians, despite the British advance, still showed little enthusiasm for the Hashemite cause, attacks on the railway were concentrated in the area of Maan – already well known to Lawrence's forces.

Soon after his return from his November raid, the situation in the Middle East and his relationship with Hussein and Faisal was seriously complicated by two revelations. First, the British government made a grave and significant declaration. There had been a serious shortage of explosives on the Western Front which could have brought about the Allies' defeat. The crisis was resolved by the discovery of a new way of manufacturing explosives cheaply and on a huge scale. The discovery was made by a Jewish research chemist, Dr Chaim Weizmann, one of the Zionist leaders. Conscious of their debt to him, the government published the Balfour Declaration, which proposed the setting-up of a national home for the Jews in Palestine, provided the rights of the existing non-Jewish population were safeguarded. This declaration totally compromised Lawrence's plans and hopes for the Arab cause – Jerusalem was a holy city for Jews, Muslims and Christians alike. Almost simultaneously Lenin, who had led the Bolsheviks to victory in the October Revolution, discovered, in the archives of the Kremlin, details of the secret Sykes–Picot Agreement, by which France was to have control over the Lebanon and Syria, and Britain control over Jordan and Iraq. Lenin, who had his own agenda for the ruins of the Ottoman Empire, published these details – to the horror of supporters of the Hashemites. These revelations put immense pressure on Lawrence's loyalty and discretion, and there is no doubt that when there was a conflict of interest between his duty as a British officer and a senior agent of government on the one hand, and his loyalty to the Hashemites on the other, the Arab cause nearly always prevailed.

Despite these complications, in January 1918 Lawrence was back in action against the Turks. A small town, Talifa, about halfway between Aqaba and Jerusalem, had been captured, but the Turks were preparing a counter-attack. The Arab commander panicked at the approach of the Turkish troops, so Lawrence intervened. He quickly changed the position of one defending group, brought heavy machine-gun fire to bear on the Turkish battalion, and then led an attack from the flank. The Turks soon broke ranks and fled. Lawrence received the DSO for his bravery in this action. In fact it was a fairly minor incident, and the Arabs have played it down. Like many of Lawrence's actions, when he was the sole reporter of an incident, it remains controversial. Fairly soon afterwards, when Lawrence was elsewhere, a force of Turkish and German troops reoccupied Talifa, and showed clearly that they were still using the railway. Throughout most of February and March 1918, Lawrence spent much time at Allenby's HQ planning the next phase of the campaign. Towards the end of March there was heavy fighting in and around Amman, which was captured and lost, and in which British and Australian units lost 1,500 dead and wounded. The contribution of the Arab troops was deplorable – a fact which Lawrence tried to cover up.

Early in April 1918, soon after the fighting in Amman, Lawrence was involved in another incident which illustrated his rather odd attitude to sexual matters. He and his bodyguard were approached by a group of five prostitutes. At Lawrence's instigation they held the prostitutes, and he and a friend dressed in the clothes of two of the girls and went with the other three back into the town, to make a reconnaissance. This nearly ended in disaster as they were importuned by some Turkish soldiers and only just managed to escape. In view of the events or allegations of what happened in Dera, this incident appears rather strange.

During the rest of April there was heavy fighting around the area of Maan with British and Egyptian troops seeing most of the action. They had the support of artillery, armoured cars and even of aircraft, but the Turkish garrison at Maan still held out. Most British officers considered Faisal's troops to be unreliable and useless, and there was severe tension, especially when Lawrence was not present to smooth things over.

The build-up for Allenby's final attack took until September 1918. Then on the 19th a major onslaught drove several Turkish and German divisions back towards Dera, where the German commander von Sanders had concentrated his defences. The irregular forces were ordered to sweep round to the east to cut off the retreating enemy. Faisal's force made a very bad start. At Aqaba in early September there had been a mutiny and soon after that all his officers took offence and resigned their commissions. Lawrence and Faisal smoothed over the difficulty, but the situation remained volatile. More problems arose when a local Arab commander demanded £10,000 to release supplies from a store he was guarding, but despite these setbacks the attack on Dera proceeded. A battle developed in which aircraft played a significant role. German aircraft briefly gained supremacy, but Lawrence was able to call on reinforcements including a large Handley Page bomber, and thus contributed to the enemy's defeat.

Lawrence had the difficult dual role of liaising with British and Australian troops and personally leading Faisal's troops into battle. As the advance continued, pressure on him increased dangerously. Faisal's units were now operating more closely with Allied troops, and this produced alarming tensions. Most Allied soldiers respected the Turks as brave professional adversaries, but felt complete contempt for the Arabs. The Bedouin were conspicuously absent from any fighting, but as soon the fighting was over they swarmed in to attack and murder survivors and to scavenge for loot. Even wounded British soldiers were attacked and robbed. Lawrence had constantly to make excuses for Arab atrocities, and the pressure on him built up until he was in a hysterical condition and close to a breakdown. At the village of Tafas Arab troops were almost out of control after they had defeated a Turkish unit and it appears that in the pandemonium after the battle Lawrence ordered machine–guns to be turned on the prisoners. Both at that time and later Lawrence denied this, though it was attested by other witnesses.

These events put Lawrence under almost unbearable pressure, but he was also keyed-up further by the plan he and Faisal had hatched for Faisal to appear as the conqueror of Damascus. There was still a possibility that this could happen because the diplomatic scene was changing quickly. The USA, which had joined the Allies in 1917, was opposed to the old imperial powers carving up the Ottoman Empire, and this could help Faisal's cause. As his troops approached Damascus, Allenby received conflicting instructions from Whitehall. Finally he was ordered to appoint French officers to any temporary administration, within the terms of the Sykes–Picot Agreement.

On the ground Allenby's offensive had been remarkably successful. He directed a mounted column to veer round and attack Damascus from the east, while the 4th Cavalry Division made the major attack from the south. On 30 September 1918, only eleven days after the campaign had begun, his forces were close to Damascus. An Australian unit reached the city first, and, virtually unopposed by Turkish or German forces, advanced into the centre of the town and received a jubilant welcome from the people. At the town hall the commanding officer received the formal surrender.

Lawrence arrived soon afterwards and immediately set out to impose his scheme to establish Faisal as the captor and rightful ruler of Damascus. In the chaotic aftermath of the battle, Faisal's forces swarmed all over the town, and were almost completely out of control. They indulged in a wild orgy of looting, rape and murder. After a day of mayhem, the Australian commander, General Chauvel, put armed military guards on all hospitals to prevent Arab troops murdering Turkish prisoners. Lawrence - very close to breaking-point – had several hysterical clashes with the guards and with the doctors in the hospitals. His espousal of the Arab cause had cost him dear. By 2 October 1918 order had been restored. In a victory parade an Arab unit was allowed to lead the march past, but when the local people watched the Australian, British, Indian and French troops with their guns and armoured cars, they realised who the real captors were.

Lawrence had planned a triumphal entry for Faisal, but Allenby, who reached Damascus on 3 October, said 'Triumphal entry be damned', and merely sent a staff car to fetch him. They had a lengthy discussion after which Allenby imposed a temporary administration under the terms of the Sykes–Picot agreement, appointing a governor with a French adviser, both nominally under Faisal. As a temporary measure France would control the Lebanon, and Allenby retained authority over the area south of Damascus. Lawrence had undoubtedly deluded himself about the position of the French in Syria, and had deviated dangerously from government policy. The nervous and emotional strain of the campaign had brought him close to a breakdown and, after a firm rebuke from Allenby, he was sent on a month's home leave. There he continued his passionate support for the Arab cause and wrote the first of many descriptions of how Faisal's forces had captured Damascus.

Lawrence had always deluded himself about the chances of the Hashemites taking over Syria, but he was an expert publicist with powerful connections and he did his best to uphold Faisal's cause during the Versailles discussions on the settlement of the Middle East. He became increasingly bitter as, one by one, his hopes for Faisal were dashed and his disillusionment was complete when French forces drove Faisal out of Damascus in 1920. Lawrence consistently – first from the security of All Souls in Oxford and then from his temporary position under Churchill at the Colonial Office – maintained the view that the Arabs had revolted against the Turks to gain independence, not just to change one master for another.

In the difficult and complex problems of the post-war settlement of the Middle East, Churchill as Colonial Secretary, while aware of Lawrence's prejudices, employed him for his knowledge and experience. For several years he operated at a high level both in London and the Middle East. He constantly warned that there would be unending tension between the Arab states and what they saw as Jewish interlopers. As late as 1921 he was sent out by the British government to attempt to get Hussein to agree to British policy towards Palestine. He felt so strongly about what he saw as the British betrayal of the Arab cause that, when invited for an audience with King George V, he refused the order for his CB and DSO – an empty gesture which did no good either to him or to the cause.

In his mercurial and troubled mind, conflict raged between exhibitionism and withdrawal. In the years after the war an American journalist,

Lowell Thomas, fascinated by the story of Lawrence, and using the new medium of film and cinema, launched an effective propaganda exercise both for him and the Arab cause. This caught the public mood in Great Britain and in the USA and contributed substantially to the build-up of the Lawrence myth. Lawrence appears almost as the noble and heroic young knight, as the maverick anti-militarist, in contrast to the red-faced blimps of the war, few of whom had caught the public imagination.

Yet the growth of the myth failed to solve his personal problems. As a Fellow of All Souls he could have chosen a number of fields in which to pursue a career, but he rejected these opportunities and enlisted in the RAF under an assumed name. Next, he served briefly in the Royal Tank Corps, but through high-level contacts was able to return to the RAF. Although he had deliberately sought the anonymity of service life, he successfully overcame the social gulf between himself and most of his barrack-room comrades, and gained their respect and affection. He was, at the same time, appalled at the crude language and constant obscenities with which he was surrounded. He developed a passion for speed though he never learned to fly. He was an early enthusiast for the motor-cycle, and in the RAF he was involved in the development of speed boats for air-sea rescue. As the Lawrence myth developed, he appeared, thinly disguised, in many thrillers and stories as a brilliant and eccentric spy. In 1928 he was posted to the North West Frontier Province – albeit as Aircraftsman Shaw – but this prompted more thrillers centred on a remote and romantic figure playing a modern version of the Great Game.

In the 1920s he had purchased a cottage, Clouds Hill, in Dorsetshire. Here he entertained friends from his service units, and many famous people. Although he abhorred the idea of a heterosexual relationship, he enjoyed close friendships with Lady Astor, Mrs Bernard Shaw and others. He retained the friendship of Churchill, Robert Graves and of Captain Liddell Hart who wrote his biography. Lawrence also wrote a book, *The Mint*, which described his life in the RAF.

He finished his service in the RAF early in 1935, the year in which *The Seven Pillars of Wisdom* was published. This brilliant, romantic but inaccurate description of the Arab Revolt, ensured the continuation of the Lawrence myth and again made him a household name, but soon afterwards the country was shocked by the news of his death. He was killed when his Brough Superior motor-cycle crashed near Clouds Hill. He was forty-six.

For sixty years since then the life, character and achievements of Lawrence have continued to fascinate the public. Books, plays, and films, often creating fierce controversy, have centred on Lawrence the Man and Lawrence the Myth.

VON LETTOW-VORBECK
AND SMUTS IN EAST AFRICA

On 28 June 1914, the Austrian Archduke Franz Ferdinand and his wife, who had been attending a function in Sarajevo, were being driven to a neighbouring castle for lunch, when the driver took a wrong turning. Gavrilo Princip, a student revolutionary, had planned to assassinate the Archduke at the ceremony but had been prevented by the crowds from getting close enough. He was walking home disconsolately when the royal car drew alongside him. He immediately opened fire, killing them both. These shots reverberated around Europe, but they had serious consequences in many parts of Africa as well – not least for the German and Austrian settlers in German East Africa (modern Tanzania).

Germany had annexed this territory as recently as 1885, after the German nationalist Karl Peters had travelled through the country, which was nominally under British suzerainty. By offering crates of guns or gin, Peters had obtained the thumbprints of many chiefs on bogus documents which purported to hand over their land to Germany. For political reasons in Europe Bismarck decided to accept these outrageous proposals. At the same time he consolidated his hold on German South West Africa (Namibia) and the Cameroons in West Africa. After only thirty years of German occupation and development, as soon as war was declared in 1914 all these territories were suddenly vulnerable to British attack.

While the British had begun to develop Kenya, and had built the Mombasa–Nairobi railway, the Germans had developed the port of Dar es Salaam, and had built a railway from there to Tabora, and on to Kigoma on Lake Tanganyika. They built another line from the port of Tanga along the mountain range which led up to Taveta and Moshi close to Mount Kilimanjaro, and it was here, where the majority of German settlers lived, that the most significant initial fighting took place.

The war, precipitated by the Sarajevo shootings, had not been entirely unexpected, and across Africa there had been serious discussions as to whether the colonies would remain neutral, though such a prospect must have seemed unlikely. In January 1914 Colonel Paul von Lettow-Vorbeck arrived in Dar es Salaam to take over the defence forces of German East Africa. He immediately set out to reconnoitre the entire country, and to work out his strategy. Almost at once he went to Tanga and travelled up the railway to Kilimanjaro. Here he found many prosperous German settlers, who were keen to help if war came. There were many sporting and rifle clubs, and he urgently considered how best to incorporate these into his forces. He inspected his African troops (referred to by both sides as 'askaris'), and found they were armed with rifles from 1870. He realised that with the

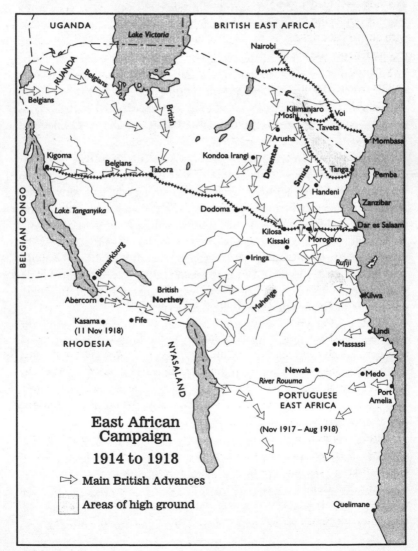

East African Campaign 1914 to 1918

⇨ Main British Advances

▢ Areas of high ground

much larger British settlements in East Africa and South Africa, and with the Royal Navy controlling the sea, he had no chance of defeating the British. Instead he decided that his greatest service to his country would be to occupy as many enemy troops as possible, for as long as possible, in order to prevent them being used against Germany in other theatres of war. To ensure this he must make certain that he never suffered a decisive defeat. In this single-minded aim he was brilliantly successful, and in spite of losing territory and being totally cut off from home supplies, he was still operating with an effective fighting force when the armistice came in 1918. In his first reconnaissance, he realised that the Mombasa to Nairobi railway, which was very close to the German border, would be vulnerable to guerrilla attacks, and its defence would hold down many British troops.

In April 1914 he travelled down to the small southern port of Lindi, and in May went by railway from Dar es Salaam to Tabora and up to Kigoma on Lake Tanganyika. From here he sailed along the lake to Bismarcksburg. Having completed his reconnaissances, he assessed the strength of his forces. The Protective Force, intended more for internal security than for modern war, amounted to about 200 Europeans and 2,000 askaris. In addition there were 45 European police officers and another 2,000 police askaris who could be enlisted to help.

He quickly saw that for the type of warfare he envisaged, he needed small, well-disciplined units, and he organised his entire force into independent companies, each with sixteen Europeans, 160 askaris, and two machine-guns. Each company had 250 'carriers' or porters. This may sound excessive, but until 1914 every European official would travel with eleven carriers, and each askari had a 'boy'. By concentrating on mobile units using carriers, Lettow-Vorbeck gained an immediate advantage over the British who used motor transport, which confined them to the execrable roads, or horses and mules which succumbed in thousands to the tsetse fly which plagued most of the area. He saw that communication and supply would be key factors, and even before the war started he had organised the transportation of rice from the area around Lake Tanganyika down to the coast.

Lettow-Vorbeck was well-suited to his task. Commissioned in the successful German army moulded by von Moltke, he had experience of bush-warfare in German South West Africa during the suppression of the Hottentot and Herero revolt of 1904–6. During that campaign he had been wounded and taken to Cape Town to recuperate. There, in the years before the Union of South Africa in 1910, he had observed and assessed the

Anglo–Boer situation, which was to assist him later. After returning home, he commanded a unit at the great naval base at Wilhelmshaven, and became familiar with naval supplies and transportation.

Almost as soon as the war started, he faced a serious crisis when British naval units approached Dar es Salaam. The Governor, Dr Schnee – who was to be despised by British and Germans alike – had immediately discussed surrender. Lettow-Vorbeck overruled him, and then hurried north to take command of military operations along the northern border. Soon there were brisk clashes with British detachments from Kenya in the area around Kilimanjaro. His newly organised companies were then involved in action along the border and towards the Nairobi railway line. He described one encounter when a contingent of British and Dutch farmers, armed mostly with sporting rifles, sustained heavy casualties – 20 killed out of 60 – at the hands of a disciplined company of askaris.

On 2 November 1914, several British cruisers and transports arrived off Tanga – the port and terminus of the German rail link with Kilimanjaro. They demanded immediate surrender. The commander on the spot prevaricated, and this gave Lettow-Vorbeck time to bring his companies down by rail to oppose the anticipated landings.

When he arrived in Tanga, he received conflicting reports about a British landing, so he grabbed a bicycle and rode into the town in bright moonlight. The place was deserted. The landing-party had obviously withdrawn, but he could see the ships lying offshore in a blaze of lights, and regretted that he had no artillery. He quickly organised his companies to repel another attack. Although he had already decided that he must avoid a decisive defeat, he was also determined to hold Tanga as his base for all operations in the north of the country. 'To gain all', he said, 'we must risk all.'

Early next morning an Indian expeditionary force with one British battalion, 1st Loyal North Lancashire Regiment, 101st Grenadiers (Indian Army) and 1st Kashmir Rifles came ashore. Their attack made some progress in the centre, but Lettow-Vorbeck's best company opened effective fire from the flank. Very soon the attackers panicked, broke ranks and fled to their boats, leaving behind nearly 800 casualties, including 141 British officers and men, and masses of equipment. It was an amazing victory against overwhelming numbers. Later in the day a British officer, Captain Mein-ertzhagen (later to be involved with T. E Lawrence) came ashore to arrange a truce, and the removal of badly wounded troops. The British had clearly hoped that a powerful pre-emptive strike would bring about the surrender of the colony which was prevented only by Lettow-Vorbeck's outstanding leadership.

This defeat at Tanga changed the whole situation, and led to four dreary years of warfare and countless deaths. The Germans, cut off from home supplies, were delighted to have captured stores, modern weapons, half a million rounds of ammunition, sixteen machine-guns, telephone apparatus, and enough equipment to rearm three more companies. The assault on Tanga coincided with sporadic and rather amateurish attacks along the northern border, but these were quickly defeated.

A substantial lull ensued during which Lettow-Vorbeck with dynamic energy made preparations for a long campaign. He foresaw that transport would be the key to his strategy of opposing British advances, while refusing major engagements. He had recruited 8,000 carriers and organised camps at intervals of a day's march. These men would bring supplies and food, not only from the plantation areas around Kilimanjaro, but even from Lake Tanganyika. He set in motion the production of key materials. Women, black and white, eagerly took to spinning and weaving locally grown cotton, tyres were manufactured from locally produced rubber, boots and shoes were made from hides, and even motor fuel was developed from cocos. The Masai, whose lives centred on their cattle, gladly traded meat and hides. All the German plantations willingly increased their output, and the manufacture of quinine was systematically developed. During 1915 more than 60 companies were formed throughout the colony, totalling 3,000 Europeans and 11,000 askaris.

While the build-up of supplies and transport was under way, Lettow-Vorbeck kept up attacks on the Nairobi railway by patrols of about ten men who destroyed bridges, mined the permanent way and always sought to capture horses and equipment. Their success in the latter enterprise was such that a new mounted company was able to be formed.

Early in 1915 British forces moved towards Jassin, just north of Tanga and close to the border. Lettow-Vorbeck decided this advance must be challenged, and he faced it with nine companies. The ensuing battle at Jassin lasted several days. British losses were estimated at 700, and in the end four companies of Indian troops with their European officers surrendered. German losses were equally heavy. Lettow-Vorbeck, who had lost six experienced regular officers, realised that such losses could not be sustained, and determined to stick to guerrilla warfare in the future.

During the year there were increasing rumours and reports of the arrival of Rhodesian and South African troops, and at the end of the year the Rhodesians took part in their first battle. As the enemy numbers built up, Lettow-Vorbeck decided that the main attack would probably come along the railway, and in the settled areas between Kilimanjaro and Tanga. He therefore arranged for as many supplies as possible to be taken south, and even got an enterprising planter to build a light railway from Wilhelmstahl towards Handeni at the rate of two kilometres a day.

Sporadic fighting took place at sea, where the Royal Navy had massive superiority, and from time to time it bombarded the coastal towns of Dar es Salaam, Tanga, Kilwa and Lindi. A German cruiser, the *Königsberg*, managed to slip through the British blockade, and in July 1915 took refuge in the lagoons at the mouth of the River Rufigi. The British attacked with flat-bottomed boats, but the German commander threw the breach-blocks of his guns overboard and scuttled the ship. The breach-blocks were later retrieved, all the guns were dismantled, carried away, and used again throughout the campaign. The crew, with guns, ammunition and equipment, were a valuable addition to Lettow-Vorbeck's forces.

Elsewhere in the colony sporadic clashes took place. British steamers dominated Lake Tanganyika, and the Belgians made several forays, driving eastwards from the Belgian Congo. At the southern end of the lake, the garrison of Bismarcksburg fought with units from Abercorn, but no decisive results were obtained.

The build-up of Lettow-Vorbeck's forces for the anticipated attack was influenced by events elsewhere in Africa, and by one man in particular – General Jan Smuts. When war had been declared – an event which Smuts called 'a catastrophe without cause or reason' – the government of South Africa had to decide whether or not to attack German South West Africa. Deep and bitter resentment still smouldered among the Afrikaner people who had been defeated in the Boer War, and there were armed uprisings against the proposals to attack German territory. This opposition was suppressed. Then Smuts and Botha, showing considerable military skill, led the South African campaign, and by July 1915 had defeated the German forces. Against continuing Afrikaner opposition, it was decided to send a South African contingent of 20,000 men to take part in the campaign in German East Africa, and after considerable hesitation Smuts agreed to command it.

An experienced British general, Smith-Dorrien, had been appointed to overall command, but he was taken ill in Capetown, and Smuts succeeded him. In East Africa in February 1916, Smuts took over an army of 45,000 men, including 19,000 South Africans, 14,000 Indians, plus Rhodesians, and West Africans. This mixed bag of races and regiments had suffered a series of failures, and morale was low. From the start Smuts faced serious problems. The Nationalist press in South Africa fiercely criticised the cost of the campaign in men and money, and many British officers were snobbish and patronising. They objected to serving under an 'amateur' and a 'colonial'. While Smuts's biographer, Hancock, described Lettow-Vorbeck as 'a man of superb resolution and skill', Lettow-Vorbeck, Botha and Francis Brett Young, the novelist who served in the campaign, all testified to Smuts's outstanding ability. A balanced view of Smuts's strategy was given by Meinertzhagen. Where Smuts favoured a campaign of manoeuvre – to prevent an outcry at home over casualties – Meinertzhagen believed that he should have brought the Germans to battle and crushed them whatever the casualties.

The forces under Smuts's command had assembled in February 1916, along the spur of the Nairobi railway from Voi to Moshi and Taveta, just south of Kilimanjaro, where Lettow-Vorbeck had established a strong position. He had decided to hold Taveta because, while determined to avoid a pitched battle, he thought that here he could exploit his advantage of being able to move his troops swiftly by rail.

On 12 February 1916 the British attacked, but were quickly repulsed, and retreated in confusion. Lettow-Vorbeck who supervised the burial of more than 60 of the enemy's Europeans, commented that many were very young and untrained, and it seemed that they had been encouraged to join up by the promise of farms and plantations.

By March Smuts had two divisions under his command, and he launched a strong assault on a German fortified position near Kilimanjaro. The attackers suffered heavy casualties, but advanced in such force that the Germans were driven out, and then reverted to their tactic of well-chosen ambushes. For several weeks constant fighting took place in the Moshi–Taveta area, and along the line of the River Pangani and the Tanga railway which skirted the Pare Mountains. This area of dense bush made communications difficult for both sides, and resulted in confused and unexpected clashes at close quarters. Lettow-Vorbeck tried to keep tight control of his retreating forces, and complained that reports on enemy movements were wildly inaccurate. While Smuts commanded the forces advancing down the railway, and then southwards past Handeni, he sent a mounted force under the South African General Deventer to thrust on towards Kondoa Irangi. Lettow-Vorbeck faced acute difficulty because he had no wireless communication with his other units, and he had to divide his limited forces in order to harass and delay both Deventer and Smuts.

The Tanga railway ran through Buiko and Wilhelmstahl, a heavily populated area of German plantations, and during his withdrawal Lettow-Vorbeck received constant help from the people. He and his officers spent much of their time on reconnaissance, and he recalled that on the frequent occasions when he accepted engagement it was 'because I was familiar with the ground' – the true test of a good commander.

When the British advance divided into two separate prongs under Smuts and Deventer respectively, Lettow-Vorbeck took over the forces south of Kondoa Irangi to delay Deventer's advance towards the railway from Dar es Salaam. During prolonged clashes in this area, Lettow-Vorbeck stayed very close to his leading units, and ensured that although the British were able to bring forward more and more troops, they were never able to bring him to a decisive battle. Because millet was grown extensively in this part of the country, and the railway to Dar es Salaam was still available to him, his troops were well fed and healthy at this time.

He now had to face difficult strategic problems. While he was delaying the enemy advance at Kondoa Irangi, strong detachments of British and Belgians were advancing eastwards from Lake Tanganyika, and southwards from Lake Victoria towards Tabora, the main town on the Dar es Salaam railway. At the same time, the forces under the direct command of Smuts were also advancing southwards past Handeni and towards Morogoro, another big supply depot on the railway. Knowing that he could not hold this vast territory, and that his highest priority was to keep his forces in action so as to keep the enemy occupied for as long as possible, Lettow-Vorbeck began to withdraw his battle groups – while still adopting delaying tactics – farther south towards the valley of the River Rufigi. This would allow the railway and the main settlement positions in the north, as well as Dar es Salaam and the railway to Kigoma, to fall into British hands, but they would still have to keep large forces in the field to pursue him. The country south of Morogoro was most suitable for guerrilla warfare and if necessary he could retreat still farther south to the Portuguese border and even beyond.

By now Smuts had two divisions, and a separate mounted brigade under command. Despite the continuing off-hand attitude of some British regular officers, Smuts's leadership and dynamism injected a necessary drive and confidence into the whole force. From the British point of view, Smuts's original intervention had brought immediate and tangible results. Within a few weeks of the main actions in the Taveta area, the German threat to the Mombasa–Nairobi railway had been removed, the large German settlements and plantations around Kilimanjaro had been cleared, and the German railway between Tanga and Moshi had been cut and overrun. There now followed a slow British advance along the railway and down the Pangani valley towards Tanga. Smuts's planned advance had been intended to encircle and destroy the German forces, but he had overlooked problems posed by the start of the rainy season which played havoc with the British motor, horse and mule transport. The roads became impassable, the men succumbed to fever and dysentery, and tens of thousands of animals were lost to tsetse fly. Lettow-Vorbeck had foreseen this and had deliberately chose local carriers who were fairly immune to fever.

It might be thought that Smuts's advance was brisk and businesslike, but in fact his troops suffered severe privations. The campaign was vividly described by Francis Brett Young – author of the successful novel *The House Under the Water* – who served as a doctor in the campaign along the Pangani. He described their tortured progress through dense waterless thornbush, 'with thirst and fatigue and endless marching under a hot sky, and wondering whether the animals and men would hold out or collapse'. Their painful advance was further slowed by small machine-gun detachments which inflicted casualties from ambush and then fled into the bush. After losing heavily to these and to sickness, Brett Young's unit reached the fairly important centre of Buiko, where they rested briefly. This beautiful place proved pestilential to man and beast. Hundreds succumbed to fever, and thousands of beasts died from tsetse fly, one cavalry unit recording the loss of forty horses a day; impossible to destroy, their carcasses were left to the lions and vultures.

After Smuts's troops passed Handeni they were involved in heavy clashes along the River Lukigura. A wide mix of Commonwealth forces took part, including two South African battalions, which captured Handeni, but were reduced to half strength by fever. Other units included Gurkhas, Dogras, Pathans from the 17th Indian Cavalry, a Sikh Mountain Battery, and several battalions of the King's African Rifles. In the dangerous and confused fighting, Smuts alarmed his staff by his frequent forays to the front line 'in the big Vauxhall car in which he daily risked his life'. His drive and determination achieved success, and in the Lukigura battles some fairly substantial German units were captured with a quantity of weapons. It was reported that enemy morale was very low.

After weeks of marching through waterless thornbush, the rains reduced the terrain to an impassible quagmire. Brett Young returned to Handeni, where, with hopelessly inadequate resources, he did his best to care for the thousands of sick and wounded brought into his casualty clearing station. The fit and the sick alike were emaciated from lack of food and water. He purchased sixty cows from the local Masai to provide milk for the wounded, and had a great thorn stockade built to keep out both the lions and the Masai. Referring to the local people, he wrote: 'Why should we break in on their hallucinated happiness with our alternate frenzies of religion or bloody war?' He added that amidst all the suffering, the masterful courage of Smuts dominated the whole of the war in East Africa.

The British campaign continued, and during July and August 1916 Deventer led his forces against effective opposition under Lettow-Vorbeck himself, and reached Dodoma on the main Dar es Salaam railway. At about the same time Smuts, advancing southwards roughly parallel with Deventer, reached Morogoro, another supply depot on the railway. In September 1916, after these long and difficult campaigns, British forces captured Dar es Salaam, with very little fighting. A few weeks later the British surrounded a large German unit which was attempting to rejoin Lettow-Vorbeck and more than 100 Europeans and 1,500 askaris surrendered.

Towards the end of 1916 Smuts was recalled to South Africa and most of the South African troops went too. They had been decimated by casualties and disease, and 'were of no more use – absolutely used up'. The mounted troops had hardly any horses left.

Generous tributes were paid to Smuts for his attractive character, and fiery, fearless leadership, but what did he actually achieve? His forces captured the important German settlement area in the north between Tanga and Kilimanjaro, and the railway which connected them. They drove Lettow-Vorbeck's troops southwards and captured Dar es Salaam and the southern railway. Smuts had overwhelming strength, but he never moved his brigades swiftly enough to inflict a decisive defeat on the enemy. Both Smuts and the senior South African officers appeared to be unduly conscious of the effect of the campaign at home, and therefore tried hard to avoid any serious loss of life. Consequently, opportunities were lost – especially in the initial fighting around Taveta, when the Germans could have been defeated. Two further criticisms must be levelled against Smuts. When he left for home, Lettow-Vorbeck was still at large, his forces posing almost as great a threat as when he started. He had not set out to defend towns or railways, but to keep his force intact. Against this criterion, Lettow-Vorbeck succeeded where Smuts failed. Smuts actually left at the end of 1916, and naturally reported on all the territory captured, giving the impression that the issue of German East Africa had been resolved. This most unfortunate impression caused immense difficulty to his successor General Hoskins, because thereafter the home authorities were reluctant to send sufficient supplies or reinforcements. Finally, Meinertzhagen, in a muddled tribute, described Smuts as a brilliant and attractive character, but added that he was a bad tactician and strategist, an indifferent general, but a remarkable soldier.

As Smuts and the South Africans pulled out, a new factor entered the East Africa campaign. In 1914, Germany had held two colonies in West Africa – Togoland and the Cameroons. Well-trained troops of the Gold Coast Regiment had quickly captured Togoland, but in the Cameroons had been involved in nearly two years of severe fighting. They returned to the Gold Coast (modern Ghana) in April 1916, and after a very short break left for East Africa in July. They landed at Mombasa in September, and marched to the Kilimanjaro area. Here in the cold and the wet, many experienced soldiers succumbed to pneumonia, as did many members of their regiment who were shipped around the Cape in 1943 to fight the Japanese in Burma. During 1917 as Lettow-Vorbeck retreated ever farther south, his main opponents were the battalions of the Gold Coast Regiment and the Nigerian brigade which followed.

The Gold Coast Regiment, with its well-disciplined, well-trained and experienced troops, quickly gained a good reputation among the Allies. By the end of 1916 its leading battalion had clashed heavily with German units in the hilly country just south of Morogoro on the southern railway. In one engagement in December 1916 the unit lost 140 killed, including Captain Butler who had won the VC and DSO in the Cameroons. During weeks and months of campaigning in the rainy season, there were constant reports of transport problems, shortage of food – weeks on half-rations or less – and shortages of everything 'except water which was present in odious superfluity'. When the rainy season ended the tactics of both sides changed, and most clashes centred on control of wells and water-holes. In September 1917 the Nigerian brigade inflicted heavy casualties on Lettow-Vorbeck's main force, after which he again moved his HQ farther south.

He was now facing a serious strategic situation. Deventer's troops had reached the railway at Dodoma and were advancing along the line in both directions. British forces already held the eastern end of the line and had captured Dar es Salaam. At the same time, a predominantly Rhodesian group under General Northey was advancing north-westwards from the northern tip of Lake Nyasa. Clearly, these three prongs of attack were intending to corner his force in the Morogoro area. 'It would surely be madness', he wrote, 'to await the junction of the hostile columns, each one of which was superior to us in numbers.'

With this decision, Lettow-Vorbeck personally commanded his forces in a very difficult withdrawal from Morogoro and Kilosa, past the Uluguru Mountains to Kissaki. This was a large German settlement with very substantial stores. The local Africans realised that the Germans were pulling out, and it proved difficult to obtain enough labour to transport all the stores farther south, though they did manage to drive herds of more than 1,000 cattle towards a tsetse-free area in the Rufigi valley. Even now Lettow-Vorbeck looked for every opportunity to attack and delay the enemy advance. From Kissaki, because he knew the ground, and had anticipated the British move, he was able to ambush and defeat a large mixed force of cavalry and British and Indian infantry, capturing many horses and taking thirty European prisoners. Some of these, who took an oath not to fight again, were returned to the British commander who, suspecting a trick, did not reciprocate this humanitarian gesture.

After the severe fighting around Kissaki, German units withdrew to the Rufigi valley. Now Lettow-Vorbeck had to consider the effect of increasing British activity from a base they had established on the coast near Kilwa. Although there were periodic and occasionally costly skirmishes, he succeeded in gradually disengaging during the early part of 1917. His reminiscences of this period concentrate more on the problems of food and supplies. He had to reduce the cereal ration, but encouraged all units to supplement their diet from the plentiful game, which included buffalo, antelope and elephant. He also issued instructions on how to shoot a hippopotamus, and then use the meat and fat. A very real problem in providing food for the fighting units was that, because the supply lines were so long, most of it was eaten by idle mouths along the way. He therefore drastically reduced the number of carriers. Early in 1917 he was holding positions in the Rufigi valley, and hoping to maintain these until the rains started in March. Then, knowing the British could not move swiftly in the wet season, he planned to relocate his HQ at Massassi, which lay inland from the small port of Lindi. With remarkable forethought, he had crops sown around Massassi, hoping for the harvest when his troops arrived.

Having retreated to the extreme south of the German colony, Lettow-Vorbeck now carried out a detailed reconnaissance of the entire territory from the port of Lindi to the shores of Lake Nyasa. His main preoccupation remained the provision of food and supplies to sustain his troops. He personally experimented with making bread without wheat flour, and taught himself, and then instructed others, how to make boots from antelope hide and from captured saddles. Shortage of salt was alleviated by boiling sea water at the coast, and sugar was replaced by plentiful supplies of wild honey. The staffs of the German hospitals gladly adapted themselves to the role of field hospitals, even though they had to make bandages from bark. When supplies of quinine ran low, a ghastly tasting but effective alternative was obtained by boiling Peruvian bark. This became known as Lettow schnapps.

Throughout 1917 the British forces advanced on several fronts with the Gold Coast Regiment, the Nigerian brigade, the King's African Rifles, and units of Indian Infantry and cavalry. There were months of fighting and evasion, of endless marching on short rations and little water, of sharp fire-fights and severe casualties. Slowly the German forces fell back to the area around the ports of Kilwa and Lindi, and then further on to Massassi. At this stage the German units which had opposed Northey and his Rhodesians, and had then withdrawn eastwards to the Mahenge hills, continued their eastward march, and joined up with Lettow-Vorbeck around Massassi. In September 1917 a major battle took place there, and the Germans captured a large supply of weapons and ammunition.

Although he was constantly retreating, and being attacked by vastly superior numbers, Lettow-Vorbeck was always seeking the chance to inflict a decisive blow on the enemy. In October, having gleaned intelligence about the Nigerian brigade's general, he set up a powerful defensive position, knowing that his opponent usually persisted with frontal assaults. His tactics proved correct. For four days wave after wave of attacks were broken on the German defences. The Nigerians and other units in the battle lost nearly 2,000 men out of a total of 5,000. The Germans also captured a dozen guns, machine-guns and other supplies. Lettow-Vorbeck considered this to be the most significant defeat of the British since their initial débâcle at Tanga. Involved in this serious reverse were the Gold Coast Regiment, the King's African Rifles and 25th Indian Cavalry. For their part the Germans lost a number of able and experienced officers, and once again withdrew.

By the end of October, despite his victory, Lettow-Vorbeck realised that the severe shortage of food, supplies and ammunition meant that he could no longer maintain a large force in the field. He found that his ersatz quinine would only last another month, and after that he would quickly lose all his Europeans to malaria. In this situation, the civilian governor of the southern province suggested surrender, but Lettow-Vorbeck brusquely rejected the idea.

There was a fairly large hospital near his HQ and in order to cut down his numbers he left almost 1,000 European and African soldiers there. Some of these were eager to fight on, but Lettow-Vorbeck admitted that 'even among the Europeans there were those who were not unwilling to lay down their arms'. In the fighting at this time, the Gold Coast Regiment captured a number of prisoners. Documents and letters seemed to reveal that the situation among the Germans was far from happy. Evidence from captured prisoners is always suspect, but there were clear statements that Lettow-Vorbeck was admired by his African troops, but feared and disliked by his officers. There were references to 'the disgusting greediness, gross selfishness, and predatory character of Lettow-Vorbeck', and a clear statement that 'European officers and men were sick to death of the futile resistance'. These views are not supported by most other evidence. His memoirs and other documents show a kindly, considerate and humane man, who won the admiration and respect of his own officers and of his enemies.

On 21 November 1917 Lettow-Vorbeck set off with a group of 300 Europeans, 1,700 askaris and 3,000 bearers, to march up the Rovuma valley – the border between German and Portuguese territory. There were fairly frequent clashes with small enemy detachments. In one incident thirty horses were captured from a South African cavalry troop – useful both as chargers and as food. Food supplies were again eked out by the abundant game. On 25 November he had a stroke of luck when a large Portuguese garrison was sighted while his forces were crossing the Rovuma. He immediately decided to attack, and sent several companies round to approach from the flank and the rear. The garrison comprised newly assembled and untrained recruits. Assaulted from all sides, they quickly capitulated. The Germans counted more than 200 enemy dead, and took 150 Europeans and several hundred askaris prisoner. The garrison was generously stocked and when the troops moved in there was an orgy of looting which even Lettow-Vorbeck himself had difficulty in stopping. His booty included modern rifles and machine-guns, equipment, horses and a million rounds of ammunition – enough to re-equip his entire force with new rifles. He commented: 'With one blow, we had freed ourselves from a great part of our difficulties.'

The luxury of the captured supplies galvanised the German column, but unfortunately it did not provide food for the askaris, so for many weeks they had to continue marching, constantly on the look-out for food. The smaller, well-disciplined column established a cheerful march routine, which survived largely on game from the bush. During this period the British commander General Deventer sent a demand for immediate surrender. Lettow-Vorbeck took this to mean that the British must be at their wits' end, and just ignored it. Several Portuguese garrisons were captured, and each provided weapons and food to last for a considerable time. Lettow-Vorbeck was delighted to learn from his African soldiers the secrets of feeding from the bush, and he described the system they evolved of obtaining the maximum amount of meat and fat from the hippopotami they slaughtered in large numbers along the river. This relatively relaxed progress continued throughout the rainy season from November to February 1918. Sometimes they reached a Portuguese settlement where they were able to stay for several weeks in relative comfort.

In January 1918, the Germans began to come under more pressure, because a large British force, including two battalions of the King's African Rifles and a battalion of Cape Coloured troops, approached, moving east-wards from Lake Nyasa, roughly along the border of Portuguese East Africa. The British achieved some success in getting the German askaris to desert. In an attempt to corner the Germans, the British had also shipped the Gold Coast Regiment and a battalion of the King's African Rifles down to Port Amelia. They used this as a base, but only probed slowly into the interior. There was now closer co-operation between the British and Portuguese to put more pressure on the enemy. For months during 1918, Lettow-Vorbeck marched and countermarched over large areas of Portuguese territory (modern Mozambique), and travelled more than 200 miles, nearly down to Quelimane close to the Zambesi, continuing to taunt and delay his pursuers the while. Much of his movement was dictated by the need of food, but there were occasional severe clashes, with both sides losing heavily. As the

Germans reached the more fertile areas farther south, their supply problems diminished. The local people regarded the Portuguese as unjust oppressors and were usually helpful and friendly towards the Germans. In July 1918 Lettow-Vorbeck personally led an attack on a mixed British and Portuguese force and defeated them. They had been based at a railway junction, and the capture of this once again solved his supply problems for some time.

In September Lettow-Vorbeck had to make another serious decision. If he continued to move southwards, he would reach the great Zambesi which would be impossible to cross, and where he could be trapped. He decided to change direction completely, and head north as quickly as possible, hoping at the same time to put his pursuers off the scent.

At this time he discovered that the Gold Coast Regiment, which had endured months of heavy fighting, had been sent home. These brave men from the northern tribes of Ghana – the Moshi, Dagarti, Fulani and Fra Fra – had won more than 40 DCMs and MMs, as did their equally brave successors who fought against the Japanese in Burma during the Second World War. No one seemed to raise the ethical question of taking these young men from their homes, and carting them halfway round the world to fight someone else's war.

As the Germans hurried north they did not entirely elude their pursuers, and they still had to fight fairly frequently. Early in September 1918, they sustained more than 100 casualties in a fight with two battalions of the King's African Rifles. By mid-September Lettow-Vorbeck had only 170 Europeans and 1,400 askaris left. Then his force was hit, surprisingly, by the influenza epidemic which caused such havoc elsewhere in the world, but which was hardly to be expected in central Africa. In September 1918 alone, more than twenty men died of influenza. Despite their prolonged suffering over many months, Lettow-Vorbeck describes even this last part of the campaign in quite a light-hearted way. On the march, the columns stopped for their lunch break, and Europeans and Africans alike pulled out a piece of bread and hippopotamus fat and sat down to eat it – 'a very jolly gathering'.

He had many reasons for hastening to the north. He was losing many carriers who were now close to their homeland, and who were tired of campaigning in strange lands. As he marched off – roughly parallel with Lake Nyasa but about fifty miles to the east – he realised that the British could rapidly move reinforcements by boat along the lake. On the other hand, his force was now back in German territory, the country was fertile, and supplies readily available. By October he had become aware of an increasing build-up of British troops, and he again changed direction to elude their pursuit. With intelligence of enemy movements, and with detailed reconnaissance of the ground, he made a swift and spirited march westwards, and crossed into Rhodesia, approximately halfway between Lake Nyasa and Lake Tanganyika.

He reached the small settlement of Fife on 30 October, but continued his vigorous march against only light opposition, through fertile and prosperous areas with much European settlement and many well-developed mission stations. His leading troops captured Kasama on 11 November. Next day he was hurrying off by bicycle on another reconnaissance when one of his officers caught up with him. An English despatch rider, under a flag of truce, had just reached their HQ. He was carrying an urgent message from General Deventer to Lettow-Vorbeck saying that an armistice had been agreed.

He and his officers received the message with mixed feelings. Having been cut off from all news of Germany, he could hardly believe that the Kaiser had abdicated, and that there had been a revolution in Germany. The situation of his own force was better than it had been for some time, and he felt he could have fought on for another year. He soon received a more detailed despatch from Deventer, giving him the terms of unconditional surrender. He was ordered to release all British prisoners, and to march to Abercorn to surrender. It was an abrupt message, but it did say that, in view of their gallant fight, European officers could keep their personal weapons. Next day he was invited for coffee in the mess by the colonel of the King's African Rifles, and was treated with respect. Then at Abercorn, the British commander, General Edwards, treated him courteously and hospitably. He was assured that his askaris and carriers would go to a camp, where their back pay would be dealt with.

At Abercorn his force of 150 Europeans, 1,000 askaris, and 1,500 carriers handed over 40 machine-guns and 1,000 rifles – nearly all British or Portuguese. He and his officers were well treated by the British and by the Belgians. They were taken by boat along Lake Tanganyika to Kigoma, and thence by train to Dar es Salaam, where they arrived on 8 December. Here again they were well treated, though they complained that they were not prisoners of war. General Deventer entertained Lettow-Vorbeck to lunch, and he was treated with respect and admiration. He was amazed at the thousands of troops and hundreds of motor vehicles at Dar es Salaam.

Here too influenza struck again, and he lost a tenth of his officers who had survived the rigours of the campaign. He finally left Dar es Salaam on 17 January1919 – five years to the day since he arrived – and the ship took him to Rotterdam.

Back in Germany, he and the other survivors were warmly welcomed. He was pleased to hear from English sources that altogether during the four years of war in East Africa, 137 generals had served there with 300,000 troops, who had suffered 60,000 casualties. It is difficult to verify these figures, though the map illustrates the large number of British and Belgian troops which were pursuing him all over East Africa. There is no doubt that Lettow-Vorbeck brilliantly achieved his aim of keeping his force in being, in order to occupy as many enemy troops as possible, to prevent them being used elsewhere against the German army. In fact, although some Indian troops did fight on the Western Front, most of the units used against him in East Africa would not actually have been deployed in the European theatre. The Gold Coast Regiment, The Nigerian Regiment and the King's African Rifles were not likely to have taken part in the fighting on the Western Front.

Lettow-Vorbeck's strategy succeeded admirably, but in addition he proved himself to be an outstanding guerrilla commander, with personal leadership and tactical acumen of the highest order. At the end he felt he was welcomed home because he and his troops had upheld Germany's soldierly traditions.

HEINZ WILHELM GUDERIAN

My most vivid memory of May 1940, as a sixteen-year-old schoolboy, was hearing the news that the Germans had reached Abbeville. I had visited the town on a school trip early in 1939. I recall the sense of total disaster that I felt, realising that it heralded a catastrophe for the Allied armies. I did not know then that this brilliant drive by three armoured divisions, which advanced more than 200 miles in eleven days from Sedan to Abbeville on the Channel coast, was the outstanding achievement of Heinz Guderian, one of the truly distinguished German generals of the Second World War. This dazzling achievement – a major factor in the downfall of the French army and nation – delighted Hitler, but caused him to make some dangerous assumptions about the power of swift panzer advances to overthrow nations.

Guderian was born in 1888 into a Prussian family, deeply imbued with feelings of loyalty, duty and discipline. After attending several cadet schools, he was commissioned in 1907 and served in his father's battalion. The young Guderian was a dedicated and serious-minded professional, who deplored the casual and unprofessional attitudes of most of his fellow subalterns. He was stationed at Goslar, a delightful town in the Harz Mountains, and then was posted to Koblenz for a specialist wireless signals course. He did outstandingly well on this course, and also became fluent in French and English. Already marked for promotion, he gained a coveted place at the Berlin War Academy in 1913. In Berlin he married Gretel – an ideal wife who was calm and balanced, while he was mercurial and impetuous. This characteristic, allied to his radical views on military issues, made him a true maverick, treated with ill-concealed hostility by the traditionalists.

When war began in 1914 Guderian was one of the few officers trained in the new systems of wireless communications, and was in charge of a unit working with the cavalry. He was involved in some of the early battles during the advance into Belgium, but because the new system did not work properly, many opportunities were lost. He later discovered that the French had broken his secret code within two days and were receiving all their messages. During these clashes he witnessed the slaughter of the infantry by machine-guns, which rapidly led to the stalemate of trench warfare.

In 1916 he became intelligence officer at Fourth Army HQ, and consequently missed the first appearance of British tanks at the opening of the
battle of the Somme. The British had developed tanks more swiftly than
the Germans, and Guderian – whose career was to be bound up in the
development of tank warfare – also missed the battles around Cambrai,
where the British again gave an indication of the tank's potential. During
the autumn of 1918 when the German army were in full retreat under pressure from British troops supported by massed tanks, he observed and
absorbed the lessons.

Given his severe Prussian upbringing, with its emphasis on duty and
honour, Guderian was disgusted at the breakdown of discipline and order as
the German army retreated, and he grieved that all Bismarck and von
Moltke had achieved appeared to be lost. The German people became
increasingly disillusioned as Freikorps groups and left-wing soldiers' councils contributed to the overall chaos, while the threat from both the Poles
and the communists from the east could not be contained.

Guderian, like all German officers, faced difficult challenges to his
loyalty and integrity. The Freikorps, a ruthless right-wing group, had considered launching an offensive to establish control over Latvia and the Baltic,
while at the same time the threat of the Bolsheviks grew more menacing.
The Treaty of Versailles destroyed any hope of rebuilding a sound and patriotic army, and Guderian went through a period of near despair, during
which his impetuous nature could easily have jeopardised his future career.
He was highly thought of by many senior officers, who were trying to
convert the army to its new role, despite left-wing upheavals, attempted
right-wing coups such as the Kapp revolt, or Hitler's *putsch* in Munich in
1923. Guderian loyally supported General von Seekt who was trying to
build up the army within the restrictions laid down by Versailles, and to
plan as far as possible how to expand it when the opportunity arose.

In 1921 Guderian returned to his favourite town Goslar to train an
infantry company for co-operative action with mechanised troops. His
innovative and demanding training under a regime of firm discipline
produced a superbly efficient unit, which responded enthusiastically to
his leadership.

Guderian approached his work with almost fanatical determination, and
he protested, as any ambitious officer might have done, when he was sent to
a staff appointment near Munich to carry out research into logistics and
motorisation. He dreaded being shunted into a backwater, but he discovered

that his post at Munich gave him a great opportunity to develop his interest in tank warfare. He had already studied the ideas put forward in England by Fuller and Liddell Hart, and he had looked on enviously at the formation of the British Tank Corps in 1923. He brought enthusiastic dedication to the whole concept of mobile and motorised warfare. The Treaty of Rapallo (1922) had enabled Germany and Russia to co-operate in the development of new types of warfare, based on aircraft and tanks. Guderian seized the chance which this gave to skate around the restrictions imposed by Versailles. With the backing of Krupp in Germany, Bofors in Sweden, and the Russian military powers, he developed pilot schemes to design different types of tank. He began to make his name with erudite articles, putting forward revolutionary proposals on the conduct of modern war. He inevitably incurred the hostility of old guard cavalry leaders, who resented the mechanisation process. Many generals in high places considered him a dangerous maverick.

He gained more publicity and more support by his brilliant and witty lectures – usually on the theme of 'the dynamic punch in modern warfare'. His crusade was helped by the acceptance of Germany into the League of Nations (1926) and the withdrawal of the Allied Control Commission in 1930. In the late 1920s he had further opportunity to develop his ideas on co-operation between infantry and tanks, and went to Sweden to witness major exercises which included infantry and tank co-operation, and the tactical use of smoke-screens.

Several European powers were now experimenting with new tactical ideas, and the British, thanks to Fuller and Liddell Hart, were generally in the lead. Gradually the idea took shape of an armoured division complete with tanks, infantry, armoured cars and artillery. Ironically, in view of the events of 1940, Guderian based many of his plans on the official British manual for tank training. Fortunately for him there were senior officers whom he had convinced, and they nurtured his progress. He was now encouraged to develop his original ideas and carry forward his experiments to produce a balanced force – the precursor of the armoured division.

From his training and experience in signalling at the end of the First World War, he was also well equipped to tackle the main problem facing tanks – namely effective communication from a command set to subordinate squadrons or troops. Guderian ultimately aimed to have effective communication with each individual tank as the basis for the deep penetration of enemy terrain. He also concentrated on solving the problem of security for radio messages relayed to and from tanks in battle.

While the wider question of the role of the tank in future warfare was being actively debated, Guderian, who had been appointed in 1930 to command a Motor Transport Battalion, used the opportunity to practise every type of action envisaged in his concept of an armoured division. He had to improvise and use replicas of armoured cars and dummy tanks, but gradually he convinced his colleagues that his views were sound.

Like all German officers of the time, Guderian's loyalty and integrity were severely tested by the increasing problems of the Weimar Republic during the early 1930s. His Prussian outlook and his nostalgia for the days of Bismarck made him view the rise of the Nazis with considerable unease. Yet, with the social upheaval, six million unemployed, and the continuing threat from the east by the Poles and the communists, he, like most Germans, began to think that perhaps Hitler was their best hope. Hitler went out of his way to gain the support of the officer corps and of the army. When he became Chancellor in January 1933, he appointed von Blomberg and von Reichenau, who were sympathetic to his aims, to high command. Guderian, while still believing personally that the army should keep clear of politics, accepted the situation.

In 1934, while still a colonel, he had the great opportunity to demonstrate to Hitler his revolutionary concept of the armoured division. Hitler seemed impressed by the co-ordinated action between reconnaissance cars, light tanks and motor cycles, together with aircraft and artillery. Little came of this immediately because Göring was ensuring that most of the available resources for rearmament went to the Luftwaffe. At this stage most German military thinkers, including Guderian, were concentrating on purely defensive notions to protect the German heartland from possible French incursion – such as the Ruhr occupation of 1923 – or the aggressive stance of Poland in the east.

In practical terms the greatest obstacle to Guderian's notion of the panzer division lay in the hostile attitudes of the traditional cavalrymen who resented the entire mechanisation programme; and of the gunners who still clung to the idea of their relatively static role of infantry support. They found it hard to adjust to the swift mobile advance with self-propelled guns envisaged by Guderian.

His hopes received a major boost in 1934 when he became Chief of Staff of the newly established Panzertruppe, and in the following year he was able to conduct manoeuvres for what was virtually an armoured division. These exercises succeeded admirably, but also illustrated the continuing problem of radio communication. Frustrating obstacles still remained through the attitudes of the military hierarchy, although a panzer command was established in 1935. This contained three panzer divisions – albeit with very few tanks. Guderian was given command of one of the new divisions, but still had to face the official view that the panzer division should support old-style infantry and cavalry formations.

He had been deeply involved in the debate in Germany about the future role of the tank. The debate centred on which type was to be preferred – a light tank for rapid reconnaissance, armed with a 20mm gun; a medium tank of about 18 tons with a 75mm gun; or a heavier tank which could face the powerful French tank that was being developed. Constraints included the strength of roads and bridges and the vehicles' capacity for cross-country deployment. Thanks to Guderian's obsession with signals communication, German tanks were greatly superior in this field compared to their rivals. As Chief of Staff Panzertruppe he had wielded great influence, but as a divisional commander he had to watch in frustration as his successor allowed many elements of his co-ordinated force to be handed over to other arms.

The struggle to establish effective armoured units was taking place simultaneously in Germany, France, Great Britain, the USA and the Soviet Union, all against a background of inter-service rivalry, limited funds, and long-held prejudices of the military establishment. In Germany in the late 1930s a totally new factor was added to the equation. After his success in marching unopposed into the Rhineland in 1936, Hitler confidently set out to challenge the Versailles settlement and to prepare for war. The military were encouraged to develop ideas for a sudden swift attack – the *Blitzkrieg*. Most German military leaders were opposed to this, but Guderian saw that it could bring valuable support for his ideas. In 1937, with official backing, he wrote his book *Achtung – Panzer!* in which he outlined his policy and presented it in a light that would find favour with Hitler. At this time Hitler was increasingly staffing the Wehrmacht with pliant personalities such as Keitel, so as to reduce the influence of the old army staff, many of whose leaders were forced to resign.

In 1938 Guderian was to become more deeply involved with Hitler, who after his successes of 1936 had moved quickly towards his next target – Austria. Prompted from Berlin, the Austrian Nazi Party put tremendous pressure on the government of Chancellor Schuschnigg, and Hitler backed this with blatant military threats. When the Austrian government called for a plebiscite in the hope of stalling a German take-over, Hitler prepared to invade (Operation 'Otto'). On 12 March 1938 German troops marched into Austria and that afternoon Hitler spoke to enthusiastic crowds in Linz, the town where he had been brought up. Standing beside him was Guderian, who had commanded the panzer troops for the invasion. While he shared the euphoria, Guderian was seriously displeased that so many of the military vehicles had broken down, and he immediately set about correcting this weakness in the three panzer divisions now under his command.

While Hitler was in the throes of reducing the Wehrmacht to a compliant tool, the German officer corps was deeply and dangerously divided; opponents faced a difficult situation, and overt opposition to Hitler by senior military commanders virtually ceased when the elderly and respected General Beck was forced out in 1938. Guderian, despite his growing involvement with Hitler, was still facing opposition to his ideas from within the army. In various theatres of war – notably Ethiopia and Spain – Fascist forces had experimented with tanks, and the results had not been impressive. The Spanish Civil War had also given an opportunity for experiments in aerial bombing, notably at Guernica, and this appeared to be a more powerful weapon for winning wars.

While these struggles were continuing, events again favoured Guderian. After the Munich crisis of September 1938, when Czechoslovakia was abandoned by the Allies, Germany was once more able to occupy a country without any serious fighting. Again it fell to Guderian, commanding XVI Corps, to be in charge of the military operation. He vividly described the take-over of the mountainous defences in the Sudetenland, after which the rest of the country was indefensible. He was carried away with admiration for Hitler's brilliance in achieving such a great victory without bloodshed. He declared enthusiastically that, thanks to Hitler, everyone was delighted that war had been avoided, and the Sudeten Germans had been rescued from their unjust oppression by the Czechs. It would be easy to assume that Guderian had been duped by Goebbels's propaganda, but, up to 1938, the majority of Germans, unaware of what was to come, revered Hitler for giving them back their self-respect, for solving unemployment, for apparently creating prosperity, and for correcting the injustices of the Treaty of Versailles.

Guderian remained in command of XVI Corps, but his rapid rise and his close association with Hitler did not prevent his opponents in the army – especially traditional cavalrymen – from attempting to undermine his position or side-track his career. Several months of scheming and frustration were suddenly terminated by Hitler's new moves in the summer of 1939. In August Guderian was posted to command XIX Corps, which consisted of 3rd Panzer Division and two motorised divisions. During a summer of hectic manoeuvres it became clear that Poland was to be their next target.

In the German attack on Poland on 1 September 1939, Guderian led XIX Corps in a swift advance eastwards across the Polish corridor. The defenders fought bravely, but, massively outnumbered in both tanks and aircraft, they had little hope of success. Many witnessed the sickening sight of galloping cavalry being mown down by tanks and machine-guns. In the area of the corridor there was more fighting than farther south where Guderian's old corps, as part of 3rd Army Group, were able to advance quickly over open country – ideal for panzer movement.

With only one panzer division under his command, Guderian kept his HQ close to its leading tanks, and established his reputation as a brave and intrepid leader, who had no time for incompetence or failure. By his dashing example he drove his units forward and kept up their momentum. Not only did he provide inspiring leadership, he recorded every deficiency in the tanks and motor vehicles under battle conditions, so that they could be promptly remedied. After four days, at his HQ close to the front, and in sight of Polish artillery positions which had been destroyed, Hitler, accompanied by Himmler and Rommel, came to see him. Hitler assumed that the guns had been destroyed by Stuka dive-bombers, but Guderian bluntly told him they had fallen to the panzers. He added proudly that in the entire advance his corps had suffered only 150 casualties.

The southern advance, though swift, had been effectively held up at Warsaw, and one panzer division had lost half its tanks. This delay gave Guderian a remarkable opportunity. His corps was ordered to drive east and south towards Brest-Litovsk, nearly 100 miles east of Warsaw. The popular image of the Polish campaign as an easy walk-over is belied by the heavy fighting and serious losses which many German units sustained. Many untried troops and untried leaders made serious blunders, but Guderian, by insisting that all commanders be at the front of the advance and as close as possible to the action, kept up the momentum. He himself was so close to the rapidly moving front that on one occasion he was cut off and had to be rescued by motor cyclists.

On 14 September, two weeks after the start, XIX Corps reached Brest-Litovsk. The garrison was well dug-in and defended bravely. For Guderian it was another opportunity to show that his well-trained units could adapt to a new situation, using the concerted fire power of tanks, artillery and infantry in a formal attack on a defended town. This combination quickly overcame Brest-Litovsk. Then Guderian had a bitter clash with the High Command when they proposed to split his corps – an idea which offended every principle of war that he held dear. Despite this disagreement, he was awarded the Knight's Cross of the Iron Cross. He had shown that effective training and vigorous leadership could win victories and reduce casualties.

When Poland capitulated, the German army hurriedly repaired its vehicles, handed over large areas to the Russians under the terms of the Russo–German non-aggression pact, and hurried westwards for the expected attack from France – which never came. The Germans had learned valuable lessons from the Polish campaign. The infantry were criticised for being ineffective, and the artillery showed that they needed to be more mobile. But the most important lesson was proved by the armoured division: that they could advance and seize territory, and move so quickly that the enemy could not re-establish an effective front. Some critics of Guderian maintained, erroneously, that Polish resistance was pathetic and that his tactics would not work against a more formidable enemy.

Hitler, however, was so delighted with the results that, almost at once, he ordered preparations for an attack in the west. Most German officers were horrified. They regarded the invasion of Poland as a minor war, and hoped that now it was over it would be possible to prevent a world war. Hitler's idea seemed so dangerous and fanatical that a small group of officers planned to assassinate him. Initially, Hitler proposed to attack France on 12 November 1939, but there was such strong opposition by nearly all the senior army generals that it had to be postponed.

For Guderian this was a particularly unhappy time. In the autumn Hitler ranted at his service chiefs, maintaining that he could rely on the air force and navy but was opposed at every turn by the army leaders. Guderian deplored the backbiting and intrigues among the senior generals, but they prevailed upon him to put their case to Hitler. A brave man! The interview, described in the admirable biography *Guderian* by Kenneth Macksey, achieved little, but Guderian's integrity and character enabled him to put the case firmly, and obviously he gained Hitler's respect. But he left the interview feeling that Hitler had still not grasped the proper role of the panzer division. He returned to his HQ near Koblenz, miserable and frustrated, lacking even facilities to train his troops.

Deep and bitter debate over the strategy of the attack in the west continued into 1940, but towards the end of February Hitler decided on what was essentially Guderian's plan for the attack on France. In the centre aiming at Arras, von Runstedt's Army Group A, including Guderian's XIX Corps, had ten panzer and motorised divisions, and 34 infantry divisions. In Army Group B, operating farther north, von Bock commanded three panzer and 24 infantry divisions. Von Leeb's Army Group C, covering von Rundstedt's left flank in the south, had another 44 divisions in reserve. Never was there a better illustration of the basic maxim of the concentration of force. In their scattered commands, the French had about 100 divisions, the British ten divisions, and the Belgians and Dutch about 30 altogether – approximately the same number as the Germans. The Allies had about the same number of tanks but rather fewer aircraft.

After the frustrations of the winter, Guderian was delighted to be training his panzers for the big attack. A brilliant all-round officer, he was perhaps at his best training his troops for a role in which he had total conviction. He showed really superb leadership in his warm, cheerful and positive supervision of training exercises both in his corps and throughout the army. The urgent manoeuvres centred on rapid movement, swift co-operation between infantry and tanks, and efficient river-crossing. Guderian studied all the available intelligence sources, and was heartened by the lack of positive French activity. His aim was to crash through the good defensive country of the south Ardennes, and break out into more open country beyond Sedan and the Meuse – names redolent of past battles. After several postponements, but within days of the German success in Norway, on 10 May 1940 - the day Churchill replaced Chamberlain – the Germans launched their attack with more than 100 divisions.

Guderian was not the brutal and insensitive Nazi general that might be supposed, but a totally professional officer, deeply concerned about the blacker side of Hitler's policies, which he was now beginning to understand. He worried about his sons who were serving elsewhere, and in the days before the attack wrote touchingly to his wife about the beautiful cherry blossom and the colours of the spring countryside.

The Germans, ruthlessly thorough in their preparation, had infiltrated agents across the border to safeguard bridges and key traffic junctions, but as division after division moved across the frontier, serious hold-ups took place. Guderian's XIX Corps led the advance towards Sedan. Always as close as possible to the front, his reconnaissance aircraft once got lost and nearly landed among the French. After several days of confused but occasionally severe fighting, his corps faced its first major test when it had to cross the Meuse against a well-prepared enemy. Now thorough and efficient preparation came into play. The formal assault started with several hours of bombing by heavy bombers and dive-bombers strafing the French defenders. In addition, Guderian had brought up the formidable 88mm anti-aircraft guns to fire directly at the defences. A weak, poorly trained and demoralised French division cracked under this assault, and soon the German infantry gained a foothold. This they quickly exploited during the night, and even before the leading tanks had crossed the river, they had secured a bridgehead six miles deep.

The French had motorised divisions with tanks and more than twenty independent tank units for infantry support, but these were scattered along a wide front. Their serious deficiencies in training, organisation, communications and overall grasp by the higher command, were soon exposed. One division alone did fight well and engaged Guderian's forward troops in very heavy fighting. Some French heavy tanks, which could outgun the German tanks, briefly held sway and recaptured the important village of Stonne, but they paused, and fresh German infantry with effective anti-tank weapons drove them out. Guderian's corps not only destroyed the French guns, but

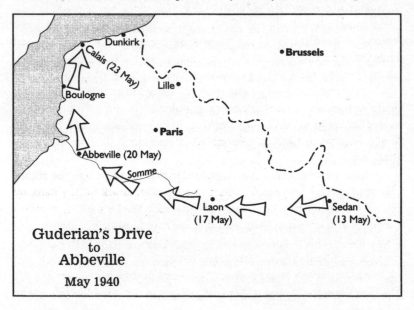

Guderian's Drive
to
Abbeville
May 1940

their morale as well. He had had some worrying moments when as a consequence of his swift advance his flank became vulnerable to French counterattack, but his calm and cheerful confidence kept the momentum going and overcame the doubts of his superior, Field Marshal von Kleist. Few commanders in any army gained such respect and affection from their troops, and after the first hectic days, when much French armour had been destroyed, Guderian had the satisfaction of knowing that his corps had played a decisive role.

After a period of total involvement in the fighting, Guderian was suddenly caught up in high-level disputes over both the tactics and strategy of the advance. Having crossed the Meuse near Sedan on 13 May, his HQ was just north of Laon on the 17th. On that day von Kleist came to his HQ, countermanded Guderian's order to advance, and accused him of disobeying orders. Guderian immediately offered to resign. This is a good illustration of the vicious in-fighting between commanders on the same side which occurred so frequently even during what appeared to be the most successful campaigns. In a similar case, the Japanese commander Mutaguchi sacked his leading divisional commander, Sato, immediately after the battle of Kohima; and on the same day Grover, who commanded the British 2nd Division throughout the battle, was also sacked – to the fury of his division.

Guderian's threat of resignation went at once to von Rundstedt, commander of Army Group A, who had been worried about the speed of the advance, and the danger of French counter-attacks on the flanks. He refused Guderian's resignation and sent an intermediary. This tense stand-off shows not only the pressure on commanders in battle, but the military and political factors which influenced the final decisions. Hitler shared von Rundstedt's worries, and started interfering in military decisions. Von Rundstedt tended to give in to Hitler's importuning, but his solution to this crisis was to allow Guderian to make reconnaissance in force – an opportunity he gladly grasped.

Von Rundstedt's concern was understandable, and just as the reconnaissance in force was about to start there was an attack on the flank by three French tank battalions under Brigadier de Gaulle who, as a consequence of the German hold-up, found himself confronting not rear echelon troops but front-line units of 1st Panzer Division. After a fierce fight the panzers, with help from the Luftwaffe, drove the French back.

Now the High Command allowed Guderian to advance. By 19 May his XIX Corps was ready, and on the 20th, in one of the most successful tank advances of the war, its thrust reached the Channel at Abbeville. This amazing advance had cut the Allied armies in half, and von Kleist had three panzer divisions close to the Channel ports and poised for further attacks.

Guderian's dazzling achievement took the Allies as well as the German High Command by surprise, and there was some dithering about the next step. Guderian had hoped to send three panzer divisions to attack Boulogne, Calais and Dunkirk respectively. The British were planning to defend all of these, but had Guderian been able to push ahead as he had wished, his panzers would have reached Boulogne and Calais before the defences were in place. As it was, because of the need to safeguard his lines of communication, only one division was available, and this was sent to Boulogne on 22 May. It met strong resistance from French units and from British units in the port area, but the town was taken after thirty-six hours. After this Guderian was keen to strengthen the ring around the Channel ports, so he by-passed Calais and sent 1st Panzer Division towards Dunkirk to strengthen the barrier between the retreating British and French forces and the sea.

At this critical moment, Hitler, for a mixture of military, political and ideological reasons, and because he and von Rundstedt had become nervous, ordered the advance to halt. In his book, *Panzer Leader* (p.117), Guderian writes: 'We were utterly speechless.' It appeared that Göring had influenced the decision so that the Luftwaffe and certain Nazi formations could share in the glory by completing the operation. Hitler's intervention boded ill for Germany's forces. For Guderian, his frustration was mellowed slightly by his promotion to command Panzer Group Guderian, consisting of two army corps, but – partly because of the envy of senior commanders – he was denied the accolade of 'Army Commander'. He was still regarded by some generals as being an insubordinate individual, but his brilliant success could not be denied.

On 10 June, after a short period of re-organisation near Sedan, he set off with Panzer Group Guderian, heading almost due south. His fast tanks overran or by-passed the tragic sites that had suffered the pyrrhic slaughter of static trench warfare during 1914–18 – none more so than Verdun – and in less than a week his group had overrun Châlons-sur-Marne and Chaumont. Then, on the 16th, in one of the most brilliant manoeuvres of the campaign, he wheeled his entire force on the pivot of Besançon and drove eastwards through the Belfort gap. On the 18th he joined up with Seventh Army and continued the drive into Alsace and Lorraine. Nearly half a million French troops were taken, including the garrisons of the Maginot

Alexander the Great

Shaka

Stonewall Jackson

Garibaldi

Lawrence of Arabia

Von Lettow Vorbeck

Guderian

Patton

Stilwell

Wingate

Skorzeny

Giap

Line which had proved quite useless. His forces reached the Swiss frontier on his birthday. Four days later, on the 22nd, France signed an armistice, and because of his brilliant leadership throughout the campaign Guderian had become a national hero.

In the brief lull after the victory he was able to meet both his sons, one of whom had been wounded in the campaign. He also put forward a remarkable assessment of the strategic situation (*Panzer Leader*, p. 136). He proposed that the German forces should immediately advance down the Rhône, seize the French Mediterranean bases, take Malta with the available airborne divisions, and transfer panzer divisions to North Africa to join up with the strong Italian forces in Abyssinia. The weakness of the British in Egypt was well known, and he reckoned they would pose no serious obstacle to a swift advance to the Suez Canal.

These proposals, however, did not find favour with Hitler. Guderian, while fuming at the loss of immediate opportunities which victory had brought, enjoyed a brief posting to Paris – where he was promoted to colonel general – and then to Berlin. In a scathing observation about the proposed invasion of England (Operation 'Sealion'), he said it was never taken seriously, and the inadequacy of the air and naval forces made it a hopeless undertaking. As one of the outstanding trainers of troops, he took over the training of the many new panzer divisions which Hitler had ordered to be established. Guderian observed, ruefully, that while the numbers of divisions doubled, the number of tanks did not, 'which was after all what counted!'

In November 1940 Guderian, who at this time was not privy to high-level discussions, heard about Hitler's plan to invade Russia (Operation 'Barbarossa'). He was amazed and appalled. Hitler had violently denounced those leaders who had involved Germany in a war on two fronts in 1914, and Guderian found it hard to believe that such a disastrous step would be taken. At the same time, to Hitler's fury, Mussolini made an unco-ordinated attack on Greece, and also suffered a major defeat by the British at Sidi Barrani on the border of Egypt. As a consequence, panzer divisions had to be diverted to the Balkans and North Africa. So much for the concentration of force.

A dedicated officer, Guderian devoted himself to training his panzer divisions for the tasks which lay ahead, but he was concerned at the poor quality of the motor vehicles coming from the captured French factories. Reading the histories of Charles XII and Gustavus Adolphus of Sweden, and of Napoleon, and of the defeats they suffered in Russia, he increasingly sensed disaster.

In June 1941, the count-down for 'Barbarossa' drew nearer, Guderian was commanding Panzer Group 2, consisting of nine divisions, mostly armoured but including some motorised and some infantry divisions. This group was to spearhead the main advance on the central Russian front from Brest-Litovsk – which, as Guderian said, he had to capture again – towards Smolensk. He took part in fierce arguments about the role of the tank in any breakout, and pointed out that if infantry headed the attack, the roads were always clogged up and the tanks could not advance. As a senior commander he refused to circulate in his units the Nazi-inspired directives about the treatment of captured Russians and stressed that a soldier had to follow the dictates of a Christian conscience.

As the preparations reached a climax, Guderian expressed his concern on several important issues. He believed that Hitler and the senior commanders had seriously underestimated the supply of tanks enjoyed by the Russian forces, and their ability to fight effectively. He thought it absurd to imagine that Russia could be defeated in a few weeks, and he criticised the failure to issue his troops with winter clothes. He began to realise the danger of Hitler's insane ambition, and the further menace posed by his interference in military decisions. Like many front-line commanders, he appeared largely unaware of the proposed activities of the SS extermination squads which were to follow the military advance.

On Sunday 22 June 1941, the invasion began and appeared to take the enemy by surprise. Air superiority was achieved almost at once, and the panzer divisions drove forward sweeping aside most opposition. In *Panzer Leader* Guderian's diary vividly portrays the hectic days of the initial advance, and his constant emphasis on the need to keep the momentum going so as to prevent the Russians assembling effective lines of defence. Guderian's successful advance was achieved partly by his exploitation of the disagreements among more senior commanders and even Hitler himself. As his drive to the east continued, he was threatened with court-martial by von Kluge – the first move in a feud which lasted throughout the war. Within seven days his leading forces had reached Minsk and had inflicted a serious defeat on the Russians – for which the Russian commander Pavlov was executed. Early in July Guderian faced another clash with von Kluge, who forbade him to cross the Dnieper. He evaded this order because the operation was too far advanced to stop. Then, in mid-July, by another dramatic advance under his personal leadership, his Panzer Group reached Smolensk.

By the beginning of August the headlong advance was beginning to slow, and worrying factors emerged. The Russians had improved their defensive tactics by destroying bridges, mining roads and, while not challenging the advancing panzers, making determined attacks on the follow-up troops. For the first time the new Russian T34 tank appeared. This had more powerful armour and a much better gun than any of the current German tanks. In the wider strategic context, serious disagreements arose among the German leaders.

Guderian and most commanders favoured a concentration of force for a drive in the centre to reach Moscow as soon as possible. Hitler visited the front, and sowed dissent among the generals, and between them and the Nazi hierarchy. He proposed that both Leningrad in the north, and Kiev and the Ukraine in the south should first be captured, and then Moscow would inevitably fall.

Against this increasingly uncertain background, Guderian maintained the success of his Group by his overwhelming energy, personality, confidence and determination. He inspired complete devotion from his troops by his care for them and his constant appearance at the front where the fighting was fiercest. Once he was so far forward that he drove through a Russian unit whose troops claimed to have killed him; later he radioed a message to the Russians to tell them they were mistaken. At this time all his operations were conducted with what he saw as the desirable strategic aim firmly in mind; that the campaign be terminated before the onset of the dreaded Russian winter.

From now on the indecision and back-biting among the High Command, and the increasing anger at Hitler's autocratic and unpredictable interference in military decisions, clouded the confidence which the first successful weeks of the campaign had induced. Guderian's success had created antagonism among some rivals and some superiors, but there was also a move to elevate him to the highest command in place of the ineffectual Field Marshal von Brauchitsch.

Hitler's proposal to halt the drive on Moscow, caused near despair among the generals, and they prevailed on Guderian to go with the Chief of Staff, General Halder, and try to get Hitler to change his mind. Guderian had already spoken out boldly against the Kiev/Leningrad plan on the grounds of logistics, maintenance, tank supplies and the impending danger of a winter campaign.

He was taken, without Halder, to see Hitler in the presence of General Jodl and Field Marshal Keitel. He argued strongly against the Kiev proposal, but it was made clear to him that a decision had already been reached. Hitler added that generals never understood the economics of war. Guderian had little alternative but to acquiesce, though later, Halder bitterly criticised him for doing so. From now on Guderian became almost a pawn in the strategic confusion. He had hoped that, after a brief halt at Smolensk for supplies and maintenance, his Panzer Group would advance on Moscow before the Russians could organise effective defences. Instead, his Group was ordered to move due south to support the slower Second Army, and to surround a vast Russian army east of Kiev. During this time it appears that

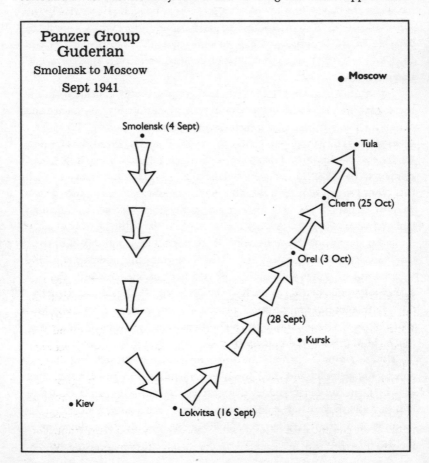

Panzer Group Guderian

Smolensk to Moscow
Sept 1941

Moscow

Smolensk (4 Sept)

Tula

Chern (25 Oct)

Orel (3 Oct)

(28 Sept)

Kursk

Kiev

Lokvitsa (16 Sept)

Halder was waging a personal vendetta against Guderian, and deliberately souring his relations with other senior commanders.

In early September Guderian's Panzer Group left Smolensk and advanced more than 200 miles to Lokvitsa; by the 16th it was assisting at the capture of Kiev which fell on the 26th, Russian losses including 600,000 prisoners and 2,500 tanks. Hitler now changed his mind again. Having despatched substantial forces from the central thrust to go south to Kiev, and others to go north to attack Leningrad, he decided that the attack on Moscow should go ahead after all. This decision ignored the ominous arrival of the September rains and the stiffening resistance of the Russians, soon to be commanded by the formidable Zhukov.

Hitler's absurd change of plan presented Guderian with another challenge and another opportunity. In the ten days after the fall of Kiev he had to reorganise Panzer Group 2, replenish ammunition, food and fuel, repair his worn-out tanks and vehicles, and prepare for another hectic drive north-eastwards towards Moscow. This feat of administration – only feasible because of the intense devotion and loyalty of all his troops – ranks with the most brilliant of his other achievements. It provides a valuable background to his remark, 'The troops must think we're crazy.'

Still inspired by his confidence and his leadership, the first tanks of Panzer Group 2 set off on 28 September, covered 130 miles in three days, and reached the important town of Orel on 3 October. Then to the anger, dismay and frustration of all the army leaders, Hitler again intervened and diverted forces for a local victory rather than keeping up the momentum towards Moscow. On the 5th Guderian's Panzer Group was renamed 'Second Panzer Army' – though this brought little solace and no additional tanks. The announcement coincided with more sinister developments. On that day the leading troops of 4th Panzer Division first encountered the Russian T34 tanks. Guderian remarked on the vast superiority of this tank, and added: 'The division suffered grievous casualties.' Even more worrying, that night it snowed and the roads 'became canals of bottomless mud'. He asked again for winter clothing and was told not to make unnecessary requests.

Here in the area of the town of Tula, Guderian's swift progress was finally halted. Russian resistance greatly increased, the temperature dropped to minus 20°, the snow deepened, and German losses in tanks became higher than the Russians'. In late November on the southern front, von Rundstedt was forced to withdraw under strong Russian pressure. When

Hitler ordered him not to do so he resigned. At almost the same time, Guderian and other commanders facing Moscow withdrew their forces in the face of a strong Russian advance.

By the end of November it had become clear that there would be no swift advance on Moscow, and the commanders became increasingly concerned as to whether they would be able to extricate their units from the grip of the Russians and of the winter. Von Brauchitsch allowed Guderian to withdraw from Tula to the line of the river around Orel. He wrote movingly to his wife of his concern: 'for my poor men. It is frightful, unimaginable'. On 17 December he received a personal call from Hitler, who promised him massive aid by air, but ordered him to stand fast.

Matters deteriorated rapidly, and on 20 December Guderian went to see Hitler. He was met by a harsh, hostile glare. Hitler had not been informed of the withdrawal to Orel and ordered it to be stopped at once. Guderian explained that the withdrawal could not be stopped because the earth was frozen five feet deep and it was impossible to dig trenches. Hitler was impervious to logic, reason or reality. Guderian hung on grimly to his factual arguments. They could not stop the withdrawal and the troops had to have winter clothes. He added that they were losing more men from frostbite than from enemy action. The long and acrimonious discussion went on for hours, and Guderian also suggested that officers from the front should be put into the decision-making councils of the army and the party. Hitler was furious.

Guderian then had the dismal task of returning to give his divisional commanders the new orders from Hitler. Already the Russians were pushing back his leading units. Then on 26 December, after unpleasant clashes with von Kluge who blamed him for the withdrawals, Guderian was dismissed. He issued a loyal and touching Order of the Day to his troops. Gradually the army learnt that Hitler had become the new Commander-in-Chief.

Sudden release from almost impossible tensions led to physical and psychological problems both for Guderian and his wife. He was always something of a hypochondriac, but he did suffer from continuing but slight heart problems, though not enough to influence his effectiveness. After his dismissal he was offered a large estate in East Prussia, and, ever the optimist, started planning for the future with enthusiasm. Like other commanders sacked by Hitler, he watched with apprehension as Himmler's SS units increased in size and power, and Göring claimed the highest priority in supplies for the Luftwaffe. After a lengthy period of frustrating idleness during which Germany suffered defeat at El Alamein and complete disaster at Stalingrad, by the beginning of 1943 Hitler was at last convinced that he must recall Guderian.

In February 1943 he was appointed Inspector General of Armoured Troops with direct responsibility to Hitler for every aspect of armoured warfare. The vested interests of the gunners, and of the SS units, prevented him obtaining the overall responsibility, but in March 1943 he did set out to introduce an effective system into the chaos of tank production. He soon re-established contact with many of his previous rivals, but von Kluge never forgave him and even challenged him to a duel. Guderian was approached by a group of conspirators who were considering the elimination of Hitler, but he gave cogent reasons for not joining them.

Respected as a man of ability and integrity, his enthusiasm and efficiency contributed to the rapidly increased production of new Panther and Tiger tanks, with improved armour and the more powerful 75mm gun. In July 1943 he ensured that he was close enough to the action at Kursk on the south Russian front, to assess their effectiveness, though the technical shortcomings of the new tanks were not the main reason for the disaster German forces suffered there. Guderian worked closely and enthusiastically on the supply of tanks and munitions with Albert Speer who had overall charge of war production. There were great achievements in the supply and technical field, but Guderian was still seriously frustrated – usually by Hitler's interference – in developing and carrying out effective defensive tactics for the panzer divisions.

By the beginning of 1944, Guderian became aware of various plots to remove Hitler, but he appears sincerely to have held aloof from them. At the same time, he had frequent clashes with Hitler over the strategic conduct of the war. On one occasion, voicing the feelings of many, he suggested to Hitler that he should hand over the direct conduct of the armed forces to a general with experience of war in action. Hitler did not agree. Like Rommel, another popular and successful tank commander, Guderian agonised over the damage done to the German cause by the Hitler's disastrous interventions.

In July 1944, when the Allies were already advancing from the Normandy bridgehead, the conspirators aiming to remove Hitler stepped up their activities. Rommel could have been a popular figurehead, and he had been directly sympathetic, but he was removed from the scene when he was injured in an Allied air attack. Although he was approached, Guderian still refused to compromise his oath of loyalty, either on the issue of Hitler's assassination, or the concept of a separate peace with the West. On 18 July, two days before the bomb plot, he was told that von Kluge, then Commander-in-Chief, was planning an appeal to the Western Allies. Guderian was horrified. That information and how he handled it could have dangerously compromised him. On 19 July he was asked to postpone a divisional exercise, which nominally aimed to deal with enemy air landings and civil unrest. On 20 July he inspected troops in the morning, and spent the afternoon at home on his estate. He was recalled from a long walk to hear the news of the failed bomb plot. In *Panzer Leader* (p. 339) he states: 'I knew nothing about the assassination attempt' – and he reiterates, defensively, details of his alibi for the day. Some critics believe he arranged his alibi at home on 20 July deliberately so as to avoid suspicion of implication. More severe critics maintain that Guderian betrayed the conspirators in order to obtain the highest army post for himself. This allegation is unjust and totally unfounded.

Such criticism was doubtless prompted by his summons on the following day to be appointed Chief of the Army General Staff – hardly a post anyone would have angled for at that moment. While Guderian took up this high office, Hitler exacted terrible vengeance on anyone connected with the bomb plot – even von Kluge and Rommel were to pay with their lives. Guderian took on his task with the greatest reluctance, and only because he wanted to defend all he held dear against the surging advances of the Russian armies.

Guderian's appointment soon involved him in the clash between the army and the Nazi, SS and Gestapo forces under Himmler. This became clear in the battle for Warsaw, when the SS units perpetrated horrendous crimes against Polish soldiers and civilians alike. Guderian still hoped to be able to defend his beloved homeland, but soon realised that this would be impossible. He was not involved in the Ardennes offensive in December 1944, except that his plans to stem the Russian advance were weakened when valuable panzer units were taken away from the eastern front.

During the following months, Guderian, often at the risk of his life, openly challenged Hitler's decisions on the conduct of military operations. To the amazement of other commanders on the council, Guderian stood up to Hitler and finally forced him to back down. Guderian increasingly felt that the destruction of Germany was now inevitable and had been brought about largely by Hitler's insane policies, and the military incompetence of

Himmler and his Nazi stooges. During March 1945, as enemy forces rampaged over Germany from both east and west, Guderian had a final bitter clash with Hitler. At the end of the meeting he was sent on six weeks' sick leave. He travelled with his wife to Munich, where he spent a week in hospital, and then joined a panzer unit in the Tyrol where he was captured by the Americans who interrogated him. No charges were brought against him and he was released in 1948. He spent his last years working on his memoirs and preparing *Panzer Leader* for publication. In 1952 it became a best-seller in America and was widely translated. He died in 1954.

Dubbed 'This maverick General' by his biographer, Kenneth Macksey, Guderian by his integrity and high principles pursued his career in commanding positions throughout the whole of the Nazi period from 1933 to 1945, without once compromising his honour or his loyalty to his ideals. Furthermore, he was the earliest military leader of his time to envisage the potential of the new weapon – the tank – and to mould its deployment to his own concepts. That alone justified his place as a great military leader, but he had, as well, the ability to train and enthuse his troops, and to lead them brilliantly in action. Few commanders have the ability to develop new methods of warfare, or to train men to use new weapons efficiently. Guderian excelled at all three, and despite the numbing degeneracy and corruption of the Nazi system, he imprinted his ideas on modern warfare. His training of the panzers, his brilliant drive to Abbeville, his eastward advance to Smolensk at the start of Operation 'Barbarossa', and finally his defensive plans for the panzer army, certainly make him one of the outstanding generals of the Second World War. He was, too, a warm, kind, thoughtful human being – the very reverse of the image of the Nazi ogre. He concluded *Panzer Leader* with the motto: 'I shall do what I believe to be right and honourable.'

PATTON

The image and the memory of General George Patton – one of the
most colourful characters of the Second World War – owes much to
the media. The popular press in the war years created 'Old Blood
and Guts Patton', and subsequently, the Hollywood presentation with
George Scott popularised this leading tank general. His love of flamboyant
uniforms to match his character, and his joint symbols of the pistol and
the tank projected an image that the press and the public relations were
eager to endorse.

Born in 1885, like Alexander the Great he was nurtured on the tales of
Troy and brought up in the military tradition. Totally dedicated to the art of
warfare, he excelled at the Virginia Military Institute as had his grandfather
and Stonewall Jackson, and entered West Point in 1904 together with many
others who were to make their reputations during the Second World War.

At West Point, although he was an outstanding horseman and a very
fine athlete, he was boastful and not at all popular. Later he stated: 'War is
the supreme test of man,' but such a view came from an extremely confident and, indeed, arrogant character. In spite of his athletic and sporting
prowess, he made very few friends, and this characteristic stayed
throughout his life. He did achieve his ambition of becoming a general and
a distinguished war leader, but he would have been wiser and more tactful
not to boast of this to his fellow West Point cadets. He intimidated some,
and alienated many more. His upbringing, with emphasis on heroic exploits
from Alexander to the American Civil War, helped to get him through his
course, but intellectually he was less than average and he resorted to much
learning by rote. He became well known for his ingratiating attitude to the
college staff and for never stepping out of line, but even so he had to repeat
a year of the course and took five years to graduate.

Having done so, in 1910 he married. His wife Beatrice was from a
refined and cultured Massachusetts family and brought some intellectual
balance to their lives, but she accepted his primacy in the family and the
crudity of some aspects of life as an army wife. Soon after their marriage,
the Pattons sailed to a posting in Hawaii in an old yacht. In 1912 Patton
represented the USA in the pentathlon at the Stockholm Olympics and

acquitted himself well. Then the couple drove through France, and Patton made contact with the French Military Centre for *épée* and sabre fencing. Beatrice, a strong Francophile, encouraged him to learn the language and to share her interests.

In 1916 he took part in Pershing's punitive expedition against Mexico. Pershing started with a small force which rapidly built up into an army of more than 150,000, with infantry, cavalry, artillery and air squadrons to crush Pancho Villa – who was virtually a bandit. Patton flourished in this Wild West type of activity and managed to get himself noticed by Pershing.

In 1917 he was given command of Pershing's HQ troops, and they sailed to France in May of that year. Patton, almost alone among the American military leaders, was an enthusiast for the tank. Initially he spent some time travelling to the various sectors of the Western Front with Pershing, but was then delighted to be chosen to lead a small US team to visit the leading French tank school. Soon afterwards he set up the first US tank unit near Nancy, and then a larger tank training centre. He relished this new responsibility, and spent the winter of 1917 assembling his vehicles and weapons, and training his crews. He liaised closely with the French – helped by his fluency in the language – and at the same time passed the General Staff College course. In May 1918 he witnessed one of the first tank battles when the French put in a counter-attack with tanks in a sector of their line which was under pressure. By August his tank unit was ready for action and took part in a battle near Verdun. After this initial action, his tanks were transferred over 40 miles to another sector of the front near Rheims. Ironically, these places, the epitomy of static trench warfare, where Patton first saw real action, featured again in his victorious drive in 1944 when his tanks swept past towards the German frontier. At the end of September 1918, as a major, he led the 304th Tank Brigade into action. His tank came under heavy fire and the supporting infantry were mown down. Patton himself was wounded by shrapnel and was taken to hospital. When the war ended he had been promoted to colonel, and had received the DSC, the DSM and the Purple Heart. In March 1919 he returned home.

Unlike most men who served on the Western Front, Patton, who was not a popular officer, appears to have been disappointed when the war ended and chances of further glory and promotion were curtailed. There followed nearly twenty years of rather dull postings – including two to Hawaii. His wife and their two daughters and son followed the routine of army families everywhere. The two girls married army officers and their son went to the Virginia Military Institute and West Point.

Patton's experience of the tank in battle in 1918, and his dedicated study of the tactics and strategy of tank warfare – similar to Guderian's in Germany, and Montgomery's in England – created new opportunities as war approached. When Pearl Harbor jolted the USA into war, Patton was already being groomed by the media as an heroic character. As a major general he had gained prestige if not notoriety for his command of the 2nd Armoured Division in massive military manoeuvres which were held across many of the southern states, and did something to bring home to the American people some of the realities of modern war. His flamboyant antics and colourful panache were taken up by a public relations system in dire need of a reassuring character. He played up to the press and nurtured his tough-guy image. His phrase: 'Grab the enemy and kick him in the arse,' was widely reported. Then in October 1942 he was given overall command of the expeditionary force which was to cross the Atlantic and capture Casablanca in French Morocco. His address to his assembled troops: 'Kill the lousy Hun bastards, and cut out their living guts', was not well received in the wider community, but it reinforced his reputation as an aggressive commander.

His force, more than 37,000 strong, crossed the Atlantic in more than 100 ships. Commanding three divisions plus naval and air units, Patton made a fairly straightforward plan for the assault at Casablanca. He estimated that the French North African troops would not fight too strongly, but did anticipate sterner resistance from the French Vichy naval and marine units.

Before the landings could take place, the Americans fought a battle with the pro-Vichy French navy. The battle lasted more than twenty-four hours, and at the end US battleships, cruisers, destroyers and dive-bombers had sunk or damaged the French battleship *Jean Bart* and eight destroyers. Patton in his flagship *Augusta* was caught up in the naval battle which delayed him getting ashore.

When he landed on 9 November the 3rd Division had already landed near Casablanca, but had been held up by heavy fire from French batteries of 75mm guns in and around the town. Nearly 90 miles farther north, the 9th Armored Division made a determined attack on the French defenders of an old Moorish fort. After a brisk fight in which a number of casualties were sustained, the garrison surrendered. More than 100 miles south of

141

Casablanca the 2nd Armored Division landed with little opposition and quickly drove north.

With so many untried officers and troops, there was confusion and fear on the beaches. When Patton himself landed – almost in a mood of exultation – his calm, brave and aggressive demeanour quickly took control and infused life into the attacks. He personally organised a tank attack on an enemy gun battery and then drove his forces towards Casablanca itself.

As 2nd Armored Division was approaching Casablanca from the south, the French asked for a truce. It had been a valuable baptism of fire for the untried US forces, and the surrender came on 11 November – Patton's birthday.

Patton's main aim was to take Casablanca, and develop it as a main supply base for the US forces in North Africa. Initially, after its capture, he trod the diplomatic path. Stressing support for *'La belle France'*, he got on well with the existing French Vichy administrators – many of whom had happily co-operated with the Germans – as he did with the Sultan of Morocco whom he hoped would lend Arab support in attacking the German lines of communication.

Having dealt diplomatically with the French, Patton was still faced with the problem of Franco's pro-Axis Spanish Morocco. Here he changed his technique. He moved the whole of the 2nd Armored Division and some of the 9th Infantry Division up to the Spanish Moroccan border, and invited the Spanish military governor to witness a military review. The parade of massed tanks with fighter-bombers flying overhead appeared to pass on the necessary message.

Already Patton was showing his deep knowledge of military history by quoting the clashes of Romans and Carthaginians on the very ground they were now crossing. His new regime in Casablanca was successful and the town was chosen for Roosevelt's and Churchill's conference in January 1943. Meanwhile he had received more decorations - an Oak Leaf Cluster to his DSM, and the *Légion d'honneur* from the French.

In March 1943 Patton was appointed to command all US troops in Tunisia – two infantry divisions, 1st Armored Division and a Ranger battalion. From this modest beginning, US forces in the European theatre rose to seventy divisions in seven armies. Since November 1942 1st Armored Division, which now came under Patton's command, had been harried and defeated by Rommel's 10th Panzer Division. It had been poorly led, outgunned, outmanoeuvred and hammered by Stukas, Messerschmitts and even by its own Lightnings. Its final humiliation had come at the Kasserine Pass just before Patton arrived. This battle-hardened division deeply resented the blood and guts exhortation with which its new commander greeted it.

While Patton was taking over the US Command, Montgomery and the Eighth Army were attacking Rommel's defensive position along the Mareth Line. Patton's equivocal feelings for 'Limeys' were exacerbated when he had been guaranteed air cover and then his HQ was plastered with bombs and raked with fire by Messerschmitts. Allied strategy had been for US forces to advance to the sea just west of the Mareth Line and cut off Rommel's forces. The Germans had anticipated this and Rommel therefore withdrew from Kasserine, a move which was not followed up swiftly enough by the relatively inexperienced US troops. The Allies had planned an attack on 17 March, and Eisenhower, Alexander and Patton were present. Before the full attack could go in, Rommel had withdrawn and then three days of heavy rain bogged down any advance. The US advance on the small town of Gafsa illustrates some of the problems that Patton was facing. Although there had been a big build-up of forces, and the presence of the top brass, the approach to Gafsa by relatively untried troops was slow and tentative and their reconnaissance inefficient. Then came the rain and more hesitation. Eventually the leading troops reached Gafsa only to discover that the Germans had left but not before thoroughly booby-trapping the place.

By the end of March Montgomery's Eighth Army had assaulted and overcome the Mareth Line, but Rommel had had time to withdraw to another strong defensive line which in three weeks of attacks Patton could not break. His forces did achieve one encouraging success when 1st Infantry Division held and repulsed a strong attack by 10th Panzer Division which retreated having lost more than half its tanks. On 7 April 1943 the leading units of Patton's II Corps met the advancing units of Eighth Army at Wadi Akarit, and the armies advanced together with British First Army. In July 1943 Patton was given command of US Seventh Army for the invasion of Sicily .

After the elimination of the Axis from North Africa, the next likely target for the Allies was Sicily, though strenuous efforts were made to deceive the enemy and suggest other possibilities. In one of these, Operation 'Mincemeat', the British dropped the body of a supposedly British officer in the sea off the coast of Spain. Documents recovered from the body and passed to the Germans indicated that the Allies intended to occupy Sardinia, and that the attack on Sicily was a feint.

Although the invasion did succeed and the island was conquered in thirty-eight days, a major opportunity was lost. Sicily was held by ten Italian and three German divisions, and though most of the Italian divisions were eliminated, the majority of the Germans got away to the mainland, to continue a long and bloody defensive campaign up the length of the peninsula. The Strait of Messina, that crucial stretch of water, little more than a mile wide at its narrowest, which had featured the Scylla and Charybdis of Greek mythology, and witnessed the equally crucial crossing of Garibaldi and the Thousand after they had vanquished the island, was itself a formidable obstacle. It seems remarkable that, given the overwhelming Allied control of both air and sea, the German divisions were allowed to escape. There had been serious disagreement at a high level over the proposed tactics for the Sicilian campaign, but there appears to have been little imaginative planning, and little intention in the final proposal of bagging all the German divisions.

The Allied attacking forces comprised Patton's US Seventh Army with six divisions, and Montgomery's British Eighth Army with five divisions. These battle-hardened divisions under overall direction of Eisenhower and Alexander, were backed up by 3,000 ships, many new weapons and equipment – landing-craft and DUKW amphibious vehicles known as 'ducks' – and by overwhelming air forces. Again one asks, why were the Germans allowed to escape across the Strait of Messina?

Patton was already notoriously outspoken, and given the need for close co-operation with Montgomery and Alexander, Eisenhower had warned him to count ten before he spoke. Patton tended to be critical of the British, although he never reached the level of offensiveness of Stilwell in Burma – and he had a serious clash even before the Sicily invasion started. He had proposed a plan based on speed and surprise, but the British plan for two major advances from the south coast was adopted, and Patton accepted it.

Operation 'Husky' began with airborne landings on 10 July 1943. The Italian divisions rarely fought hard, but the Germans, including the Hermann Göring Division, resisted stubbornly. The US advance, brushing aside Italian opposition, swept on and reached Marsala (where Garibaldi and the Thousand landed in 1860) on 22 July. Some 50,000 Italians surrendered. The Allies had suffered few casualties until now, though some of their troop-carrying planes were shot down by friendly fire. Patton had hoped by speed and surprise to prevent the German divisions escaping to the mainland, but the more ponderous British plan did not achieve this.

After capturing Marsala, Patton drove his forces even harder. He became obsessed with the need to reach Messina and Palermo before Montgomery, and this resulted in a bitter clash between Patton and his assistant commander, Omar Bradley, who argued that to achieve his ambition he was prepared to sacrifice the lives of his soldiers. Patton ignored Bradley's criticism and thrust on. Always in the front line, on one occasion he shot some mules that were blocking a bridge and threw their carts over the edge. Bradley's criticism did affect Patton and he anguished over the heavy casualties sustained in the advance to Messina.

The Allied advance continued, although the main German defence line running from the north coast to the south of Mount Etna held up many attacks. Eighth Army, advancing along the east coast, met very firm resistance from the German troops who were highly skilled in every aspect of defence and withdrawal. An experienced Canadian division, and well-known British divisions – 5th, 50th, 51st and 78th – were held up, particularly at Augusta and Catania. Creeping artillery barrages went ahead of the unfortunate infantry as they scrambled along the foothills of Mount Etna.

In the north Patton achieved a valuable success when he by-passed the German defence line with an amphibious landing at Sant Agata on the coast closer to Messina. Eventually, on 17 August, Patton's advance guard reached Messina only to find that the Germans had already left.

The Sicilian campaign progressed against a background of upheavals on the political front. The Allied advance precipitated an Axis crisis, and Hitler flew to northern Italy to bolster Mussolini. Then the Allies bombed Rome, and two days after Patton had entered Palermo on 23 July 1943 the Fascist Grand Council arrested Mussolini. King Victor Emmanuel asked Badoglio to take over the government and make peace moves. Hitler furiously opposed this, and sent several additional German divisions to Italy.

Eisenhower had hoped that Patton would emerge from the Sicilian campaign as a successful and mature army commander with enough battle experience to offset the greater experience of Alexander and Montgomery. Patton was still unpredictable – witness the incident of the mules on the bridge, and the sacking of the successful and popular commander of US 1st Division in mid-campaign. Eisenhower still nurtured these hopes, when news came to him of an incident – trivial in itself – but which in the eyes of the American public, was to overshadow the significant military achievements of the campaign.

Patton was visiting a field hospital in Sicily full of badly wounded men. He was under great stress, conscious perhaps that his strategy of rushing towards Messina had caused very high casualties. He went from bed to bed having a quiet word with the men, when he came to a man who was shaking with nerves and who said, 'I can't take it.' Patton lost control, struck the man in the face and ordered him out of the tent with such phrases as 'yellow-bellied son of a bitch – not fit to lie in bed next to brave wounded men'. In another incident a few days later he assaulted another soldier and abused him as 'a cowardly bastard'.

These incidents presented Eisenhower with a grave dilemma. He had three alternatives: relieve Patton and send him home for court-martial; order a field court-martial; or arrange some other punishment. He told advisers who were severely critical that they were asking him to get rid of his best general. In the end, Eisenhower, declaring Patton's conduct to be despicable, ordered him to apologise publicly to the soldiers he had struck, to the medical staff who had witnessed the incidents, and to all the officers and men in Seventh Army. Censorship was removed and soon the whole of America knew what had happened. This issue raised intense debate: in the Seventh Army where Patton was extremely unpopular, and at home where after lurid press reports, his family suffered much abuse, but it appeared that a large majority of the people supported him.

This was at a critical stage of the war, when Italy's surrender was expected in a matter of days, and when senior command posts were being allocated prior to the Second Front. Patton's real punishment was to be side-lined just at this moment. He was relieved of his command of the Seventh Army, and saw Omar Bradley promoted over his head to command US First Army for the invasion of Normandy. Patton was sent to Corsica where he used his fluent French to talk about his pride in the recapture of the birthplace of Napoleon. He performed a similar function in Malta, where he displayed his amazing knowledge of the wars and civilisations of antiquity, and the ancient sieges of Malta.

These trivial achievements could not hide his deep hurt and frustration. Then he was posted to England, furious that he was not getting a battle command. From their days in Tunis Rommel had been fascinated by Patton, and he could not believe that one of the best US generals could be sacked for striking a soldier. Eisenhower – profiting from this information – used Patton as part of a significant deception plan. He was given a well-publicised HQ at Knutsford in Cheshire, and the command of twelve divisions – dummy divisions complete with dummy huts and dummy tanks – which were preparing to land in the Calais area. This deception succeeded in diverting some German forces from the Normandy area, but all the divisions were phoney, and Patton, ever the action man, began to feel that he, too, was phoney.

He continued to remain close to controversy. In a minor engagement – opening a joint Anglo-American forces' club – he made a light-hearted aside about the grand days to come when Germany had been defeated, and America and Britain would rule the world. Patton had checked that the press was not present, but this trivial remark caused a serious diplomatic incident and a formal Russian protest. In the end the issue was referred right to the top, to General George Marshall. Patton was again reprimanded. He suffered further frustration when the D-Day invasion took place and he was not part of it. He was still arrogant and conceited, and during this period he continued to make indiscreet and destructive criticisms of Montgomery, now commanding 21st Army Group.

Omar Bradley, who had been Patton's 2 i/c in Sicily, now played a significant role in Patton's career. Bradley, commanding US First Army, proved himself to be one of the ablest strategists on the Allied side. Quiet, efficient, determined, he contrasted with Patton in every way. In June 1944 he saw the need for the US forces, with their huge inventory of tanks and guns, to be prepared for a fast-moving breakout from the Normandy beach-head. Thus was formulated the plan that, while the main US, British and Canadian forces fought and destroyed the German armies in the area of Caen, Falaise and Alençon, another US army should be ready to drive south from the Cotentin peninsula, and sweep round eastwards towards Le Mans and make a swift breakthrough which the Germans would be unable to contain. US Third Army would fulfil this role and Bradley chose Patton to command it. Post-war intelligence has revealed that, at that time, the Germans still believed Patton and his supposed twelve divisions were about to land and break through at Calais.

After ten weeks of fierce, bloody and constant fighting, from the beaches and through the Normandy bocage – those narrow, closely wooded groves, ideal for defence, which the Germans used brilliantly – at last a hole began to appear in the German defences west of the Cherbourg peninsula. By the end of July, Patton's Third Army had been assembled, and on the 28th he was ready to order his tanks forward in Operation 'Cobra'.

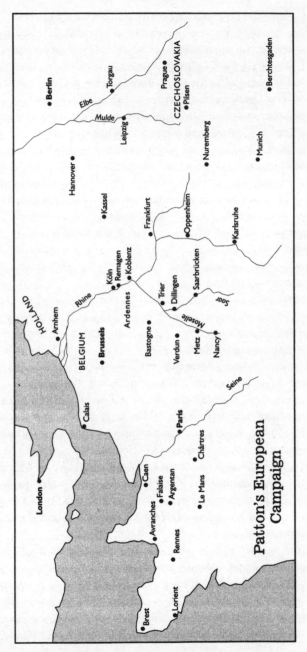

Patton's European Campaign

Third Army's tanks and guns had started crossing in July when the Normandy beaches were packed with guns, vehicles, equipment and supplies. Patton, delighted to be again part of the action, established his HQ in a village and, remembering Sicily, was punctilious in handling the press. He gave a clear outline of his intention to break out and advance as swiftly as possible. Bradley's VII and VIII Corps in First Army fought prolonged battles around La Haye du Puits, and massive bombing strikes preceded each advance, on one occasion 2,000 aircraft dropping 4,000 tons of bombs; but as Fourteenth Army discovered in Burma, well dug-in defenders can survive the heaviest bombardment of shells or bombs, and remain operational. The Germans did just that, and fought ferociously as the ground troops moved in. In the western sector where Patton's breakout was planned, von Rundstedt still had twelve divisions. As the Allies slowly drove forward, the German high command had to decide whether to withdraw from Normandy. Then, to the Allies' advantage, Hitler intervened, and forbade any withdrawal. Von Rundstedt, who saw the urgent need to regroup, resigned, and von Kluge took over. After more massive attacks accompanied by 'carpet bombing', the Allies began to advance, but their progress was neither swift nor easy. The Germans, masters of defensive tactics, left mines and booby-traps everywhere, even on dead bodies.

On 30 July 1944 Patton's Third Army, led by 4th Armored Division, began to move. No formation had ever been better prepared or better equipped for this type of advance. Coutances was reached and passed and the tanks and armoured personnel carriers set off down the wide straight roads of Western France. By 31 July, Avranches, the hinge of the entire operation, had been captured. Then part of the formation veered west into Brittany while the main body turned south-eastwards towards Le Mans. Leading this advance was one of the outstanding divisions of the European campaign – and Patton's favourite – 4th Armored Division. The rapidly moving tanks not only broke through towards Le Mans, but by the end of the first week of August the western probe had advanced successfully against little opposition, occupying most of Brittany and reaching the ports of Brest and Lorient, though the latter held out until the end of the war.

Although the advance was swift, there were many clashes. One of the early successes of 4th Armored was achieved when a small unit ambushed the HQ of an SS panzer division and completely annihilated it. They discovered afterwards that the Germans were absolutely weighed down with loot – wine, cheeses, cigars, fur coats and silk underwear. As the German troops broke, the world witnessed a new sight – German military refugees pushing carts and perambulators, trying to escape and being harried from dawn to dusk by Allied fighters and bombers. A contrast to 1940, when Guderian had led his troops through the same country.

Third Army advanced so swiftly that the Germans had difficulty in anticipating its real objective. They moved troops towards Brittany, and then it was too late to counteract Patton's main drive, which was intended to wheel north from Le Mans and trap the whole of German Seventh Army. In the breakout, Patton – no longer a mere blustering, flamboyant tank leader – had controlled one of the most successful operations of the war. By the middle of August his three corps had occupied Brittany, advanced south to St-Nazaire and were thrusting eastwards. Most crucially, on 13 August he reached Argentan, the southern point of the Falaise gap, less than fifteen miles from Falaise. If the gap could be closed the German Seventh Army was doomed. The German commander von Kluge who, against Hitler's wishes, had ordered his troops to withdraw from the Falaise pocket, was summarily dismissed, and committed suicide in the plane taking him back to Berlin. On 21 August, the Falaise gap was closed, and the Allies took 50,000 prisoners and found 10,000 dead. Simultaneously Patton's leading tanks thrust on, capturing Chartres and Orléans on 16 August, and coming close to Paris.

Patton's brilliant advance had totally confused the German High Command. Initially they assumed his main drive would be to Brittany, to secure the ports of Brest and Lorient. Then when his main force wheeled east, they assumed he would thrust towards Paris, and moved their defending troops accordingly, only to find Third Army's tanks pushing north to Argentan – to seal the fate of Seventh Army.

Hitler ordered that Paris be razed, but the German governor, von Choltitz, who had already been in touch with French resistance forces, ignored the order, and on 25 August French and US troops arrived to take over the city. De Gaulle arrived that evening. Third Army, determined to keep up the momentum, drove relentlessly onwards.

It had taken but a few days from Hitler's order forbidding von Rundstedt to withdraw from Normandy, to the capture of Paris. While Third Army's headlong advance caused chaos and confusion, and occupied vast areas of country, it had the additional effect of making it impossible for the German High Command to regroup or control the situation. This paralysis of command and control of the German forces in northern France at this time, because of the rampaging advance of Patton, appears remarkably similar to the disintegration of the French Command in the summer of 1940.

After Paris had fallen Patton continued his drive to the east, taking a leadership role in which he excelled. Third Army advanced nearly 500 miles in two weeks, and Patton was there driving them on, cheering, cajoling, providing the leadership, but showing as well his amazing skill in organising the logistics for this remarkable advance. The Third Army drive raised significant strategic issues. While they drove east of Paris, the German Seventh Army still faced Bradley and Montgomery. How far could Patton be allowed to advance, with such substantial enemy forces still unsubdued in his rear? Patton, ever suspicious of Montgomery and the British, was outraged at any curb on his progress. In the initial breakout, Bradley had ordered him to halt at Argentan, the southern jaw of the Falaise trap. Now, after the fall of Paris, another factor emerged. From Le Mans – captured on 8 August – Third Army's leading tanks reached Rheims on the 29th. Patton was buoyed up by the thought that in a few weeks he could be leading the victorious Allied advance across the border and into the heartland of Germany. Any curb on this, he tended to blame on the machinations of the British and especially Montgomery. In fact, Patton's brilliant advance had in some ways created the main problem – an adequate supply of fuel.

On 3 September 1944 his tanks ran out of fuel. He begged and implored for more fuel to keep the momentum going. He offered to give up supplies of food and even ammunition if only he could have more fuel. He was the main instigator of The Red Ball Express, which involved thousands of US heavy trucks driving night and day to bring fuel and supplies across France from Cherbourg to the advancing units approaching the German border, but even this effort could not sustain such a huge force. The US armies came to a halt.

Fuel was not the only problem. Eisenhower had other strategic and political issues to consider in deciding priorities. At this time one of Hitler's last desperate gambles had been the V1 attacks on London and, from September, the more deadly V2 rockets. Churchill had alerted Roosevelt and Eisenhower to the suffering and devastation in London, and Eisenhower had properly given priority to British Second Army to clear the area from which the V1 'doodlebugs' were being launched. This decision could not be gainsaid, but there were those who thought that if Patton had been adequately supported and supplied, his rapid advance could have continued into Germany before any major defence could be organised, and he might have been able to force a German capitulation before the winter. Eisenhower carried the overall strategic responsibility, and had to balance the needs of all the Allied armies – not just Patton's.

The high hopes of early September of finishing the war before Christmas depended on a massive breakthrough into Germany. The Joint Chiefs of Staff decided that this should be attempted not by Patton but by Montgomery's brainchild, Operation 'Market Garden', in which British 1st Airborne Division, 101st and 82nd US Airborne Divisions and the Polish Parachute Brigade were dropped in Holland to seize the bridges over the Rhine. They were to spearhead a swift advance through Holland and into the flat plains of north Germany. This gamble came to a halt at Arnhem. By 21 September, when the Germans recaptured the bridge at Arnhem – the 'Bridge Too Far' – Patton had already continued his advance eastwards from Rheims. His rapidly moving tanks crashed through many places whose names, like Marne and Verdun, were redolent of static trench warfare. He had reached Metz in the upper valley of the Moselle. At this stage, Montgomery was arguing for a single thrust into Germany, but Eisenhower insisted on a broad front approach. Supplies remained a paramount issue, since Cherbourg was still the only major supply port, and Eisenhower rightly gave priority to the forces attempting to clear the estuary of the Scheldt and to open the great port of Antwerp.

The US armies' enforced halt for lack of fuel, when they were probing beyond Nancy, Metz and Luxembourg, gave the Germans a breathing-space of which they took full advantage. Somehow they regrouped their scattered units, hastily organised defences along the Siegfried Line and along the Rhine, and called up all able-bodied males, including old men and school-boys. Secret weapons and new jet planes appeared and gave the German people renewed hope. Where Patton had faced disintegration and chaos, suddenly there were fiercely defended strongholds to overcome. In Metz the defences were manned by cadets from an army training school and their fanatical resistance was to cost many American lives. From the high days of summer, suddenly an early wet autumn brought swollen rivers and acres of mud in which tanks just wallowed. In this dramatically changed situation, Patton had to prove his quality in a totally different type of war.

Allied strategy now changed, the destruction of German industry taking priority. US First and Ninth Armies set their sights on the Ruhr, and Third Army had the complex and difficult task of overcoming the Saar industrial complex. In the east, the Russians were advancing even faster, aiming to destroy Silesia, while industrial targets in Czechoslovakia were allocated to home-based heavy bombers. High priority was given to the destruction of

V1 and V2 bases, and the factories manufacturing jet aircraft. The Allies were seriously concerned about the speed and power of the jet fighters which were now appearing, and they feared even more the jet bombers which they knew were nearing completion. The Saar industrial complex, built up on its plentiful supply of iron, had been deliberately developed by the Nazi scientists because the key components and most factories could be located underground. The whole complex stretched through the Saar and into Lorraine and Luxembourg. This became Patton's first objective.

He quickly developed new tactics for the totally changed situation. Now each cleverly defended town or village presented another challenge. He usually attacked from the most difficult, and therefore the most unexpected, direction, and this secured a number of useful advances. Nancy fell on 15 September. As the advance reached the Moselle and the Saar rivers and their tributaries, and approached the Siegfried Line, the fighting became fiercer and casualties increased. Bridges had to be constructed under fire, despite the use of dense smoke-screens to conceal the work.

Patton suffered severe frustration at this time even though the logic of the High Command's strategic decisions was obvious enough. While US First and Ninth Armies were heading for the Ruhr, Canadian First and British Second Armies would advance over flatter, open country, where northern Holland merged into Germany. US Third Army, however, was confronting a wet mountainous area ideal for defensive delaying tactics. Bradley's HQ coined a new phrase for Patton's situation, 'active defence'. Patton stated publicly that he did not understand it, and continued his aggressive pressure along the swollen rivers of the Saar. Every day his fighting patrols pushed forward to overrun another village or cross another tributary of the Moselle. Then Hitler recalled von Rundstedt and he took over the defences around the Saar. Still Patton drove forward. No spectacular gains were made, but even in mid-September – soon after the costly enforced halt for lack of fuel – Patton, using sound armour, infantry and artillery tactics, defeated the German 16th Division, and by a swift flanking drive ambushed and destroyed a panzer brigade. One of the marks of a great commander is that he dominates the enemy in his theatre and dictates the action. This Patton achieved.

By the end of September he was facing a formidable proposition – the fortress city of Metz. For centuries this had been the guardian of the eastern ramparts of France, and the main communications centre controlling the routes up the Moselle valley to Luxembourg and into the Rhine valley, and from Switzerland westwards into France. From the 5th century onwards it had stood virtually impregnable – throughout the wars of religion, the Napoleonic Wars, the Franco-Prussian War and the Great War. At the beginning of the month, during their brief respite from Patton's advance, the Germans had reinforced its medieval bastions with the most up-to-date weaponry.

Patton knew that if Metz were not taken his progress into Germany would be rendered substantially more difficult, but he also reckoned that it would require three divisions to besiege the city. So on 1 October he launched a direct frontal assault. Most of the defensive systems were interconnected by a maze of tunnels, deep underground, with command posts co-ordinating fire from every type of gun. The defenders appeared immune to the heaviest bombardment, and the US infantry and engineers attempting to scale the walls or to dig tunnels made scant progress. At Fort Driant, one of the most powerful of the defensive towers, the Americans broke in and began to probe along the tunnels. They were impeded by mines, booby-traps, steel doors, collapsed roofs and enemy fire. Artillery and aerial bombardment did nothing to help the attackers in this weird subterranean struggle. After nearly two weeks when negligible progress had been made, Patton appeared to give up, but he claimed that valuable information had been gained.

Having apparently decided not to continue the assault on Metz, he resumed his drive further into the Saar, beginning with that most difficult of military operations, a river crossing against a powerfully entrenched enemy. With the autumn rains the Moselle was a formidable obstacle in itself, but the leading infantry units of 5th and 95th Divisions, despite grievous losses, got across and resumed the advance. This was a remarkable feat of bravery and determination, rightly commended by Patton, but its true purpose soon became apparent, when by the end of November Metz was encircled and all the fortresses had surrendered. This was a significant military victory and illustrated yet another aspect of Patton's ability as a general. When the city fell senior SS and Gestapo officers were taken prisoner. One SS general, who was in fact the senior Gestapo officer for the entire region, and who was detested by the regular army colonel who had conducted the defence, was caught trying to slink away in disguise. Fuming with contempt, Patton told him he was the lowest form of animal life.

Patton now resumed his systematic assault on the Saar region with a three-pronged advance to Saarbrücken, the main industrial and route centre. By the end of November, in atrocious weather, his divisions were through the useless Maginot Line and had reached the River Saar. They were now menacing Saarbrücken, Dillingen and other industrial centres on the very border with Germany, and Patton felt that he was poised to break into the German heartland. Before doing so he had to breach the Siegfried Line. Here skilfully prepared concrete tank traps, carefully co-ordinated fire power from every type of gun, with underground communications, and powerful tactical reserves, proved a daunting obstacle. Patton started his attack on 29 November with eight divisions. His forces made six crossings of the Saar and in three weeks of bitter fighting had drawn close to most of the industrial towns of the Saar, and had fought their way into Dillingen. At this crucial moment Patton was called upon to show his greatness as a commander in another and unexpected way.

When the rapidly advancing Allies ran out of fuel in early September, Hitler had already been planning a counter-stroke, and had some factors in his favour. He had raised nearly a million more fighting troops, and the Volksturm, men aged sixteen to sixty, had been established. Despite the Allied heavy bombing campaign, armament production had been brought to a peak under Minister Albert Speer. By the beginning of October Hitler's plans for Operation 'Watch on the Rhine' had been completed. This aimed to hit the US forces in the Ardennes with thirty-one divisions, crash through their relatively weak defences, grab the bridges over the Meuse, and drive on to Antwerp, thus splitting the entire Allied force. Hitler reckoned, correctly, that an attack in winter would be helped by fog and rain which would curb the gigantic Allied air superiority. The main attacks would be launched by three panzer armies. The Americans considered the Ardennes to be a quiet sector, and it was held by a couple of weak divisions, and one newly arrived from the USA.

On 16 December 1944, in heavy fog which precluded all flying, I Panzer Corps broke through fairly light defences and made for the Meuse bridges. In this crisis, further confusion was caused by Skorzeny's ploy of infiltrating saboteurs in American uniforms, an operation which proved remarkably successful. After thirty-six hours of fairly rapid advances, skilful defence and the blowing of bridges, gradually slowed the panzer momentum.

Within three days it became clear that the town of Bastogne was the key to the Ardennes offensive. At Verdun on 18 December Eisenhower, Bradley and Patton conferred urgently on how best to hold the southern sector of Hitler's attack. This was not the time for recriminations, but the Ardennes offensive created dangerous tensions among the senior commanders.

Clearly, Eisenhower – kept isolated by the Skorzeny threat – bore responsibility, but Bradley, commanding 12th Army Group, and, more specifically, Hodges, commanding US First Army, had to shoulder the blame for the reversal. Patton was in no way implicated, but he was destined to play an important role in the defeat of von Rundstedt's Ardennes break-out. Eisenhower's plan included moving major US units southwards, and giving Montgomery the responsibility of destroying the advance in the north and west, while Patton held the southern sector. Patton, bitter that his advance through and beyond the Saar was being frustrated, and still harbouring his old resentment of Montgomery, when told to hold the southern sector, is alleged to have burst out that he would stuff von Rundstedt down Montgomery's throat. Nevertheless he undertook to do what few commanders would have even considered. He agreed to disengage his forces from their positions beyond the Saar, change the direction of his advance by 90 degrees and rescue the beleaguered US troops in Bastogne. At the conference, British representatives just did not believe that this could be done, or that Patton could do it.

As soon as he left the conference his orders flowed through his excellent communications system to such effect that units began to move off immediately – told that they would receive details later. The US 101st Airborne Division was rushed into Bastogne next day – 19 December. In appalling conditions of snow, ice, rain and fog, hampered by inadequate roads through difficult hill country, Patton's favourite 4th Armored Division covered one hundred miles in thirty-six hours. Other divisions moved as quickly. Bastogne was a crucial focal point of the network of roads and railways. It was besieged by von Manteuffel's Fifth Panzer Army, part of which had by-passed the town and advanced a further thirty miles to Dinant in the upper Meuse valley. Patton's rapid and powerful advance from the south towards Bastogne with armoured and infantry divisions posed a serious threat which von Manteuffel and von Rundstedt could not ignore. At the same time, Montgomery detached XXX Corps from British Second Army and hurried them south to defend the lower Meuse bridges.

Manteuffel's move to Dinant on 24 December proved to be the farthest point of their advance. To the north of the Battle of the Bulge, Sixth Panzer Army had ground to a halt by 24 December and then was forced to divert troops to the Bastogne area to counter the obvious threat from Patton. The fierce and prolonged fighting in and around Bastogne took place in continuing snow, rain and fog which neither side were properly prepared for and which itself added to the horror. Patton introduced an element of grim humour by publicly appealing to God to put a stop to the rain and fog. Almost at once fine weather appeared, and the overwhelmingly superior Allied air forces were able to set upon and destroy the panzers now uncomfortably isolated across the whole area of the Battle of the Bulge. Patton's divisions continued to pound northwards and on 26 December relieved Bastogne. His advance, his threat to the southern flank of the German drive, and his relief of Bastogne played a most important part in the defeat of the dangerous Ardennes offensive.

After Hitler's final throw in the Ardennes, Eisenhower reverted to his strategy of a broad advance towards the Rhine, and throughout weeks of savage fighting the Allies pressed on towards the German heartland. In this situation, Patton realised that his Third Army would not have a high priority for supplies, because the prime target would be the Ruhr and the flatter reaches of the Rhine farther north. Starting in January 1945, Canadians, British, Poles, French and Americans, from Arnhem in the north down to the Swiss border, slowly advanced.

Following the spectacular success of Third Army's relief of Bastogne, and their role in the German defeat, Patton's prestige remained high. Having from Sicily onwards rarely been popular with his troops, his personal success at Bastogne greatly improved his image, and his colourful exhortations received a better response. In January and February Third Army's twelve divisions probed forward through the hilly area of the Eiffel and down the river valley towards Koblenz where the Moselle joins the Rhine, at the famous spot where a memorial celebrates the foundation of the German Empire by Bismarck in 1870. By the end of February the Allied forces were approaching the Rhine along its entire length. Hundreds of divisions were now operating on German soil, happy that they were no longer destroying the towns and villages of Holland, Belgium, Luxembourg and France.

Patton's divisions were not the first to reach the Rhine, but after some unspectacular progress at the beginning of February his armour – once again 4th Armored Division – managed to break through the main German defences and begin a more rapid advance. On his flanks to the north and south (US First Army under Hodges, Seventh under Patch) the tanks began to roll, and with close co-operation between the three, large numbers of German prisoners were rounded-up. The greater publicity given to the capture of the bridge at Remagen – by Hodges' First Army on 7 March –

tended to overshadow the equally significant advances and successes of Patton's armour and infantry. They slowly advanced eastwards from Koblenz and up the historic Middle Rhine to Mainz, where the Maine joins the Rhine, and onwards to Mannheim and Karlsruhe. Here Seventh Army linked up with French First Army under General de Lattre de Tassigny, operating from the Swiss border northwards.

As the Allied armies approached the Rhine, Patton engaged in a slightly mischievous ploy. Still pursuing a rather foolish grudge against Montgomery, he was determined to claim that his forces crossed the Rhine before Montgomery's. He knew that Montgomery was planning a major assault backed up by the largest concentration of tanks, guns and aircraft since D-Day. The attack was due at midnight on 23 March. Patton therefore gave orders that the leading units of 5th Infantry Division, using rubber boats, but not supported by any artillery build-up, and in total silence, would cross the river at 23.30 hours on 22 March near Oppenheim. The rubber boats set off at the exact time and reached the far bank completely unobserved. The enemy was only alerted some twenty minutes later, and it took them more than two hours to locate the exact landing-place. By this time a substantial bridgehead had been achieved, and was strong enough to repel the expected counter-attack. This crossing was hardly significant in military terms, but with Patton's jaundiced view of Montgomery, it gave him some satisfaction to announce to the world that his forces had crossed the Rhine before Montgomery's rather heavy-handed approach had even started.

Once the Allied armies had crossed the Rhine, and swift movement became possible, difficult political and strategic decisions had to be taken. This created renewed tension between the senior commanders, and between them and the politicians. The parameters for many of these problems stemmed from Eisenhower's message to Stalin – on his own initiative – that the main Allied advance from the west would aim at Leipzig and Dresden – not Berlin. Churchill, who had a far more critical view of the Russians, was horrified at this suggestion. He demanded that the Allies drive as far east as possible, arguing, correctly, that the Russians would not give up territory they had conquered. Montgomery, whose relations with the Americans had deteriorated since he had spoken publicly of bailing out the Americans in the Ardennes, was equally aggrieved that his target was not to be Berlin. Eisenhower's decision was based partly on the supposed need to prevent a Nazi last-ditch stand in an Alpine redoubt, though later it was discovered that the Germans had no such plan. The idea of a swift drive to Leipzig and

Dresden at least pleased Patton, for the rolling countryside of southern Germany was ideal for his type of blitzkrieg warfare.

From the tentative crossing of the Rhine at Oppenheim on 22 March 1945, it is remarkable how quickly the Allied advance followed. By 28 March the leading Third Army units had captured Frankfurt am Main and wheeled north to link up with Hodges' First Army, trapping a complete German army corps. This became a repeat of the style of the Normandy breakout. Tanks roared ahead with little opposition, and infantry followed along the open highways in fast-moving trucks, almost in holiday mood. They all became adept at locating hidden stores of wine and food, and valuable souvenirs.

On occasion the headlong advance was halted – as at Kassel – which Third Army captured on 4 April after two days of stubborn fighting. Kassel was an important centre at a junction of the autobahn. It illustrated other aspects of the sudden collapse of the Wehrmacht. Most German soldiers readily gave themselves up, but some SS units and especially the fanatical members of the Hitler Youth were always liable to snipe or lay booby-traps.

Patton now spent days driving hectically in his jeep, trying to keep control, though all his headquarters were moving just as rapidly, and communication was very difficult. Once again, supplies were the key problem, not so much the supply of ammunition, since not much was being used, but of fuel. Hitler, in yet another insane order, had demanded a scorched earth policy, with the destruction of every house, road, bridge, railway, factory or warehouse, but fortunately most German commanders ignored this, and generally as the troops moved through the towns and villages of southern Germany people seemed to be going about their normal lives. In contrast, in towns where a determined SS unit decided to fight on, those towns were systematically destroyed.

The top-level fears of the mythical Nazi redoubt in the Alps certainly favoured Patton. Third Army now received priority for fuel and reinforcements, so that it could drive unimpaired across the country towards Czechoslovakia and Austria, thus completely dividing the German armed forces. It also had to ensure that it would be in a position to prevent die-hard Nazi divisions and the Nazi hierarchy from reaching the Alpine redoubt. With its reinforcements Third Army's strength built up to twelve infantry and six armoured divisions.

During April 1945 the Allied armies drove relentlessly eastwards, meeting occasional firm resistance which was quickly overcome. In the east the Russians continued their drive on Berlin, and soon each side had to consider strategic and tactical issues for the division and control of Germany after their armies had joined up. In the west there was friendly rivalry between American armies over which famous cities they would liberate. Patton was sandwiched between Hodges' First Army on his northern flank and Patch's Seventh Army to the south.

The names of new rivers now appeared on the maps and in the head-lines – replacing the Rhine, Moselle and Saar. The Weser was crossed and Hanover taken on 10 April, and Magdeburg on the Elbe fell to US Ninth Army on 11 April. After Patton's troops had captured Kassel on 4 April, they reached the Mulde, the main western tributary of the Elbe on the 13th. New frustrations surfaced. Third Army had been ordered to veer south-eastwards towards Czechoslovakia and Austria. The problems facing Eisenhower and his Russian counterparts Zhukov and Konev are vividly illustrated by the question of Czechoslovakia. Patton, his tanks already on the move, wanted to advance directly to Prague, where Czech patriots had already begun to revolt. They were eager to welcome American forces, but Eisenhower had agreed that Prague be reserved for the Russians. So Patton obeyed orders, advanced as far as Pilsen – which had its compensations – and halted. At this time his more southerly prong entered Linz in Austria, which Hitler, in an emotional moment, had entered in 1938.

The rapid military advances brought about the total collapse of Germany, and created a situation of massive and indescribable chaos. Millions of people – refugees, prisoners of war, Wehrmacht deserters, concentration camp victims and slave labour victims – took to the roads. Prisoners of every nationality were desperate to get home. German soldiers were desperate to hide themselves in the flood of refugees. From the east, hundreds of thousands fled to the west, fearful of the advancing Russians. The Allied armies did their best to cope with this tide of human flotsam, but soon they had another grave and horrific task to perform.

It fell to the battle-weary Allied troops during April1945 to overrun the Nazi concentration camps. From Belsen near the Luneberg Heath, where Montgomery was shortly to receive the surrender of the northern German armies, through the extermination camps of Poland, to Dachau outside Munich, the advancing troops found more than fifty camps where the worst excesses of the Holocaust and Hitler's insane Final Solution had been perpe-trated. The effect of such horrors on hardened troops accustomed to the horrors of modern battle was instantaneous and permanent. This was the final evil they had been fighting, and it confirmed and clarified the reason for all the sacrifices and the loss of so many friends and comrades.

Patton gave a personal lead in this grim task when a concentration camp was discovered; he had all the local people rounded-up and taken in to see the gas chambers, the ovens, the piles of rotting corpses, and the pitiful survivors, often unable to walk and scarcely able to breathe. In one camp 4,000 prisoners had been starved or clubbed to death, and their corpses slung into a wood and barely covered. Patton forced the local people to dig a proper covering over the mass grave. In another small innocent-looking town, 300 Polish Jews had been killed. Patton ensured that the local citizens, who pretended that they knew nothing of it, dug the graves to complete a dignified burial. All over Germany grim Allied soldiers were to face up to the real horror of Nazi rule. Patton's personal involvement in these macabre but necessary rituals somehow confirmed his relationships and his reputation with his soldiers. In contrast to their feelings in Sicily, they now respected and revered him, and this quickly spread through the media to a wider public.

Patton's forces had dutifully halted at Pilsen, about sixty miles from Prague. Then desperate and urgent appeals for help came from the Czech patriots in the city. The SS and the Luftwaffe had decided to wreak one final savage vengeance on their victims in Prague. They murdered all the men they could find, blew up or bombed as many buildings as possible, and herded women and children in front of them into the firing line. Patton's tanks were the nearest available and they hurried forward to help. The SS, having slaughtered women and children, had no wish to take on Third Army, and they slunk away into the swarms of refugees or into the prison camps.

Patton's supporters often felt that his forces had been diverted from the most prestigious assignments, e.g., the taking of Paris, or being the first to reach Berlin – and he was to suffer one further disappointment. Although Third Army had led the advance into eastern Germany, it fell to the leading units of Hodges' First Army to link up with the Russians. They met at the medieval town of Torgau on the River Elbe on 25 April 1945. The town, deeply involved with Martin Luther and the Reformation, now boasts as well the bridge and a suitable memorial, where the historic meeting of American and Russians forces took place.

Patton had paranoid views about communism and almost equally about the Russians, and he may not have regretted that he had not been the first to meet them at Torgau. Soon afterwards his strong views created another crisis, from a relatively trivial incident. At a formal dinner with senior Russian officers to celebrate the victory over Germany and the link-up between American and Russian forces, a Russian general paid tribute to Patton and invited him to drink a toast. Patton, forgetting all his warnings from Bradley, Eisenhower and George Marshall, replied that he would never drink with any Russian son of a bitch. The Russian gritted his teeth and replied in similar vein. A direct confrontation was avoided, but the press were present and an international incident quickly arose. Patton had a furious clash by telephone with Bedell-Smith in the Pentagon and said that America would have to fight the bolsheviks some time, and the best thing would be to get the Germans on our side and start on the Russians straight away. Such an opinion may have been remarkably percipient, and may have represented a view held by right-wing American opinion, but in its context it was totally unacceptable. Patton was immediately relieved of his command of Third Army which he had led so brilliantly from June 1944 in Normandy.

He returned to Boston in June 1945 to an ecstatic welcome as the conquering hero. He appeared at official functions in full-dress uniform with his shining helmet and its four stars, complete with pistol in his belt and carrying his riding whip, to conform to the image that had been built up. He was exactly the type of returning hero the American people wanted to see.

After an enjoyable leave, mostly with his family, but travelling across the United States to receive plaudits and bouquets, he returned to Germany to command, not Third Army whose task was completed, but Fifteenth Army, largely a paper organisation set up to study the wider aspects and lessons of the war. With his life-long interest in military affairs and the study of strategy and tactics, this was a fairly congenial appointment. Even in this situation he managed to cause controversy, by some outspoken remarks about the role of ex-Nazis in German reconstruction. He was again reprimanded by Eisenhower.

In December 1945, when setting out on a trip to shoot pheasants, his car was involved in a collision with a large truck. Patton appeared to be slightly injured, but soon afterwards he became paralysed, and he was flown to the American Military Hospital in Heidelberg. Here he appeared to make progress, and was expected to be fit enough to fly back to America. But his condition suddenly deteriorated and he died on 21 December 1945.

Patton's mind was always full of the great victories of the military heroes of old; of Alexander, Caesar and Napoleon, and he saw himself in this image. Even at his dismissal in June 1945 he quoted a Roman saying about returning warriors: 'All glory is fleeting'.

Of all the Allied commanders in the European campaign, he emerged most dramatically as a character who dominated every situation in which he was involved. He had proved himself in Africa and Sicily to be considered as the general *par excellence*, and it is to the credit of Eisenhower and Bradley that the command of the new army, designed and equipped to break out from the Normandy bridgehead and strike across Europe, was given to Patton. During the campaign in Europe he became the outstanding tank general; in his ability to command and direct rapidly moving forces; to create the confidence in all his divisions to grasp and implement his daring policy; and to organise the logistics for what became the largest American army in Europe. All of these were but one aspect of his remarkable talent. He showed quite different qualities of leadership in controlling strategy and tactics during the winter campaign in the Saar, and then, triumphantly, in his relief of Bastogne in December 1944 – exactly one year before he died. The slapping incident in Sicily, and his other tactless outbursts for which he was reprimanded, should not be allowed to detract from his greatness as a military commander.

Just before he left the United States for the last time, he visited a Sunday-school at the church his family attended. He led the children in singing 'Onward Christian Soldiers'. There is no doubt that is how he saw himself.

'VINEGAR JOE' STILWELL

Field Marshal Lord Slim, who shared with General Joseph Stilwell the defeat in Burma in 1942, and later the victories over the Japanese, thought that it amused Stilwell to keep up the 'Vinegar Joe – tough guy' attitude. In fact it was no pretence. The nickname went back to the 1920s when, at Fort Benning under George C. Marshall, he made his name as an outstanding teacher and trainer in the field of tactics and command problems. The irascible side of his nature, his colourful expletives, and his short-fused patience with inefficiency, stuffiness or pretension had been well known since the First World War. It was not employed solely against the upper-crust English officers he castigated in Burma.

Stilwell's experience in China dated from 1911, and he seemed destined to crown his career in the China theatre. He cared passionately about China and the Chinese people, but by 1944 his criticism of the dishonesty and corruption of Chiang Kai-shek, which Roosevelt and the China lobby did not wish to hear, cost him his job, and he was sacrificed to political expediency. Roosevelt had hoped that China under Chiang would be a stable ally in post-war Asia. Had he listened to Stilwell, the American government and people would have been better prepared for the communist civil-war victory in 1950 over the effete Chiang Kai-shek.

Stilwell, considered a maverick at West Point before he was commissioned in 1904, made his name as a serious, professional, aggressive and over-sensitive character. He hated the dull and the humdrum. With a flair for languages, especially Spanish, he volunteered for service in the Philippines. There as a junior officer he was ready to express his colourful thoughts about the chronic army inefficiency all round him. Next, he volunteered for a posting to Shanghai, but returned to West Point as an instructor in 1913. He had married in 1910, and was devoted to his wife and family for the rest of his extraordinary life.

Disliking staff-work, and eager to get into action, he went to France in 1917 as a captain in Pershing's forces. He was closely involved in the heavy fighting around Verdun when, in July 1918, Ludendorff made his last desperate push. After the war, Stilwell, foreseeing stagnation and frustration in service at home, applied for a posting to China, and with his wife and family arrived in Peking in 1920. Here, spurning the cocktail-party circuit of the expatriate community, he volunteered to work as supervisor to a road building programme as part of a famine relief scheme. He took every opportunity to observe and record details about the country, as well as the military and political situation. He travelled to Korea and Manchuria, and noticed the early moves of the Japanese to penetrate the area. He dubbed the Japanese 'arrogant little bastards', and compared them to the Germans. Returning home, he completed the staff-course at Fort Leavenworth. He did well, but Eisenhower passed out top!

After his course he was pleased to go back to China in 1926 to command a US battalion, and here he met up with his old friend George Marshall. Ever the loner and maverick, Stilwell went on a solitary expedition which enabled him to observe the period of violent devolution in China in which the Kuomintang came to the fore. Their victories led to attack on foreign interests. To gain more information, Stilwell undertook an amazing journey with a Chinese assistant through the civil war battle zone. He nearly lost his life on a refugee train when most of the passengers wanted the foreigner taken off and shot. Later he was highly commended for his intrepid conduct and bravery. As the civil war continued, Chiang Kai-shek, whose future was to be closely linked with Stilwell, split with Moscow, and carried out a brutal purge of left-wing leaders. He also assured his future by getting rid of his wife and marrying into the rich and powerful Soong family, which had strong links with Sun Yat-sen.

Like his contemporary, Slim, Stilwell, who had no private income, earned a little extra by writing articles. These showed a deep and detailed understanding of the complex issues of the civil war, the growing involvement of Japan, and its reaction to the possibility of China becoming united under Chiang Kai-shek. Stilwell witnessed many gruesome sights as the Kuomintang advanced, and he was alarmed at the uncontrolled actions of the war lords who supported it.

Well established as a China expert, Stilwell returned home in 1929, as an instructor at Fort Benning under George Marshall. The latter was revolutionising the training of officers, and had deliberately recruited Stilwell in order to shake up the system. Stilwell purposely proposed 'screwball schemes' to shake up the officers' complacency, and it was now that he became 'Vinegar Joe' – a nickname he liked. Marshall considered him 'exceptionally brilliant'.

Nevertheless, in the early 1930s Stilwell seriously considered retiring to Carmel. He was over forty, and saw little prospect of promotion, but when he witnessed the suffering and hardship of the Depression, he realised he was relatively well off in the army. Then, unexpectedly, he had the opportunity to go back to China as the US Military Attaché. There, the Japanese were already profiting from the Manchurian Incident, and their penetration of Chinese territory. Chiang Kai-shek seemed more determined to destroy the communists than to fight the Japanese, and he pursued a ruthless scorched-earth policy against the peasants who had supported Mao Tse-tung.

When he arrived back in China, now in a more senior position, Stilwell continued his countrywide search for accurate information. Increasingly he saw Japan as the real threat in the Pacific. He reckoned that Russia and China would not be strong enough to take effective action against Japan, and that the Western powers, already enmeshed in appeasement of the Fascists, would do nothing. As Japan stepped up the pressure, there were occasional outbursts by the Chinese people, but Chiang Kai-shek was not strong enough to challenge the invader. Stilwell visited the southern city of Chungking – shortly to become Chiang's capital – and he also went to Mongolia and Manchuria. Here the methods and attitudes of the communists impressed him, though he noticed that there were no effective defences. In 1937 the Japanese took Peking, and inflicted appalling brutalities on the people. Then as their armies drew closer to Nanking and Shanghai, Chiang Kai-shek put up more resistance, hoping to gain support from the Western powers.

Perhaps more than any Western observer, Stilwell realised the threat posed by the Japanese, and witnessed their senseless brutality. He fulminated against Washington for its failure to act. In assessing the Chinese army, he had little confidence in the officers, but respected the hardy, uncomplaining Chinese soldier. In December 1937, closely observed by Stilwell, the Japanese perpetrated their worst single crime against humanity – The Rape of Nanking. When the city fell, 40,000 civilians were shot, set alight, raped or hacked to death – the Japanese showing indifference to human life or to world opinion. Stilwell commented: 'Chiang cannot stop now.' In the same month the Japanese sank a US Yangtse patrol ship – but later apologised. 'Bastards,' commented Stilwell.

Early in 1938 he obtained permission to travel to the north of China. He was amazed at the indifference to human life shown by both the Chinese and the Japanese. A Chinese commander virtually welcomed heavy casualties since most soldiers were rogues and vagabonds and were best got rid of. Similarly, when the Japanese were pressing Chiang in the Yangtse valley, he ordered the main dams to be blown up, to flood the valley. This certainly delayed the Japanese armies, but it made two million Chinese homeless and caused countless deaths. Stilwell's frustration never ceased and he nearly despaired as Washington appeared to see Chiang as a bastion of democracy against Fascism.

The climax of the Sino–Japanese campaign came in October 1938 when the Japanese took Hankow and Canton. Millions of Chinese moved away from the coastal areas carrying their belongings. At that time Stilwell met Chiang for the first time and quickly summed-up Chiang's method of keeping control by causing confusion among his commanders, and never trusting any one commander. Stilwell said that the USA and China together would have to fight Japan, but that this would need massive US supplies and a US commander. Prophetic words. In May 1939 his career prospects suddenly changed when his old friend Marshall became Chief of Staff. Stilwell was on his way home across the Pacific when he heard that he had been promoted to brigadier.

Back home he found frantic activity. Two decades of isolationism, and the feeling that no power was likely to attack the USA, had resulted in severe neglect of the armed forces. Stilwell, still concerned that Roosevelt was ignoring urgent Pacific issues, now concentrated on the challenge of training new infantry divisions. In 1940 he was promoted to major general, and he worked tirelessly to bring his division and others up to an acceptable standard. His endeavours to train vast numbers of untrained recruits were handicapped by an acute shortage of military equipment, and he was trying to overcome years of neglect, while at the same time absorbing and teaching the lessons of the Germans' lightning campaigns in Poland and France.

While this urgent work was continuing, the Japanese, aiming to extend their power in the Pacific, were putting pressure on France and Holland to cut supplies to China. Secretly, they were planning the attack on Indo-China, Malaya, Singapore and Pearl Harbor. In the face of the Japanese threat, Chiang appealed to Roosevelt for 500 American pilots and planes to be based in south China under the command of Chennault, who had been advising him for some years. They argued that China was on the brink of collapse, and that an air attack from the Chunking area could drive back the Japanese armies, cause serious damage in Japan and destroy the Japanese navy. Later Stilwell was to discover the devious dishonesty of Chiang's request, and to clash strongly with Chennault. At the time, because of active lobbying in Washington, Chiang and Chennault won their point. They were helped, as Britain was, by the passing of the Lease–Lend Act in 1941. This started an avalanche of money and supplies to Chiang, the intention being to arm and equip thirty Chinese divisions, trained and led by US officers, to drive the Japanese out of south-west China, and to construct forward bases from which to bomb Tokyo. Despite this assistance, Chiang bitterly resented his exclusion from top level strategic discussions with Roosevelt and Churchill.

In 1941 the Axis appeared invincible, and this prompted the Japanese to step up their aggressive action. They forced concessions on Indo-China which enabled them to establish advanced military and naval bases. Meanwhile in Washington, Congress was still not totally convinced about the inevitability of war. Against this background, Stilwell continued his valiant attempts to train his division. Extensive manoeuvres took place throughout the summer of 1941, and he increased his reputation as an outstanding leader and was promoted to command a corps.

During November 1941 the Japanese completed their plans for the attack on Pearl Harbor which took place at 0750 on Sunday 7 December and was a complete success. This disaster led to a panic along the Californian coast with expected attacks and sightings of Japanese planes and ships occurring daily. Stilwell was responsible for the defence of a large stretch of the coast, but he had few trained troops and less ammunition. Then he was called to Washington. Marshall had a very high opinion of Stilwell who was expected to command the first US strike-force – possibly in North Africa. During weeks of frantic discussions, Stilwell was highly critical of Roosevelt as a rank amateur, and made pungent comments to his wife about the general chaos. Then he received from Marshall the first intimation that he might be given command, not in North Africa but in China. He opposed the idea on the grounds that he would be remembered as a small-fry colonel, but he would go where he was sent.

At the highest level, Churchill and Roosevelt disagreed over policy towards China and Burma, and Chiang Kai-shek hated the British who appeared to be receiving US supplies which were destined for him. Wavell, initially with lofty contempt, antagonised Chiang still further by refusing offers of Chinese help. Anti-British feelings soon rubbed off on Stilwell. On 23 January 1942 he was formally appointed, and then was interviewed by

Roosevelt, whom he dismissed as 'frothy'. Knowing the China background, Stilwell demanded that all military supplies be processed through him, but that if Rangoon fell all supplies should go through Calcutta. It was agreed that supplies should go by air to Chungking 'over the Hump' from India.

On his way to the Far East, Stilwell heard of the fall of Singapore, and the surrender of 60,000 troops without a fight. 'Christ, what the hell is the matter?' he asked. He landed in India, took offence at pompous English staff-officers who knew little, and then met Wavell whom he considered a beaten man.

He then flew on to see Chiang Kai-shek. The Japanese, after their rapid victories across the Pacific, had invaded Burma in mid-January, with two divisions, soon joined by three more. They swept forward and captured Rangoon on 6 March. The weak British opposition – 17th Indian Division and 1st Burma Division – were rapidly pushed back northwards up the valleys of the Irrawaddy and Chindwin. By then Stilwell was in Chungking, interviewing Chiang. Although Stilwell was officially Chief of Staff to Chiang, and commander of the Chinese/US forces in Burma, he soon realised that he did not have unfettered control. He was to discover that even if Chiang agreed to a plan he would be quite likely to order his divisional commanders not to follow it. Stilwell had further problems with British commanders, whom he considered snooty and incompetent, but he did establish good relations with General Slim. Stilwell always seemed ready to run down the British, and he described with relish how Chiang was more impressed with Gandhi and Nehru than 'the whole damn British raj'.

Initially, Stilwell commanded two Chinese armies, each of three divisions of about 7,000 men. Sixth Army was located near the Thailand/ China border, and Fifth Army, composed of 22nd, 96th, and 200th Divisions, was fighting in the area from just north of Rangoon up to Lashio at the start of the Burma Road. As soon as he actually got command of the forces, he tried to plan a strategy to hold central Burma against the Japanese, with the British in the centre and the Chinese holding the eastern flank. Then, after frustrating days of waiting, he discovered that he was not to have overall command of the divisions in Burma. He was to suffer this type of frustration for the rest of his service with Chiang. Next, he flew down to Burma and met General Alexander, whom he considered brusque and stand-offish. There followed more days of frustration while he tried to get the Chinese divisions to move. He realised increasingly that almost every time Chiang agreed to a move, it would be countermanded before it happened. Stilwell hoped to have other Chinese divisions to help the one Chinese division which was in action at Toungoo, but in this too he was frustrated. He was openly critical of the British, but he admitted that Slim, at very heavy cost to his own troops, did send a substantial force to help the Chinese at Toungoo. They were unable to save the Chinese, and suffered heavy losses in men and *matériel* which they could ill afford.

By the end of March 1942, the Japanese had advanced rapidly, and the British and Chinese were in full retreat. On 1 April Stilwell flew up to Chungking to see Chiang. In a furious rage, he made his point, and as a result Chiang and his wife flew down to Maymyo, the Joint Command HQ north of Mandalay, to announce publicly that Stilwell was in full command of all the Chinese forces, and the divisional commanders would obey his orders. Despite this, Chiang continued to thwart his orders behind his back. The Japanese continued their relentless advance, helped by unchallenged air superiority. One disaster followed another. Stilwell did repay Slim's help at Toungoo, by sending 3rd Chinese Division under General Sun to help Slim out of a difficult position when the Japanese attacked the oilfield at Yenangyaung. Both the Chinese and British forces were further imperilled when a Chinese division on the eastern front crumbled and allowed a Japanese attack to break through. It advanced more than eighty miles almost without opposition and reached Lashio at the start of the Burma Road. Stilwell's agitation is seen in his comment: 'Lashio? Jesus this will screw us completely.' His diary, published as *The Stilwell Papers*, gives his vivid comments almost every day for the rest of the campaign.

Now, showing his outstanding bravery and determination, he person-ally took command of 200th Division, and led a spirited counter-attack which quickly drove the Japanese out of Tounggyi. This showed that the Chinese, with sound leadership, could defeat the Japanese, but this was an isolated incident in a massive withdrawal.

By late April 1942 it had become clear that the first priority was to get the remaining British and Chinese forces out of Burma. Stilwell discussed this issue with Slim and Alexander and it was decided that the British would move up the Chindwin towards Imphal. Stilwell, still hoping to organise some resistance to the Japanese, set off towards Myitkyina, more than 100 miles north of Mandalay. In fact, the Japanese got there before him, so when he reached Indaw he decided to turn west and his party crossed the Chindwin valley. After an appalling journey, dogged by an early monsoon, they reached British lines near Imphal, where they were well looked after.

On 24 May Stilwell reached Delhi, and amidst world-wide eulogies for his bravery and guts, announced: 'We've had a hell of a beating.'

By the end of May, Stilwell had had time to assess the defeat of his Chinese divisions. He attributed it to inferior equipment, gutless command, no proper supply set-up, and Chiang's interference. By this time too, some Chinese divisions had made a stand in the Salween gorge, and there the Japanese halted. From India, where he was co-operating with Slim, Stilwell argued strongly for a US division to come into the Burma theatre, and for the re-organisation of Chinese forces under US command, in order to prevent the total waste of US aid. In a bid to hit back at Japan, 'the Doolittle raid' was launched from carriers in June 1942. The US aircraft bombed Tokyo and flew on to the Kuomintang airfields in south China. Chiang blamed Stilwell for not having informed him about the raid, and was further incensed when, in reprisal, the Japanese advanced and captured the airfields where the aircraft had landed.

From this time on Chiang constantly threatened to take China out of the war unless US supplies were increased. After the Doolittle raid, Chiang demanded three US divisions, 500 planes, and 5,000 tons of supplies per month He also demanded that Stilwell be replaced, but Roosevelt and Marshall stood by him. Stilwell had already realised that Chiang was stock-piling most of the aid to use against the communists after the war.

Stilwell had to spend weary weeks in the hostile and corrupt atmosphere of Chungking in a tense and controversial relationship with Chiang, but his determination succeeded, and by the end of 1942 there were 13,000 Chinese soldiers training at Ramgarh, between Delhi and Calcutta, having been flown over the Hump by returning supply aircraft. Slim, commenting at the time, said that Stilwell was magnificent to have achieved this. Stilwell, in contrast, wrote to his wife: 'From the manure pile [i.e. Chungking]. Don't worry about me. If I had new teeth, new eyes, and hair dye I would not look a day over 70. Relations with Chiang still bad – the little jackass.' Stilwell had still to struggle hard to ensure that US supplies went to divisions which were likely to actually fight the Japanese

Stilwell spent weeks negotiating with Chiang, with Washington, and with Wavell in Delhi, and had gone some way to achieving his aim. Already, by the end of 1942, the global strategic situation had improved. The Russians had pushed back the Germans from Stalingrad, Rommel had been defeated at El Alamein, and the US landings in North Africa had succeeded. Supplies over the Hump had increased, and Allied strategy in Burma was moving towards the idea of the British advancing from Imphal, the Chinese advancing from Yunnan down the Burma Road, and Stilwell leading the Chinese divisions he had trained southwards down the Hukawng valley. His ultimate aim was to open a road and pipeline to link up with the old Burma Road. This progress was undermined by intrigue in Washington and Chungking – partly by Chennault – who was striving to replace Stilwell, and claimed that with more aircraft he could finish the war in six months.

Early in 1943 came more frustration. Chiang pulled out of an offensive in the spring, because he said the British were not ready. Stilwell's frustration knew no bounds. He castigated the Chinese: 'Hands out for anything they can get ... and let anyone else do the fighting.' He blamed the 'indifference, cowardice, ignorance and stupidity of the Chinese leaders ... and at the top, the bloody peanut. My God!' After Roosevelt and Churchill met at Casablanca in January 1943, Marshall and others came on to confer in Delhi and Chungking. Here Marshall supported Stilwell, though Chennault was scheming with Chiang for more and more aircraft. In May Stilwell and Chennault were called to see Roosevelt. Stilwell was depressed, because Chennault made wild claims, which Roosevelt appeared to accept – he even agreed that Chennault could contact him direct, by-passing both Marshall and Stilwell.

Roosevelt and Churchill met again at the Trident Conference in Washington in May 1943, and Stilwell produced a brilliant memo pointing out Chiang's chicanery and double-dealing, and showing how much his agents were influencing the President. Soong, the key agent of Chiang's in Washington, quickly exploited this position and threatened that China would pull out of the war unless supplies over the Hump were vastly increased.

After Trident, Stilwell snatched a brief but joyous visit to his family and returned to the 'Manure Pile', and to Chiang, 'the grasping, bigoted, ungrateful little rattlesnake'. At this time the Japanese had attacked in the Yangtse valley, and had swept the Chinese aside. Then they withdrew, and Chiang and Chennault claimed a great victory. Stilwell nearly despaired. Chennault's aircraft also attacked Japanese shipping, and made exaggerated claims, but little was sunk, and in revenge the Japanese overran several more forward airfields. Simultaneously, Chiang removed trained troops and weapons intended for the advance in Yunnan, and distributed them among his warlords.

Stilwell genuinely believed that the Chinese troops trained by him and paid for by the British in India could defeat the Japanese, but his frustration during these months of negotiation and double-dealing was overwhelming. In July 1943 he wrote: 'What corruption, intrigue, obstruction, delay, double-crossing, hate, jealousy, skulduggery, we have had to wade through. What a cesspool. What bigotry and ignorance and black ingratitude. Holy Christ, I was just about at the end of my rope.'

The next conference, at Quebec in August 1943, more directly affected Burma. Mountbatten was appointed head of South East Asia Command, with Stilwell as his deputy – thus adding to his already complex roles. He then submitted an excellent plan for the strategy against Japan. He proposed that all the Chinese forces, from south to north, and including the communists, should attack simultaneously and force the Japanese to withdraw – thereby enabling all the Allied forces to advance. Chiang never seriously considered this plan, and at the same time Stilwell was close to dismissal because of backstairs intrigue by Soong and Chennault. Then to his complete surprise, because Madam Chiang Kai-shek – another arch intriguer – chose to support him, Stilwell found himself back in favour, and because of the decisions at Quebec, action in Burma appeared more likely.

Great Britain and the USA still had differing aims, but there was at least agreement that the strategy in Burma would be for the Chinese to advance down the Burma Road from Yunnan, for the British to advance from Imphal, and for Stilwell and his Chinese divisions to advance from Fort Hertz down the Hukawng valley towards Myitkyina. This would be the precursor to a gigantic engineering project by the US forces to build a road and pipeline southwards from Myitkyina to join up with the Burma Road. The Quebec Conference also gave backing to the Chindits who, supported by 1st US Air Commando, would drop behind the Japanese lines in the area of Indaw, to destroy the railway and roads and cut off all supplies and reinforcements to the Japanese divisions facing Stilwell in the north as well as those attacking Imphal and Kohima.

While such plans were slowly maturing, Stilwell accompanied Chiang to the Sextant Conference at Cairo in November 1943, with Roosevelt and Churchill. This was the most acrimonious conference of the war – much of the acrimony being caused by Chiang. He made absurd demands – e.g. 10,000 tons of supplies a month for Chennault's air force alone. He made agreements and immediately broke them. For Stilwell at least it meant that Marshall witnessed his chicanery, and also that Mountbatten now took on a share of the odious task of dealing with Chiang. After Roosevelt and Churchill went on to Teheran to see Stalin, Mountbatten called a meeting for all the commanders involved with Burma. Stilwell had to announce that all the agreements made the previous day by Chiang had now been reversed. Stilwell managed a quick trip to the Holy Land, which he considered had been a grand interlude before returning to the Manure Pile. After the Cairo Conference, a combined operations attack on the Andaman Islands – code-named 'Buccaneer' – was called off because of Stalin's demand for a Second Front. Chiang used this as an excuse to renege on almost all his agreements. Stilwell, realising this likely reaction, saw Roosevelt alone. To his amazement, Roosevelt waffled on about billions of dollars for China after the war, and totally ignored the present problem of dealing with Chiang. Almost at once, Chiang demanded a loan of a billion dollars, and double the amount of supplies coming over the Hump. Marshall, seeing Stilwell's impossible situation, offered him a command elsewhere, but he refused – though he remarked bitterly that he would prefer to drive a garbage truck. He thought again that the 'little bastard Chiang never intended to fight'.

In December 1943, after all this frustration, and the knowledge that Chiang had nearly had him sacked, Stilwell was suddenly given complete control of all the Chinese divisions assembling at Ledo, even obtaining this in writing. He arrived in the Hukawng valley on the 21st to command the Chinese 22nd and 38th Divisions. Within a few days he had personally led an attack, and captured a Japanese strongpoint. He was criticised for this, but he saw that it gave his troops confidence, though they rarely made much progress unless Stilwell was there. Chiang then reneged on the proposed advance of Yoke Force from Yunnan, so Stilwell transferred to his own command the force under Merrill which had been trained in India on the same lines and for the same role as the Chindits. With Stilwell's badgering, the Chinese had made some progress down the Hukawng valley, and he had sound expectations of progress with the two divisions and what became known as Merrill's Marauders. Stilwell planned a sound strategy against the Japanese 18th Division under General Tanaka, and nearly trapped the whole force at the battle of Walawbum.

Stilwell often had to leave his troops in the valley and fly to Delhi in his role as deputy to Mountbatten in SEAC. He felt a personal antagonism to the British commander General Giffard, and during a very tense conference suddenly agreed instead to serve under General Slim. This was an almost Gilbertian arrangement because as Mountbatten's deputy he was senior to Slim, but it worked, and this tough pair co-operated harmoniously on the

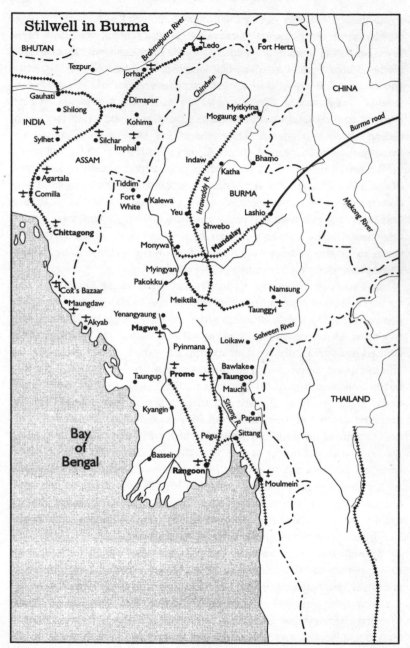

Stilwell in Burma

BHUTAN

Brahmaputra River

Ledo

Fort Hertz

Tezpur

Jorhat

CHINA

Gauhati

Dimapur

Chindwin

Shilong

Myitkyina

Burma road

INDIA

Kohima

Mogaung

Sylhet

Silchar

Imphal

ASSAM

Indaw

Bhamo

Katha

Agartala

Tiddim

Comilla

Fort
White

Kalewa

BURMA

Yeu

Lashio

Chittagong

Shwebo

Mekong River

Monywa

Mandalay

Myingyan

Pakokku

Meiktila

Namsung

Cox's Bazaar

Taunggyi

Maungdaw

Yenangyaung

Akyab

Magwe

Loikaw

Salween River

Pyinmana

Taungup

Prome

Bawlake

Taungoo

Mauchi

THAILAND

Kyangin

Papun

Bay
of
Bengal

Pegu

Sittang

Bassein

Rangoon

Moulmein

176

ground. Then, because of dithering at top level over the wider conduct of the war in Asia, Stilwell precipitated another crisis. He received information that the British were still considering an amphibious attack on Sumatra instead of an all-out effort in Burma. He therefore sent a secret emissary to Roosevelt to demand full support in north Burma; Mountbatten discovered this ploy and demanded Stilwell's removal. The clash was patched up when Mountbatten flew in to see him. Stilwell commented: 'Louis and I got along famously, even if he does have curly eyelashes.' A less generous comment than Mountbatten's: 'He is a grand old warrior.'

Months of bickering and dithering were brought to an end early in 1944, not by an overall Allied plan, but by a major Japanese attack. They launched an initial assault in the Arakan and here Slim's newly trained forces held them and, supplied by air, were able to defeat them. Then Mutaguchi, the overall Japanese commander, having failed to learn the lesson of the Arakan, launched his main attack towards Imphal and Kohima on 6 March. He planned to destroy the British forces at Imphal, and simultaneously send a powerful group under General Sato to take Kohima and then to advance rapidly to Dimapur, a huge supply depot on the railway, which supplied Stilwell's forces as well as the whole of Fourteenth Army. This remarkable plan, which had as its culmination a march on Delhi to stir up the Indian people against the British, nearly succeeded. But Sato's division was held up by the 50th Indian Parachute Brigade at Sangshak, and then by a battalion of the Royal West Kent Regiment at Kohima. From that moment the Japanese made no more advances in Burma, but they showed that they were better soldiers in defence than in attack, and most stayed in their dugouts and died rather than retreat or surrender.

The Japanese attack changed the whole situation in Burma. Although Stilwell was still criticising the Limeys' reluctance to fight, he was now to see the outstanding achievements of Slim's Fourteenth Army. At first, though, while the Japanese were threatening Imphal and Kohima, he resumed his critical stance: 'Louis has his hind leg over his neck. What a mess the Limeys can produce in short order.' In contrast, Slim made a much more generous assessment of Stilwell.

From now on Stilwell was to become substantially involved in the Chindit campaign. At the Quebec Conference of August 1943, Wingate had gained the support of the Joint Chiefs of Staff for several brigades of Chindits with 1st US Air Commando – a force of aircraft to transport and supply the entire Chindit operation. This was launched on 6 March 1944 – the same day as the Japanese attacked. The Chindits landed as planned in an area around Indaw on the railway leading north towards Myitkyina. The Chindits completely blocked the railway and all roads, and cut off all supplies to the Japanese facing Stilwell – notably Tanaka's 18th Division. In addition they cut off supplies and reinforcements to those divisions attacking Imphal and Kohima. After the war Mutaguchi blamed the Chindit operation for his failure, but Slim and Stilwell were less generous in their assessment of the Chindits.

Even with close co-operation in the field, the dissent over the higher strategy still caused friction. Stilwell held firm to his original strategic and tactical mission, which was to advance southwards to Myitkyina and its airfield, and then link-up with the Burma Road. After the Japanese had been repulsed at Imphal and Kohima, Slim aimed to destroy them completely – and this Fourteenth Army eventually did. Initially these aims did not seriously conflict.

Stilwell's successful operations down the Hukawng valley towards Kamaing and Mogaung had inflicted heavy casualties on Tanaka's 18th Division, which prompted Chiang to send him two more divisions – 14th and 50th. Throughout April and into May 1944, as the Chinese advanced slowly towards Kamaing, Stilwell discovered that Chiang was again interfering and ordering General Sun not to advance too quickly. Then orders changed again, and Sun, the best of the Chinese generals, captured Tanaka's main supply depot, and fought off a strong counter-attack.

By the middle of May, when the Japanese had begun their disastrous retreat from Imphal, Slim and Stilwell had to decide their future tactics. Stilwell's Chinese divisions, as they approached Kamaing, were coming fairly close to his objective – the town and airfield of Myitkyina. In view of this Slim agreed on 17 May to hand over command of the Chindits to Stilwell. He justified this as administratively useful, but for the Chindits it was an unmitigated disaster.

The Chindits, and particularly 77 Brigade under the redoubtable Brigadier 'Mad Mike' Calvert, had established a stronghold at 'Broadway'. They had defeated every Japanese brigade which attacked them, and with very few casualties had permanently blocked all road and rail traffic going north to Tanaka. Farther east, another Chindit unit 'Morris Force' had similarly blocked all supplies going north to Myitkyina from Bhamo. The Chindits were highly trained for a specific role – to operate behind enemy lines, and to move swiftly to different targets. They had no armour and no artillery, being trained uniquely for mobile warfare. When they were handed over to Stilwell, he needed normal infantry and artillery to attack the heavily defended towns of Mogaung and Myitkyina. The Chindits should never have been used in this role, and as a result they were slaughtered.

On 24 March 1944, twelve days after the launch of the Chindit operation, Wingate was killed. He was a tough, awkward and abrasive character, and at the same time 'a towering military genius' (Fergusson). Wingate stood up to Slim and Stilwell, and argued his case effectively. Tragically for the Chindits, he was succeeded by Lentaigne, a weak man who was no match for Slim or Stilwell. Most Chindits believe that only Lentaigne's weakness allowed them to be handed over.

Stilwell had proved himself in many aspects of command in battle, in planning, in organisation and in leadership at every level, but he still had a paranoid attitude to 'Limeys'. After May 1944, he was to show another side of his character. In addition to the Chinese divisions, he had under command not only the Chindits but also Merrill's Marauders, who had been trained to operate in the Chindit style. Unfortunately he so mishandled both these fine forces of brave, tough and highly trained men, that both units were reduced to a handful of pitiful physical wrecks. One man from Merrill's Marauders was to say of Stilwell: 'To think that I once had that bastard in my sights and did not pull the trigger.' Some of the Chindits' comments were equally pungent.

From May Stilwell had two clear objectives, the town of Mogaung and the town of Myitkyina with its vital airfield. While his main force drove stolidly southwards towards Kamaing and thence to Mogaung, he had detached Merrill's Marauders – Galahad Force – to make a wide and virtually unopposed sweep to the east in order to capture Myitkyina. By this time Merrill had had a heart attack, and the Marauders were led by Colonel Hunter, a brave and able regular soldier This operation was highly secret, but Stilwell kept in radio contact. Much depended on the success of the attack, and Stilwell agonised over it every day. He worried in particular whether the entire operation would fail if the monsoon rains started before the Marauders reached Myitkyina.

On 17 May, his diary recorded the events hour by hour. He was waiting for the crucial news that Hunter's group had reached the airstrip. At 1330 hours the code-word told him that the airstrip had been captured. 'Whoops,' he wrote, and added in block capitals: 'WILL THIS BURN UP THE

LIMEYS'. From this time onwards Stilwell's weaknesses were to have disastrous repercussions. He had been so secretive and so obsessed by Myitkyina, that he had made no plans to follow up any victory. He himself, like the Marauders, was at the end of his tether: 'One of those days you wished you were dead.' His shortcomings were to cost the Allies dear. He unwisely announced to the world that Myitkyina was captured, whereas it was only the airfield. His subsequent mistakes meant that the town was not taken until 3 August.

On 17 May, when the airfield fell, the town was defended by about 700 men – the weak remnant of two defeated battalions. Hunter urgently demanded fresh infantry units to make an immediate assault on the town. Instead anti-aircraft and engineer units were sent in. The British 36th Division were ready and waiting to fly in to relieve 77 Brigade, but Stilwell was not prepared for the hated Limeys to seize his prize. He therefore scoured units to find any available men. Some were instructed in the use of the rifle during the flight to Myitkyina. All were terrified of the Japanese.

Disaster followed disaster. On 19 May, two Chinese units attacked Myitkyina town and ended up fighting a pitched battle with each other. Then, almost unbelievably, they did exactly the same thing the next day. The Japanese, alert to the significance of the town, rapidly reinforced the garrison, which rose to 4,000 men, drawn from a division on the Salween. By the end of May Stilwell's forces had been driven clear of the town.

Stilwell's frustration and fury undoubtedly warped his judgement. The Marauders, decimated by scrub typhus and dysentery, were losing 100 men a day. A colonel, with a temperature of 103°, still led his men into action. By the end of May the Marauders were reduced to 300 fit men, and their feelings were close to mutiny. In a black mood of depression Stilwell turned on the Limeys. One Chindit brigade under Masters at 'Blackpool' had been harried and nearly destroyed by the Japanese. In desperation, and without agreement from Slim or Stilwell, Masters abandoned 'Blackpool' on 25 May, thus releasing several fit Japanese units to help Mogaung and Myitkyina. Stilwell's fury fell on the weak and inadequate Lentaigne. Another Chindit group – Morris Force – having blocked the southern approach to Myitkyina, was now close to the perimeter. They were soon to suffer from another weakness of Stilwell's command system. He tended to surround himself with yes-men and toadies who never told him the truth. Prominent among these was the egregious Boatner who, having never been in action, and never went near a unit to study the ground, issued completely fatuous orders – such as 'to the last man and the last round!'

As the long-drawn-out attack on Myitkyina continued, one major victory was achieved. The Chindits' 77 Brigade under Calvert, which had organised the Stronghold at 'Broadway', had been ordered north to 'capture Mogaung'. Calvert has been called 'The bravest of the brave'. He was recommended for the VC by his three battalion commanders, and he was the true heir to Wingate's dynamism, and the embodiment of the Chindit ethos. His brigade had been behind Japanese lines since 6 March, and were close to exhaustion, but he accepted the order and moved to Mogaung.

There, thanks to Calvert's superb bravery and leadership, and a little help at the very end from a Chinese unit, 77 Brigade of the Chindits drove out the Japanese. This exemplary achievement, by the end of which Calvert's whole brigade was reduced to 300 men able to walk, caused an interesting clash with Stilwell. One of Stilwell's sycophants at his HQ had signalled to the world that the Chinese had taken Mogaung. The fury of the Chindits can be imagined. Calvert then signalled to Stilwell that: 'The Chinese having taken Mogaung, the Chindits have taken umbrage.' Their pleasure was increased when it was heard that the wretched Boatner had said it must be a small place because he could not find it on the map. In an atmosphere of tension and anger, Stilwell sent for Lentaigne and Calvert. He started aggressively: 'You send some strong signals Calvert.' Calvert replied: 'You should see the ones my Brigade Major would not let me send.' This reply changed the whole situation. Stilwell realised that he had met a man of his own calibre, and he roared with laughter. He then realised too that his toadying and sycophantic staff had gravely misinformed him about the Chindit achievements. Stilwell immediately awarded Calvert the American Silver Star. This incident did a little to reduce the tension, but the anger remained and Mountbatten had to step in to resolve the clash. He ordered the immediate evacuation of the Chindits and the Marauders because of their pitiful physical condition.

After the capture of the airfield at Myitkyina and the Chindits' capture of Mogaung, there were few dramatic military developments, and Stilwell again became embroiled in the hateful quagmire of Chiang's HQ in Chungking. In China there was growing anger and discontent with Chiang's rule, and there was virtual civil war between him and his warlords. Then the Japanese drove strongly southwards and threatened the air bases used by Chennault who was continuing his efforts to undermine

Stilwell's position. He saw clearly the underhanded deceit and corruption of Chiang, and raged at the way the USA was being fleeced of millions of dollars worth of weapons, aircraft and supplies, which were not being used to prosecute the war against Japan. Stilwell's position depended on how resolutely Roosevelt supported him, and his strength lay in the total loyalty of Marshall who never wavered. In July 1944, in an attempt to bring Chiang to heel, Roosevelt agreed to a demand that, in return for continuing military support, Stilwell should be given command of all Chinese forces facing the advancing Japanese in south China. To reinforce this proposal Stilwell was promoted to four star general. Shortly after this he had to go to the SEAC HQ at Kandy to take over while Mountbatten was away. Here on 3 August, he heard that the town of Myitkyina had fallen, and he recorded some acid comments on the 3,000 staff at SEAC HQ. While Stilwell was away Chiang continued to prevaricate. He held back large armies in order to use them later against the communists, but he was prepared to pull out of Burma in order to hold the Japanese advancing towards Chungking: 'The crazy little bastard,' said Stilwell.

Chiang continued to obstruct so, with Marshall's support, Roosevelt sent a very blunt message. Stilwell delivered it personally. 'The harpoon hit the little bugger in the solar plexus,' he said with some satisfaction. But this proved to be the final straw for Chiang, and he demanded Stilwell's removal. In October 1944, Roosevelt agreed, and with scant ceremony in either Chungking or Delhi Stilwell departed. By then a presidential campaign was in full swing, and a major crisis over China could have damaged Roosevelt's chances. Stilwell therefore was effectively muzzled and was not allowed to say a word about his dismissal. For a general of his seniority, who had worked unstintingly for the US cause and to protect US interests, he was treated disgracefully and he was very bitter. After his dismissal his last months were far from happy. Early in 1945 he was awarded the Legion of Merit, and when the Burma Road was opened it was renamed the Stilwell Road, but this did not assuage his deep hurt.

He went to the Pacific and had a cordial meeting with MacArthur. In June 1945 he was given command of Tenth Army based on Guam, but even then Chiang's vindictiveness followed him; he objected to his setting foot on Chinese soil. He soon overcame this disappointment and had some satisfaction in being present with MacArthur at the Japanese surrender aboard the *Missouri*. He had not long to live. He arrived home in October 1945, and witnessed the atom bomb tests on Bikini in July 1946. Soon after that he was found to have stomach cancer and he died on 12 October 1946.

Stilwell was above all a tough fighting general who cared for his troops, suffered with them, and brought them victory. He had a paranoid attitude to the British, and this undoubtedly clouded his judgements about British troops and especially the Chindits. This seemed to colour his view of Merrill's Marauders as well. He usually had an apt if acerbic comment for any situation. 'In conclusion,' he said, 'if a man can say he did not let his country down, and if he can live with himself, there is nothing more he can reasonably ask for.'

ORDE WINGATE

Major-General Orde Wingate, DSO and two bars, was the complete maverick warrior: a maverick in terms of conventional military thinking, a maverick in his whole attitude to the established military system, and a maverick in his attitude to all the accepted social mores of the military community in which he served. He showed contempt for many accepted customs and conventions, and this may well be the reason why, more than fifty years after his death in March 1944 at the beginning of the second Chindit campaign, his name is still reviled by many British regular army officers. Interestingly, his reputation with the Americans, especially those in 1st US Air Commando; with the Israelis who revere him; with the RAF who worked so closely with the Chindits; and with all the Chindits who actually served with him, is unimpeachable. Only regular army officers keep up the vendetta to demean the reputation of Orde Wingate.

He was certainly the most controversial character among the British leaders in the Second World War. Bernard Fergusson (later Lord Ballantrae), who was a Chindit column commander, writes: 'Surely posterity will not grudge the memory of the great leader and military genius who fashioned us, the honour that should be his.' Similarly, Brigadier Walter Scott, describing Wingate at the launch of Operation 'Thursday', writes: 'If ever I saw greatness in a human being, I saw it in General Wingate that night,' In contrast, General Pownall, who rarely had a good word even for Slim or Mountbatten, writes: 'At any rate he is a thoroughly nasty bit of work.' (Quotes from Rooney, *Wingate and the Chindits*.) A rare, balanced comment from Richard Rhodes James, who served in a Chindit brigade in Operation 'Thursday' was that Wingate was a brilliant leader, but he was a very odd person indeed.

A very substantial cause for Wingate's extremely uncomfortable journey through life was his severe upbringing. His parents were devout Plymouth Brethren, and he spent much of his young life conscious that he suffered God's displeasure. Even when he was serving in the army, in contrast to most young officers, he pondered over the deeper meaning of life and death, and from an early age felt that he was destined for a violent death. He was born in India in 1903. As a growing child, with his brother and sisters, he was often left with aunts, while his parents went to India, but then the family was reunited in England when Wingate went to Charterhouse as a day boy. Till then he had rarely mixed with other children, and his parents were worried that as he grew up he might lose the strict tenets of the Plymouth Brethren. In the philistine atmosphere of a public school at that time, a day boy who did not play games and did not attend assemblies was inevitably isolated, and he remained a loner throughout his life. His housemaster became extremely worried when, on a games afternoon, Wingate was found in the chapel praying. He emerged from school a lonely boy, who did not share in normal school friendships, who often antagonised his peers, and was perhaps too ready to challenge authority.

He went to the Royal Military Academy at Woolwich in 1920, and a similar pattern emerged. Other cadets found him surly and unfriendly, and 'a very unattractive character'. As at school, he felt he was disliked, and again he became isolated. Officially he was considered scruffy, bolshy and unco-operative. A fellow cadet found him 'odd, anti-social and out of line with the rest of us'. After an unpleasant incident when he was punished by his fellow cadets, he harboured a grim determination to be better than his fellows, and never again to be at the mercy of the mob. Woolwich did give him a passion for horse-riding, at which he came to excel, and this brought him considerable success as a young officer, after he was commissioned into the Royal Artillery in 1923. Even then his parents pursued him with their gloomy religious views, and tried to stop him riding point to points because God might punish him.

Throughout his life Wingate seemed to enjoy easy access to distinguished people who were able to forward his career. After dinner nights and riding began to pall, a family member, Sir Reginald Wingate, formerly Governor-General of the Sudan, encouraged Wingate to learn Arabic at the School of Oriental and African Studies. He learnt Arabic fluently and in 1930 aged twenty-six joined the Sudan Defence Force as a bimbashi or major. Here he enjoyed his independent command and he liked going off on expeditions which he organised. His superiors found him interesting and impressive – his fellows found him insufferable. He organised a lengthy expedition into the Libyan desert, which gave him very valuable experience in planning and executing his own ideas.

He returned to England in 1933. On the ship he met a mother and her daughter, Lorna aged sixteen. He fell in love with Lorna and married her in

1935. Early in 1936, during a posting to Sheffield, he was disappointed not to obtain a place at Staff College. Soon afterwards, during an exercise, he went up to the CIGS and asked why he had been overlooked. The CIGS took note, and although Wingate did not go to Staff College, he was posted as Intelligence Officer to the 5th Division in Palestine in 1936. This incident illustrates very well Wingate's approach to life, and also the way he completely antagonised his fellows. Most young officers considered his action with the CIGS to have been despicable and outrageous.

Palestine in 1936 faced acute problems, which derived from the foolish and untenable settlements made for the region at the end of the Great War. While promising the area as independent territory for the Arabs under Faisal and Lawrence, the British government also agreed to the Balfour Declaration of 1917, which offered Palestine as a home for the Jewish people, provided the rights of non-Jewish people were respected. The already difficult situation in Palestine was exacerbated by Hitler's policy towards the Jews. By 1936 there was substantial Jewish immigration and this sparked off a revolt by the Arabs which two British infantry divisions were attempting to suppress.

Wingate's experiences in Palestine moulded the shape of his subsequent career. Having been brought up on the severe dictates of the Old Testament – much of which he knew by heart – he revelled in the opportunity to visit all the holy places. Near the Sea of Galilee he amazed his companions by pointing out why the prophet Saul had handled his army so badly. The impact of Palestine, and the achievements of the Jewish settlers rapidly turned Wingate into a passionate Zionist. Again he used his easy access to important people, and though he was only a captain mixed freely with Weizmann, Ben Gurion and others. His Zionist views quickly alienated most of his fellow-officers, whose general sympathies lay with the Arabs. Wingate deepened this antagonism by his revolutionary views on how the Arab revolt should be countered, and by his open criticism of current military policy.

When his own divisional HQ flatly rejected his ideas, he once again used that tactic by which he had approached the CIGS near Sheffield. General Wavell was GOC in Palestine, and one day on an exercise, Wingate waved down Wavell's car, got in, and proceeded to put forward his ideas on how to solve the Palestine problem. This again outraged all his fellow-officers, but Wavell listened, and shortly afterwards, Wingate was able to try out his plan.

This proposed a local militia in the Jewish settlements, to be trained on the British system of sections and platoons and issued with rifles and fifty rounds of ammunition. This was the earliest example of Wingate's brilliant grasp of wide military and political issues, as well as his mastery of intricate detail. Here was the nucleus of his ideas of guerrilla war, which were to be honed and sharpened in the Abyssinia campaign and brought to fruition with the Chindits. More significant than the local militia was his next idea – the Special Night Squads – which Wavell and his successor, Haining, supported. Wingate believed passionately that the Jewish settlers must be prepared to defend themselves, and to be pro-active in their attitude to the Arab terrorists. He therefore personally organised the first Special Night Squads. These were based on the area of Jewish settlements which suffered most from Arab attacks. Wingate trained the young men of the settlements and organised patrols stiffened by officers and NCOs from two British regiments, the Royal Ulster Rifles and the Royal West Kents. These patrols were an immediate success, and by the summer of 1938 the Special Night Squads had fought sizeable battles with the Arab terrorists who infiltrated into Palestine to blow up the oil pipelines.

Over a lengthy period throughout 1938 and into 1939, Wingate personally led the Special Night Squads in a tough and aggressive campaign against the terrorists. He lived in the Jewish settlements, trained their militia, and then night after night led them on fighting patrols to ambush and destroy the infiltrating Arab groups. In the best-known incident, the Arabs attacked a Jewish settlement at Tiberias near the Sea of Galilee, and massacred nineteen men, women and children. A newly arrived British battalion was nearby and did nothing. Wingate, in a towering fury, personally led the Special Night Squad to ambush and destroy the terrorist group. More than fifty were killed. General Ironside, newly appointed to command in Palestine, sacked the battalion's CO and paid tribute to Wingate's outstanding leadership. By the beginning of 1938 the Special Night Squads had destroyed more terrorists than the two British divisions combined. Of course, this did not endear Wingate to the military establishment. Colonel King-Clark, who served with Wingate, said that he was uncomfortable and abrasive at close quarters, but was a man of formidable physical courage and moral integrity. Wingate's own views on military affairs were also recorded at the time. He said: 'Great soldiers are serious, diligent and of outstanding moral character', and he added that a coarse and savage man makes a bad soldier.

Before Wingate and his wife Lorna left Palestine in May 1939, he had protested violently about his personal report by a senior officer, and had taken very grave exception to a report from the 8th Division HQ which 'opposed the idea of dressing up Jews as British soldiers'. This illustrated how far Wingate was removed from the view of the military establishment, and it was his turn to be totally outraged. His achievements with the Special Night Squads made him a founder hero of the state of Israel, and he continued his close contacts with the Jewish leaders during the fateful summer of 1939.

He returned to England, rebellious and disgruntled, but was heartened by making contact with L. S. Amery and with Churchill. After some time with an anti-aircraft unit and thanks to Amery's good offices, he was posted to the Middle East in October 1940. He thought he was being pushed into a backwater to silence him, but Wavell now commanded in the Middle East and was to give him another opportunity.

Mussolini and his Fascist government had invaded Abyssinia in 1935, and by 1936, using modern weapons, aircraft and mustard gas against half-naked warriors using spears, had occupied Addis Ababa. The Emperor Haile Selassie, a member of the League of Nations, had expected support from the great powers, but neither Great Britain nor France, at the peak of their appeasement policy, did anything. Brutal Italian rule continued – including the execution of 9,000 people for an attempt on the life of the governor. In 1940, Mussolini waited until he thought Britain and France had been defeated, and in June declared war. He had nearly 500,000 well-armed troops between Libya and Abyssinia, together with naval and air support.

By October 1940 British forces had begun to build-up. The 5th Indian Division arrived, and in Kenya there were eight brigades from East, West and South Africa. By now Haile Selassie, who had been a refugee in England, had flown into the Sudan. He had had a very cool reception from the British military especially from General Platt, the GOC, who did not wish to provide scarce weapons for the emperor's so-called Patriots. In contrast, Haile Selassie was delighted with the enthusiasm of Wingate, who had been appointed to liaise with him and the Patriots. In February 1941 Platt started his campaign. He had two divisions in the north and three in the south under General Cunningham. In addition, Wingate with 'Gideon Force', had about two battalions of Sudanese troops, to escort the emperor, and raise the Patriots in Gojjam province. In this situation Wingate had many opportunities and learned many lessons about guerrilla warfare. He

organised his force into self-contained columns, he saw the crucial importance of effective radio communication, he saw how the Italians used air
supply effectively, and he learned the value of the 3in mortar as an alternative to artillery. He also saw the value of intrepid leaders, and was fortunate to have men of the calibre of Wilfred Thesiger and Hugh Boustead to
lead his columns. Wingate realised that his main chance of success was to
use the prestige of the emperor to encourage the Italians' native troops to
desert, and then to bluff the Italians into surrender. On one occasion
Wingate called for an air strike. It never came, but it illustrated the way his
mind was working.

After several weeks of fighting by all the British divisions the Italian
forces had withdrawn from the area of Addis Ababa, and on 5 May Haile
Selassie was able to enjoy a triumphal return to his capital. To the fury and
chagrin of the regular forces it fell to Wingate to lead the victory procession.
This was not his wish, but in organising the procession he had obtained a
horse for the emperor to ride. Haile Selassie demurred, saying he would ride
in the car, and Wingate could ride the horse.

There were still battles to fight, and soon after the victory parade
Wingate scored his greatest triumph. At Agibar the Italian commander
Maraventano had drawn up a force of about 10,000 men. He was facing
serious shortages of food, water, ammunition and medical supplies for his
many wounded. On 19 May Wingate sent a demand that he surrender,
emphasising the large number of British units that were rapidly
approaching. He stressed too that British troops might soon withdraw and
the Italians would be left to the mercy of the Patriots – who were notorious
for castrating their prisoners. Wingate demanded a reply in twelve hours.
Maraventano tried to prevaricate, but Wingate set a final deadline at 1500
hours on 22 May. Major (later Brigadier) Nott who conducted the negotiations in his School Certificate Latin, presided over the surrender of 10,000
troops and 6,000 miscellaneous supporters, and arranged a guard of honour
for Maraventano. Nott added, 'As our regular troops were a platoon or so,
the joke was too good to miss.'

As commander of Gideon Force, Wingate had been a colonel, but
immediately after his great coup at Agibar he was called to HQ, told that
his unit was immediately disbanded, and ordered at once to Cairo as a
major. This was the military establishment wreaking revenge. On top of
this humiliation, in Cairo Wingate caught cerebral malaria which he tried
to treat with atabrin. It was later discovered that this combination makes

people suicidal. In July 1941 he tried to commit suicide, but was saved by the prompt action of an officer in the next room. It is hard to believe, but his enemies rejoiced, saying: 'We have got him now. It is either a court-martial or a lunatic asylum for him.' Any balanced view must agree that Wingate's treatment was scandalous and disgraceful. He had a period of convalescence and then reached England by troopship in November 1941. He returned to the warmth and affection of his family and, as always, managed to re-establish contact with some of his high-level supporters. They ensured that Wingate's highly critical report about the Abyssinian campaign was shown to Churchill.

During his leave in England he was simmering with resentment at the way he had been treated, and when he was posted to Rangoon – even though this had been arranged by L. S. Amery and Wavell – he suspected that it was to silence him. After the campaign in Abyssinia his active mind had already absorbed its lessons, and had created a fairly detailed philosophy for the long-range penetration by guerrilla groups behind enemy lines.

He arrived in India in March 1942, and Wavell appointed him a full colonel to organise guerrilla groups behind the Japanese lines. He flew to Burma, and here he met Michael Calvert, who with him was to epitomise the concept and the philosophy of the Chindits. Fortunately, these two very strong characters immediately got on well. In August 1942 Wingate addressed a conference at GHQ in Delhi in which he put forward his ideas on Long Range Penetration (LRP). His detractors and the news of his suicide attempt had preceded him, and there was hostile reaction from the top brass in Delhi. They considered he was not fit to command, and that his ideas were impracticable. Wingate believed that LRP groups of brigade strength should be infiltrated behind enemy lines, and supplied by air, while they wrought havoc on roads, railways and bridges to disrupt the enemy's lines of communication. Wavell backed him, and 77 Brigade, with a battalion each of the King's Liverpool Regiment, the Gurkha Rifles and the Burma Rifles started severe training ready for the first Chindit expedition. An initial high sickness rate was quickly overcome, and soon the whole force was fit, tough and confident. Wingate organised it into independent columns each with their own mule transport, connected by efficient radios, and supplied entirely by air.

Throughout the training, Wingate's passionate conviction and amazing attention to detail created a confident and aggressive attitude throughout the force. One officer remarked that after the savage training, the operation was a piece of cake.

In January 1943, 77 Brigade – the Chindits – moved through IV Corps' area to Imphal ready to start their first campaign, Operation 'Longcloth'. This was to be part of an advance by IV Corps, by Stilwell from the north, and by British forces in the Arakan. Early in February Wavell arrived to tell Wingate that none of the other advances could take place, and perhaps the Chindit expedition should be called off. Wingate realised that if it were called off, his vicious detractors in Delhi might ensure that it would never take place, and argued for it to go ahead. Wavell reluctantly agreed.

On 12 February 1943 the Chindits set off, two columns moving south as a decoy, while the main body of about 2,000 men moved due east. There were some initial problems. The river crossings which had been practised proved to be no preparation for crossing the Chindwin and the Irrawaddy, which in places were a mile wide. Some of the columns were poorly led and lost contact with the main force. By 1 March, despite the setbacks, and the loss of several columns, four columns had reached a fairly safe area behind the Japanese lines and more than fifty miles from Imphal. This was close to the main Japanese road and rail routes which supplied reinforcements to their divisions facing Stilwell in the north.

Calvert, who was outstandingly the best Chindit leader after Wingate, commanded the first serious Chindit attack. With his column he planned and led an assault on Nankan station to destroy both the railway and the main road. In a model operation he destroyed the station, the track, several bridges and the road, and left mines and booby-traps over a large area. His column also drove off a large number of Japanese, inflicting heavy casualties without loss to themselves. At the same time, Bernard Fergusson led his column and demolished the railway at Bonchaung gorge, though he clashed with a Japanese patrol and suffered casualties. He had to leave several wounded men behind.

There being no advance by any other British forces, the Japanese could concentrate on eliminating the Chindits. Wingate had to make a difficult decision: should they stay where they were, return to Imphal, or go farther east and cross the Irrawaddy? Intelligence had suggested, wrongly, that beyond the Irrawaddy they would be in a favourable area. This influenced Wingate's decision, which was backed by all his column commanders, to cross the Irrawaddy. The columns got across with varying degrees of success, but found themselves in a dry and inhospitable area with many roads which the Japanese now used to hunt them down. The close attention of the Japanese made air drops increasingly difficult, and several columns suffered severely from shortages of food and water. Many men were totally exhausted.

While Wingate was still pondering further options – possibly to march north towards Myitkyina, or alternatively to march farther east and hope to reach the old Burma Road and go up to China, his musings were cut short by an order to bring the entire expedition back to Imphal. Fergusson argued that they should all march north to Myitkyina, but it would not have been possible to supply such a large force at such a distance. After much heated discussion Wingate ordered all columns to abandon their heaviest equipment and most of the mules, return across the Irrawaddy, and then break up into small groups, hoping to get as many men as possible safely back to the British lines near Imphal.

Most of the columns suffered very severe privations. Fergusson in *Beyond the Chindwin* described the suffering and adventures of his column which eventually reached the Kachin Hills where the people were supportive and hospitable. They reached safety on 24 April 1943. Calvert, the best of all the leaders, was unhappy at breaking up into small groups, because there were few who could give the leadership a group required. He felt he was shelving the responsibility of a commander, just when the men needed it most. He divided his group into nine parties of forty men and gave admirable instructions to the group leaders to help them in their difficult task. Wingate and several columns spent a week in bivouac, building up their strength with large airdrops, and killing and eating the mules – 'mule for breakfast, mule for lunch, and mule for supper', as one man said. These columns suffered severely, but sometimes received help from the local villages, where the people would tell them if any Japanese were approaching. One column, which aimed to march out northwards, after several weeks found a large flat area. They called for an airdrop. Then they spelt out on the ground 'PLANE LAND HERE NOW'. The intrepid Dakota pilot landed, delivered supplies, took on all the sick and wounded and lifted them out. The rest successfully marched back to base. No. 7 Column was divided into two groups one of which decided to attempt to reach China. After eluding the Japanese, they reached the Kachin Hills and the friendly Kachin people. Here they received substantial airdrops, continued their march, and on 1 May reached a Chinese post in Yunnan. Here they were treated as heroes, and had a remarkable stroke of luck. American planes were flying supplies to Chiang Kai-shek 'over the Hump', from northern India, and one returning aircraft offered the Chindit group a lift straight back.

Wingate reached safety on 25 April, having by his unrelenting determination and discipline saved the lives of many of his group. The Chindits had suffered grievous losses: of the 3,000 men who had set off, just over 2,000 returned – and he had had to abandon much valuable equipment. On the other hand they had learnt valuable lessons about LRP. Before they returned, because none of the other Allied armies – IV Corps, Stilwell, the Chinese – had advanced, the Japanese had deployed three full divisions to attack them, the same number of divisions as attacked Imphal the following year. Mutaguchi, who commanded that attack, wrote that Wingate's first expedition changed his whole strategic thinking, and had completely disrupted his plans for 1943.

As soon as he returned, Wingate was flown to Delhi for a press conference. He made the most of this. In contrast to the series of defeats and withdrawals in the rest of Burma, here at last was something to inspire. Reuters wrote of 'The greatest guerrilla operation ever undertaken.' Years later Louis Allen in *Burma the Longest War*, wrote that the first Chindit expedition 'had panache, it had glamour, it had cheek, it had everything the successive Arakan failures lacked'. The press enjoyed their brief euphoria, but not GHQ in Delhi, where Wingate had made formidable enemies. There the fifty brigadiers and countless colonels, most of whom had never been near the Japanese, remained critical.

While the Chindits were recuperating, their *raison d'être*, about which so many were dubious, received a dramatic boost. Churchill sent for Wingate who flew back to the UK and reported to Downing Street on 4 August 1943. Wingate explained his concept of LRP to Churchill who referred to the inefficiency and lassitude on the Indian front, in contrast to 'this man of genius and audacity'. He regarded him as a man of the highest quality and invited him to dinner. He then decided that Wingate must accompany him to the Quebec Conference for which he was to set off next day. He also had Lorna Wingate taken off a train at Edinburgh and brought to Glasgow so that she could join her husband aboard the *Queen Mary*. During the voyage Wingate carefully prepared his presentation for the Chiefs of Staff. Showing a remarkable grasp of the intricacies of the strategic situation, he proposed that three large groups of Chindit columns be formed: one to link-up with Stilwell and his Chinese divisions north of Myitkyina, one to assist the advance of the Chinese forces in Yunnan, and one to concentrate on Indaw, the strategic road and rail centre for the Japanese facing Imphal and Kohima. He convinced the Combined Chiefs of Staff, as well as Roosevelt, Churchill and Mountbatten, whom Churchill had just appointed Supreme Commander South East Asia Command. Equally important, he gained the support of General George Marshall and General Hap Arnold, both of whom felt that here was one of the few British leaders who were eager to fight the Japanese. The Chiefs of Staff cabled to GHQ Delhi to provide six brigades to be trained as Chindits.

Even before Wingate left Quebec, Auchinleck had cabled that it was impossible to provide six brigades. He did offer a brigade from 81st West African Division, or even the whole division, but he objected strongly to breaking up the battle-experienced British 70th Division which had fought at Tobruk. None the less, strategic orders were given for a three-pronged assault by Allied forces in the Burma area: in the north by Stilwell, in the east by Chinese forces in Yunnan, and in the west by the IV Corps at Imphal. The most remarkable boost to Wingate's hopes came when Marshall and Arnold promised him the support of 1st US Air Commando under two outstanding leaders, Cochran and Alison, so that the Chindits could be flown in. The Commando numbered more than 50 transport aircraft – mostly Dakotas, – 30 Mustang fighters, 100 gliders and 100 Sentinel light aircraft for reconnaissance and rescue.

Wingate left his wife in Quebec; he would never see her again. She was pregnant and their son was born after Wingate was killed. After the euphoria of Quebec, his arrival in Delhi was a brutal shock. He faced petty, puerile and bloody minded opposition at every level. For example he was told there was no office and he would have to work in the corridor. He could not have a secretary and there was no staff car available. The 70th Division was being broken up for Chindit training, and the military establishment never forgave Wingate for this. Every department appeared determined not to allocate supplies for the Chindit operations. Wingate reacted violently and threatened to inform Churchill.

Churchill was not popular with the Indian Army because he made outspoken criticisms of their lethargy and defeatism. While Wingate was battling for support for the next Chindit operation, the widespread view at GHQ Delhi was that all operations in Burma should be put on hold, until the war in Europe was over, and then the troops who had beaten the Germans could come out and deal with the Japanese.

Despite the opposition Wingate set up a vigorous training programme for the Chindit brigades under the inspiring leadership of Mike Calvert, the outstanding commander from the first operation. Then Wingate was struck down with typhoid fever, but Calvert, as well as Symes, the former GOC of 70th Division, loyally carried on. Towards the end of 1943, while the Chindit training continued, high-level decisions were made about the strategy for Burma which were not communicated to Wingate. When he returned to duty in December 1943, he had to spend much time liaising with Slim, with Stilwell and even with Chiang Kai-shek.

In January 1944 Wingate discussed with Slim the detailed proposals for the next Chindit operation. Fergusson's 16 Brigade would advance from Ledo and attack Indaw; Calvert's 77 Brigade would fly into 'Broadway'; Lentaigne's 111 Brigade would fly into Chowringhee and send two columns to cut the Japanese lines between Bhamo and Myitkyina. At this critical moment Wingate was told that the main Chindit air base at Argatala could not be used, and that anyway there could be no advance by IV Corps at Imphal. Wingate exploded. He sent a cable to General Giffard, the army commander, that in view of the continuing opposition by the High Command, which would endanger the lives of his men, he suggested that the entire Chindit operation be called off and the men returned to regimental duty. Mountbatten, who supported Wingate throughout these difficult times, tried to smooth over the difficulties.

The situation was changed dramatically when intelligence came through of large-scale Japanese troop movements towards Imphal. Wingate had long anticipated this, and was ready with an alternative plan which included one of his most daring and original ideas – 'the Stronghold'.

The title was taken from the biblical phrase 'Turn to the Stronghold ye prisoners of hope'. Wingate put forward a detailed plan for the Strongholds, in his usual clear and inspiring tone. They would be sited behind the Japanese lines, would be of brigade strength located away from main roads or railways so that the Japanese could not attack with tanks or heavy artillery. It would be strong enough to defeat all other attacks, and from the Strongholds columns would go out and destroy Japanese units and road and rail communications over the whole of that area of Burma. It would be sited in suitable terrain where airstrips could be laid down for Dakotas, and the Sentinel light aircraft which would be used to ferry supplies to columns operating away from their Stronghold, and to bring back wounded. One of the most harrowing aspects of the first campaign had been the necessity of leaving wounded men behind when the column had to move on. Wingate had realised this, and now Chindits operating from a Stronghold would know that if they were wounded they could very quickly be transferred by air to hospital. The Strongholds would be garrisoned by an infantry battalion, with two troops of artillery with 25-pounders and Vickers machine-guns, and would be defended by earthworks, minefields and wire. Floater columns would operate outside the perimeter to ambush any enemy units that approached. The first Stronghold would be at 'Broadway' and 77 Brigade under Brigadier Michael Calvert would fly in.

On 19 January 1944, Slim and Giffard appeared to accept Wingate's plan, and agreed to provide garrison battalions for the Strongholds. These were necessary because all the Chindit columns would be operating away from the base. While Wingate was making last-minute preparations for the launch of what was to be called Operation 'Thursday', there was almost total confusion in the decision-making machinery at the highest level. On 25 January, less than one week after the agreement to provide garrison battalions, Slim told Wingate there would be no garrison battalions. Wingate, with the awesome responsibility of organising an operation to place 10,000 men behind the enemy lines, now felt again that this prevarication could put the whole plan in jeopardy. During these tense clashes between Slim and Wingate, Mountbatten had sent an urgent mission – Axiom – to London, to gain assurance about official backing for the operations in north Burma. Secretly Mountbatten feared that orders might come from London to cancel Operation 'Thursday'. The Axiom Conference witnessed serious divisions between those who advocated a campaign to recapture Malaya and Singapore, and others who proposed a sweep across the Pacific with the Americans and Australians. The campaign in north Burma was hardly mentioned. Anglo–American tensions reached a peak, and the Axiom mission went on to Washington. Here it seemed to the Americans that the British were reneging on all their commitments, and, again, Wingate seemed to be the only British leader who was eager to fight the Japanese. Roosevelt even cabled to Churchill to honour the pledges made at the Quebec Conference. Thus the Chiefs of Staff were still dithering and undecided when Fergusson's 16 Brigade had already started their long trek from Ledo. Lord Ismay, Churchill's main link with the military, was later to say that the waffling and dithering over the Far East strategy was one of the black spots on the British higher direction of the war. (See Ziegler's *Mountbatten*.)

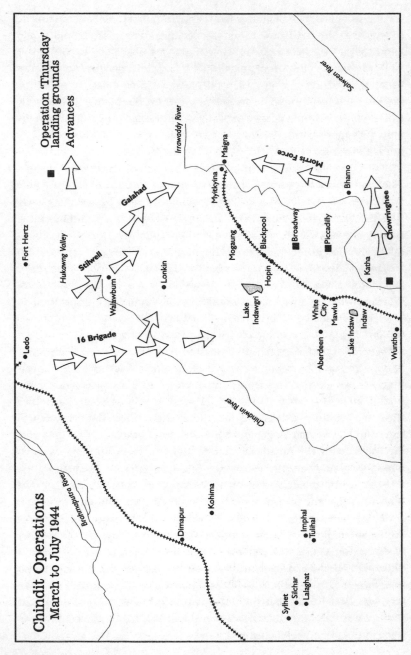

Chindit Operations
March to July 1944

■ Operation 'Thursday'
   landing grounds
⬆ Advances

Salween River

Irrawaddy River

Maigna

Morris Force

Myitkyina

Bhamo

Galahad

Mogaung   Blackpool

Broadway   Piccadilly

Chowringhee

Katha

Fort Hertz

Hukawng Valley

Stilwell

Wallawbum

Lonkin

Hopin

Lake
Indawgri

White
City

Mawlu   Lake Indaw

Aberdeen

Indaw

Wuntho

Ledo

16 Brigade

Chindwin River

Brahmaputra River

Dimapur

Kohima

Imphal
Tulihal

Sylhet   Silchar
          Lalaghat

By the end of February 1944, fairly clear information had emerged about Japanese movements. The three divisions – 15th, 31st and 33rd – comprising Mutaguchi's Fifteenth Army were moving towards Imphal and Kohima, while 18th Division was still facing Stilwell and his Chinese divisions. Wingate saw that the landing of Chindit brigades, and the establishment of Strongholds in the area of Indaw would cause the maximum disruption to the three divisions attacking Imphal and Kohima, and would cut off all supplies and reinforcements to 18th Division in the north.

The launch of Operation 'Thursday' took place on 5 March – the climax of months of urgent training and preparation. Two brigades, 77 and 111, were trained to a high pitch and ready to go. At Lalaghat airfield just west of Imphal, 83 Dakotas and 80 gliders, under the command of Cochran and Alison, were lined up, their tow-ropes laid with meticulous accuracy. The first wave consisted of 26 towing Dakotas and 52 gliders, which had to climb from Lalaghat over the mountain range to Indaw. 77 Brigade under Brigadier Michael Calvert was to lead the way. This, the biggest air operation to date, was watched by Slim, by Air Marshal Sir John Baldwin, commanding 3rd Tactical Airforce, and by senior USAAF officers.

The landing-grounds around Indaw had been carefully chosen after detailed reconnaissance, and were code-named 'Broadway', 'Piccadilly' and 'Chowringhee'. Piccadilly had been used once before during the 1943 expedition, but this was not considered a security hazard. The first flight was due to take off at 1700 hours, and until then the men were resting quietly under the aircraft's wings. To ensure security, Wingate had decreed that for the last three weeks no aircraft should go near the sites. At 1630 hours an Air Commando pilot rushed over to Cochran with photographs taken two hours earlier, which showed that the landing-ground at Piccadilly was completely blocked with tree trunks. Wingate reacted angrily because his order had been disobeyed, but then apologised because he realised that the photographs had prevented a certain disaster for 77 Brigade.

This information put Slim and Wingate under appalling pressure – illustrating starkly the anguish of command decisions when thousands of men's lives are at stake. An urgent decision had to be reached. Wingate at first had to consider whether their plans had been betrayed, and that the Japanese would be there waiting as the Chindits landed. Was there perhaps an innocent explanation? He realised too that many high-ranking officers in Delhi would be delighted if the operation were called off and then the whole concept of LRP would be finished for good. He held in his hand the lives of

77 Brigade, his most loyal and dedicated Chindits under Calvert. There was a hurried conference by Slim, Wingate, Cochran and Alison, Calvert, Scott, in command of the leading battalion, and Tulloch, Wingate's 2i/c; 77 Brigade was to have been split between Piccadilly and Broadway. Calvert agreed to go in provided his whole brigade went in to Broadway. Slim, who had to take the final decision, concurred. The admirable Cochran, whose entire planning now had to be changed, merely went to his pilots saying: 'Hey you guys, we have a better place to fly to.' The re-organised flights took off ninety minutes late.

Most of the people present have written their description of that fateful conference, including Wingate who made an official report; unfortunately there is an unpleasant aftermath. In Slim's book *Defeat into Victory*, which he wrote ten years after the event, and when he could not remember even which airfield had been used, he says that when the photographs arrived Wingate got into an emotional state and argued for the whole operation to be called off. All other evidence shows that, provided Chindit lives were not put in needless jeopardy, he argued strongly for the operation to go ahead. Calvert, Baldwin, Scott, Tulloch and Sir Robert Thompson all wrote their descriptions, which confirm Wingate's version and refute Slim's.

When assessing the significance of this operation, it must be remembered that it involved 12,000 men in gliders, which had to be towed not over the flat fields of Holland around Arnhem, but over a mountain range 7,000 feet high, to drop into small jungle clearings, and where the Japanese might well be waiting to attack as the Chindits left their gliders.

Slim, Wingate and Tulloch in the command tent waited eagerly for the first reports. These were not good. Some gliders parted from their tow-ropes. Some Dakotas ran out of fuel. One glider full of Gurkhas landed near IV Corps HQ in Imphal; the Gurkhas dutifully attacked. Two code signals had been agreed: 'Pork Sausage'– 'all's well'; 'Soya Link' (a detested ingredient of the rations) – 'trouble - do not send any more gliders'.

Calvert, always leading from the front, was one of the first to land at Broadway. There were problems. There were two trees and two ditches across the runway which air photographs had not identified. These caused the first gliders to crash. Then the next wave of gliders crashed onto the first ones. Flames from the crashed gliders lit up a lurid scene, with men struggling to clear the wreckage, screams from the wounded, and rescuers with flaming torches. To avoid a bigger disaster, at 0400 on 6 March, with morale at rock bottom, Calvert signalled 'Soya Link'.

One of the gliders had brought in a bulldozer, but had crashed into the jungle at the end of the strip. The impact threw the crew clear and sent the bulldozer through the front of the glider into the jungle. By an amazing chance – which virtually saved the whole operation – the jungle cushioned its fall and as dawn broke the American engineer calmly drove it on to the airstrip. The Americans assured Calvert that by evening they would be able to land Dakotas. His morale restored, he signalled 'Pork Sausage'.

Losses had been heavy. 37 gliders landed at Broadway, 16 did not; 30 men had been killed and 20 wounded. Fortunately the Japanese were badly confused by gliders landing over a wide area, and took a long time to identify Broadway. Baldwin flew in and returned to give an almost lyrical account of the runway under a Burma moon, with Dakotas coming in and taking off every three minutes.

Within Broadway everyone worked frantically to establish the first Stronghold, and, to their delight, on 7 March Wingate flew in. After the stresses of the launch it gave him a great boost to see the Stronghold – his personal concept – working well in practice. The Stronghold was already firmly established, with wire and mines laid, fields of fire laid down, telephone lines installed, and floater columns of the King's Regiment patrolling outside.

Broadway was some distance from Mawlu where the road and railway converged, and as soon as he felt that the Stronghold had been safely established, Calvert led a strong force of 3/9th Gurkhas and 1st South Staffords to set up a block at Mawlu. The block was based on the idea of the Stronghold, and had wired and mined defences, airstrips, a good supply of water, and was supplied entirely by air. It became known as 'White City' because of the number of parachutes festooning the trees. This derivative of Wingate's brilliant concept was swiftly involved in clashes with the Japanese. In the first clash on Pagoda Hill, Lieutenant Cairns won a posthumous VC. During Operation 'Thursday' it was remarkable what a dramatic and stimulating effect a visit from Wingate always had on the Chindits. On 24 March 1944, he flew into White City and went round the entire complex congratulating the men on their achievements, and making sound practical suggestions.

On that day Wingate also flew into Broadway and to Aberdeen where another Stronghold had been established. From Broadway, aggressive fighting patrols had fanned out across hundreds of miles of north Burma. These patrols, in addition to the impact of White City on Japanese supplies and communication, had attacked and disrupted Japanese units over an area stretching from the Chindwin, to the Irrawaddy and up to the Chinese border. This was the ideal and classic example of the Stronghold, not a defensive concept but as a base for aggressive action. Command of a Chindit unit was the supreme test of leadership in battle. Wingate and Calvert led and inspired their men at all times; others, notably Lentaigne, who commanded 111 Brigade, and succeeded Wingate, palpably failed to do so.

On 24 March 1944 Wingate returned to Imphal, where he had a discussion with Air Marshal Baldwin. He then left in a Mitchell bomber to return to the Chindit base. Shortly afterwards the plane crashed into the hills near Imphal and everyone aboard was killed.

Wingate's character and philosophy were so dominant that he remained for many years after his death as controversial as when he was alive. Because he was the complete maverick, rejecting most military conventions, and most social conventions as well, he was positively hated by large numbers of army officers who had never even met him. This paranoia continued for decades and even fifty years after his death, his critics speak of him with loathing. In contrast, virtually all the Chindits, as well as national and international leaders, considered him as a towering military genius and one of our great war leaders.

The gulf between Wingate's views and the normal was illustrated when he died and Lentaigne, who had commanded 111 Brigade at Chowringhee, was appointed to succeed him. This appointment was almost bizarre. Lentaigne's brigade had flown in a few days after 77 Brigade, and had merely marched around ineffectively. Before encountering any Japanese, Lentaigne's nerve had broken, and his brigade major, John Masters – later to become a famous novelist – was urgently trying to get a message to Wingate to say that Lentaigne had cracked up and should be flown out and hospitalised, when a message arrived saying that Lentaigne had been appointed to succeed Wingate.

Lentaigne's appointment illustrates a serious problem which bedevilled the Chindits from then on, and accounts for much of the unjust and unwarranted criticism levelled at Wingate and the Chindits. There was a group of senior officers in 111 Brigade, including Lentaigne, Masters and Morris, who did not accept Wingate's ideas and were openly disparaging about him. This was shortly to lead to tragedy and disaster for many of the men under their command.

Soon after his appointment, Lentaigne called a conference at Aberdeen – the only occasion he flew in to see the Chindits behind the lines. The change in attitude and atmosphere was obvious and immediate. Lentaigne must have realised that his crack-up when behind the lines was probably known to some of those present. He must have known, too, that most of them thought that Calvert or Symes or Tulloch should have been appointed to command. When Lentaigne suggested that Broadway and White City be abandoned, Calvert objected strongly, and from then onwards his signals to Lentaigne became so insubordinate that he had to be disciplined.

If Lentaigne's appointment was bizarre, his own appointments in 111 Brigade were almost equally quixotic. Morris, who was leading a small force up on the Myitkyina road, was promoted to brigadier and was technically in charge of the brigade, while Masters, a major, was promoted over the heads of many more senior and experienced colonels, and was put in charge of the main body of the brigade.

At a higher level, the absence of Wingate soon resulted in another disastrous decision. Before he was killed, Wingate had already anticipated the defeat of the Japanese at Imphal, and had suggested a Chindit operation further south at Pakkoku, to destroy the Japanese divisions as they retreated. When Wingate was not present to argue his corner with his usual passion and abrasiveness, things were totally different. Lentaigne, who lacked Wingate's power and conviction, could never stand up against Slim or Stilwell. He meekly agreed to Slim's plan that the Chindit brigades should be moved northwards to assist Stilwell's advancing Chinese divisions, and should come under Stilwell's command. This proved to be a death-sentence for many of them. The decision was disastrous in two separate ways.

Stilwell and Lentaigne ordered 77 Brigade, which had been made to abandon White City and Broadway, to move north and capture Mogaung. This was a scandalous order which totally ignored the role of the Chindits. They were trained and equipped for guerrilla fighting behind enemy lines. They had no armour or artillery support, and yet they were now ordered to attack a heavily fortified Japanese base. In fact 77 Brigade under the superb leadership of Calvert – who was unanimously recommended for the VC by the three battalion commanders in his brigade – did capture Mogaung at an appalling cost in dead and wounded. They felt they had to do this, because they were Wingate's brigade, and they could never let him down. After their victory, the comment they treasured most, came from Tulloch, now 2i/c to Lentaigne, who wrote: 'Wingate would have been proud of you.' That said, they were all convinced that if Wingate had been in command they would never have been asked to undertake such a murderous assault for which they were not trained or equipped.

In another field, the lack of Wingate's control and the rejection of his teaching led to a complete disaster. Masters, commanding the main body of 111 Brigade, was ordered to move north and establish a block, code-named 'Blackpool', on the road and railway about thirty miles south-west of Mogaung. Masters subsequently described this operation in his book *The Road Past Mandalay*, and he describes how he chose the site for Black-pool. It shows that he ignored or rejected all Wingate's views on the Stronghold. Wingate held that a Stronghold should be established in rough country to prevent attack by tanks or heavy artillery. Masters sited Blackpool where Japanese artillery was able to attack it from the very start. There is now massive evidence, written at the time, that experienced Chindits realised the site was totally wrong. Mr J. Milner, CBE, who was present, wrote: 'Underlying all their anger and fury was the conviction that if Wingate had been alive they would not have been at Blackpool at all.' They wondered if the Chindit doctrines had been buried with their creator. The brigade held Blackpool for seventeen disastrous days; just over 100 shattered and emaciated men survived. They had to witness the incident described by Masters, when gravely wounded men were shot to prevent them falling into the hands of the Japanese. Such were the feelings of anger that one survivor wrote: 'If Stilwell or Lentaigne had appeared they would not have lived to see the dawn.' Masters wrote a best-seller in which he described the disaster of Blackpool – but he never admitted that it was he who was responsible for the disaster by rejecting all of Wingate's precepts.

Elsewhere in Burma the legacy of Wingate continued. On the Bhamo to Myitkyina road two Chindit columns were operating. One, led by the spir-ited and aggressive Peter Cane (Lieutenant-Colonel Peter Cane, MC) was highly successful, but the column under the command of Morris, nominally a brigadier, who had openly derided Wingate's ideas, achieved nothing. It was so timidly led that it was said quite openly (e.g. O'Brien, *Out of the Blue*) that Morris was cowardly. Colonel Charles Carfrae, who gave outstanding service with the Nigerian Chindit Brigade, described how some commanders in the jungle imagined a Japanese behind every tree in the jungle and were 'reduced to pitiable ineptitude'. Morris appears to have been one of those. After the war Peter Cane's group published *Chinese Chin-*

dits and wrote: 'Wingate as a soldier was superb. Magnificently unorthodox ... he inspired all with the desire to achieve what the normal man would consider impossible ... with his uncompromising disgust at the selfish and the self-seekers, he became their enemy.'

The effectiveness of Wingate's concept of Long Range Penetration, and of the Stronghold had been amply proved at Broadway and White City, under Calvert's leadership, at Aberdeen under Fergusson, and by the better columns on the Bhamo–Myitkyina road. After Wingate's death his most destructive critics, Lentaigne, Morris and Masters, moved into positions of authority in the Chindit organisation, and worse still, Slim and Lentaigne abandoned his principles. It is an injustice that the mishandling of the Chindit brigades after Wingate's death in March 1944 should be used as a reason to abandon the idea of Long Range Penetration, and as a criticism of Wingate.

In March 1944 his widow, then heavily pregnant, received countless tributes from around the world. It is necessary to recount these in order to counteract the vendetta that is still pursued against the reputation of Wingate. Mountbatten wrote and referred to the most forceful and dynamic personality this war had produced, who had revolutionised jungle warfare. General Carton de Wiart VC wrote of an irreparable loss. Lord Ismay referred to his vivid imagination and resolute courage. Harold Laski spoke of that remarkable courage which shows that the dignity of the human spirit is unbreakable. L. S. Amery recalled qualities beyond mere intelligent grasp of war or swift daring, especially a deep compelling faith. Michael Foot paid tribute to Wingate's innermost convictions which gave him the power to perform mighty deeds, which stamped all his acts with a quality of greatness. Tributes flowed in, from General Hap Arnold in America, from the Emperor of Abyssinia, from Israel 'the noblest and sincerest friend the Zionists ever had', from famous people across the world, to dozens of modest people who were touched by his greatness. A Chindit wrote: 'He is the only man I would have followed to the ends of the earth. A King among men.' King George VI, Edwina Mountbatten, Earl Wavell, Madame Chiang Kai-shek all sent their tributes. Bernard Fergusson, who served in both Chindit campaigns, wrote: 'There are men who shine at planning, or at training, or at leading; here was a man who excelled at all three – and whose vision at the council table matched his genius in the field.' In the House of Commons on 2 August 1944, Churchill said: 'There was a man of genius who might well have become a man of destiny.'

To show that this was no brief posthumous elegy, one ironic final event confirmed his status. In 1951, Charterhouse School, which he hated, erected a memorial to Wingate. Churchill sent a message which was be read by, of all people, General Pownall, whose total misanthropy had written off Wingate, Slim, Giffard, Stilwell, Mountbatten and Churchill himself. Churchill referred to Wingate as one of the most brilliant and courageous figures of the Second World War. Mountbatten, who presided over a gathering of ambassadors and service chiefs from around the world, paid his final tribute to Wingate as: 'a great fighter, a fearless leader of men, a brilliant originator and a deeply religious man'.

These tributes and comments covering the period from 1944 to 1951 illustrate the respect and world-wide veneration for Wingate. It is necessary for them to be quoted, because from then onwards, the reputation of Wingate was assailed and deliberately undermined. This despicable move was led by a group of officers, who were in a privileged position, as compilers of the *Official History of the Burma Campaign*. These detractors gained ready support in different areas. There had been understandable resentment in the army when British 70th Division was broken up in order to undertake Chindit training. Chindit training was severe. Consequently many officers were returned to their units and they often harboured a grudge against Wingate. Some units, at a critical time in Burma, did lose experienced officers or NCOs who volunteered for the Chindits. Many units resented the priority the Chindits appeared to have in the supply of scarce equipment. When Wingate returned to Delhi from the Quebec Conference, and was met by almost total obstruction, he was aggressive and abrasive, and he deliberately used the threat of Churchill's offer to contact him directly. This caused even more resentment.

During his time at GHQ Delhi, when he was trying to cut through the obstruction and lethargy in order to set up the Chindit organisation, Wingate made a particular enemy of a General Kirby. He was a very senior staff officer who violently disliked Wingate and considered him a dangerous upstart. He retired to England, and in 1951 was appointed editor of the *Official History*. He was assisted in his task by a Brigadier Roberts, who had commanded a brigade in the IV Corps at Imphal. Roberts, who had been an officer in the Gurkhas and was an old friend of Slim's, shared Kirby's dislike of Wingate. These two officers, as the compilers of the *Official History*, had signed a commitment 'to avoid personal bias or perverse interpretation', yet they used the work in a detailed and prolonged attempt to destroy Wingate's reputation. Evidence was falsified, direct quotations were deliberately altered to reverse their meaning. This disgraceful and unprofessional attack on a brave and outstanding officer was backed up further when Roberts lectured to the Staff College in the 1960s about the Burma Campaign. The view of Wingate which he put forward was totally destructive, and thus to new generations of young officers, Wingate's image as an upstart and a charlatan was carefully nurtured.

In the *Official History* almost every comment on Wingate is petulant and destructive, although the convention in such compilations is that individual commanders are not criticised. Wingate was charged with creating a private army, and with lacking the knowledge, stability and balance to be a great commander. The White City operation was rubbished by deliberate misrepresentation, as was Fergusson's attack on Indaw. Fergusson stated that in the 1950s Kirby had badgered him to change his mind on some crucial matters, and in the end he gave in. Two further examples must suffice to illustrate Kirby's vendetta against Wingate. He wrote: 'Just as timing played so great a part in his rise to prominence, so the moment of his death may perhaps have been equally propitious for him.' (*Official History*, p. 223). Meaning it was just as well that he was killed. The Japanese commander Mutaguchi made a detailed statement about the Chindits: 'The Chindit invasion did not stop our plans to attack Kohima, BUT they had a decisive effect on these operations, and drew off the whole of 53rd Division and parts of 15th Division, one regiment of which would have turned the scales at Kohima.' In the *Official History* Kirby quoted the sentence only up to 'BUT', thus completely reversing the meaning. Eventually even Roberts became critical of Kirby's underhand and unprofessional methods. In a letter to Lewin, the biographer of Slim, Roberts described how Kirby asked loaded questions to trap Perceval the commander at Singapore. After one answer Kirby exclaimed exultantly: 'Now we've got him.' Roberts warned Lewin that Kirby had also put loaded questions to Slim.

Official histories do not provide popular reading and usually are not widely reviewed, but Kirby's volume dealing with the Chindits was roundly condemned. The *Sunday Telegraph* asked: 'Will none of the eminent commanders who worked with Wingate defend him against the outrageous conclusion of the Official History?' The *Jewish Observer* stated: 'There appears to be no end to the official vendetta against Wingate.'

Unfortunately, even Slim was caught up in Kirby's unsavoury machinations. Slim had paid a sincere and dignified tribute to Wingate in the SEAC newspaper in 1944. In contrast, when his distinguished book *Defeat into*

Victory was published in 1956, the Chindits were amazed and incredulous because Slim, whom they all revered, was totally critical and dismissive of their other hero, Wingate. The answer to their concern lies in the *Slim Papers* held at Churchill College, Cambridge. Slim wrote his book when he was Governor-General of Australia. Each chapter was sent off to Kirby or Roberts – who were then compiling the *Official History* – asking them to check details and correct him where he was wrong. The *Slim Papers* contain all these letters and the replies from Kirby and Roberts, and prove conclusively how these two men over the years managed to change the view of even someone of such unimpeachable integrity as Lord Slim.

When the *Official History* was published in 1962, supporters of Wingate were outraged. General Tulloch, Wingate's 2i/c and most loyal supporter, devoted the rest of his life to writing a book which attempted to reverse the injustice of it. He was actively supported by Calvert, by Fergusson, by Wingate's family and many more. Air Marshal Sir John Baldwin protested that the official version was unfair and inaccurate. He challenged in detail their description of the crisis at Lalaghat when Operation 'Thursday' began. Sir Robert Thompson, the great counter-insurgency expert, and military adviser to Presidents Ford and Nixon, who had served with Calvert in 77 Brigade, took strong action to have the *Official History* changed. Thompson was infuriated by those armchair critics who said that the landing of two Chindit brigades at Broadway and Chowringhee had no effect on the battles for Imphal and Kohima. He pointed out that the landings took place one day after the Japanese started their attack on Imphal, and he asked what would have happened if a German airborne division had landed on Salisbury Plain on D-Day plus one. As Tulloch, who was still a serving officer, continued to prepare his book for publication, he was called to the War Office and threatened that if his book were published he would lose his pension and could be imprisoned in the Tower of London. This may sound laughable, but it clouded the few remaining years of his life. His treatment showed the lengths to which Kirby and the military establishment were prepared to go to prevent the truth about Wingate from emerging.

'Instead of the petty, destructive and dishonest commentary of Kirby, which has had so much malign influence since it was written, Wingate should now be remembered as an outstanding wartime leader, a brilliant and original military thinker whose reputation spanned the world, a meticulous planner and organiser, and a fearless and inspiring leader.' (David Rooney, *Wingate and the Chindits*, 1994.)

SKORZENY

One of Napoleon's marshals, Philibert Sérurier, had an uneventful career except for one dramatic moment during Napoleon's campaign in northern Italy in 1796. French troops were pinned down by the Austrians and suffering casualties, when Sérurier suddenly jumped on his horse, drew his sword, and charged straight at the enemy who fled in panic. This singular act of bravery set him on the road to promotion, eventually to become a marshal of France. Similarly, the name of Otto Skorzeny, and the legend, centre for most people on his single daring act in rescuing Mussolini from captivity in September 1943. Skorzeny did, however, have many more achievements to his credit before the final defeat of the Nazis in 1945.

Born in 1908, he spent his young days in a Vienna which was suffering grievously from the effects of the Depression, and from the dislocation and dismemberment of the Austrian empire. His fairly prosperous father imposed a stern and frugal regime on the family, but like all middle-class families in Vienna at the time, inflation destroyed their savings. Otto developed harsh right-wing political views which he never lost. He studied engineering at Vienna university, and became renowned for his aggressive activities in the student duelling groups – carrying proud scars on his cheeks to prove it. Later he said that going in to action was nothing compared to his first duel. During the 1930s he built up a successful engineering business in Vienna, but soon after the Nazis took over in March 1938 he volunteered to serve as a pilot in the Luftwaffe. He was turned down, for being too old, and in disgust volunteered for the SS. After some extremely rigorous training he was posted to the Waffen SS Division Das Reich. Over six foot three inches in height, he was tough, scarred and well imbued with SS arrogance. His aggressive behaviour caused trouble during his service in Holland in 1940, and he was transferred to another unit and took part in campaigns in Hungary and Romania. As an engineer officer he did not serve in the front line, but he did win the first of his awards for bravery when his division was involved in heavy fighting during the grim campaign in Russia in the winter of 1941. He was wounded during a mortar attack, and was evacuated to Germany. He reached Vienna in December 1941 for sick-leave, but fumed at his imposed idleness, and early in 1942 he was back in Berlin at the SS depot, where he suffered more months of frustration.

Almost as soon as Churchill came to power in May 1940 he had ordered the establishment of the first commando units, and at Lochailort in the west of Scotland, a band of men assembled who were to make their name in the annals of irregular warfare in the Commandos, the Long Range Desert Group, the Chindits and the SAS. Among them were the Stirling brothers, Spencer Chapman and Mike Calvert. By 1942 the Germans too had begun to see the value of men whose panache and leadership qualities were often frustrated by the humdrum routine of regular units, and this was to give Skorzeny his chance. He was called for interview, and given an outline of the type of operations to be carried out by these proposed new units, styled on the British Commandos. He eagerly accepted the challenge, and in April 1942 at Friedenthal near Berlin he took charge of what was called the Hunting Group. He was able to recruit a number of able and experienced parachutists and linguists, but he had great difficulty in obtaining the specialist equipment and weapons such units needed. Then he had a brilliant idea. The Germans had penetrated the Dutch underground movement, and were using active double-agents. Skorzeny used one of these to signal urgent requests for supplies of explosives, radios, submachine-guns, silenced pistols and mines. He enjoyed the joke as British planes flew in these supplies especially for him.

In most armies, irregular units – notably the Chindits in Burma – suffered frustration because regular formations were reluctant to hand over equipment and weapons that were in short supply, for use in what they considered to be mad-cap schemes. Skorzeny suffered in the same way. He came up with a scheme to disrupt the Allied supply route to Russia through Persia, but had to cancel it because the authorities refused to lend him a suitable bomber to drop the necessary supplies to his agents. He proposed several other operations, including one behind Russian lines which was favoured by Himmler, but lack of accurate intelligence and reconnaissance prevented them taking place. During this period of frustration, he had, however, made some useful contacts at a high level.

In July 1943 his opportunity came. He had been drinking in a bar in Berlin, when he was called urgently to report to the Wolf's Lair, Hitler's HQ in East Prussia. He was present among a number of senior officers addressed by Hitler. Then the rest were dismissed and Hitler spoke to him alone. He explained that, the previous day, Mussolini had been arrested by the

Badoglio government which was suing for peace with the Allies. Hitler was determined to rescue Mussolini and to keep Italy in the war. He ordered Skorzeny to carry out the mission.

The Wehrmacht were still holding Rome, and Skorzeny flew in next day with about seventy men from his Hunting Group. First he had to find out where Mussolini was being held. Several weeks passed before he obtained a lead which suggested that Mussolini was on the small island of Ponza, just off the coast of Italy. He immediately began to plan a rescue operation, only to hear that Mussolini had been removed to La Maddalena – an island off the coast of Sardinia. Skorzeny flew there, and in disguise scoured the harbour and the bars for information. He soon had confirmation that Mussolini was held in a well-defended villa above the harbour. He flew back to Rome to collect his men, but on the way his plane was attacked by British fighters and forced down into the sea. Skorzeny was knocked unconscious and broke three ribs, but was rescued by an Italian boat. Despite his injuries, he flew at once to see Hitler. He had to scotch a rumour that Mussolini was in Elba, and then presented a plan for Mussolini's rescue. Hitler approved, but warned Skorzeny that if he failed he would be disowned. He flew back to the island only to learn that Mussolini had been moved elsewhere.

Skorzeny had to return to Rome and start again. Then he was lucky, when an intercepted security message suggested that Mussolini was held at Gran Sasso, a ski resort on the loftiest peak of the Apennines, about 100 miles from Rome. The resort boasted one large luxury hotel which was totally isolated except for a funicular railway. Skorzeny flew over the place in a reconnaissance plane, and could see troops guarding every approach road, but he noticed a small grassed area close to the hotel. As he flew back to Rome he was once again attacked by Allied fighters, and he witnessed waves of Allied aircraft supporting the Salerno landings. This made Mussolini's rescue even more urgent.

Skorzeny had to weigh up the various possibilities for the attack by ground troops, by parachute drop, or by glider. Against all advice, he decided to try to land his men by glider on the grass patch near the hotel. He swiftly assembled twelve gliders, each of which could hold ten men. He explained his scheme and all his men volunteered to go.

On 12 September 1943, just as the operation was about to start from a small airfield near Rome, Allied bombers attacked, but luckily none of the gliders was damaged. Skorzeny was in the third glider, and had highjacked an Italian general to help when they arrived at Gran Sasso. Almost as soon as they had taken off, some of the gliders were lost, including the first two whose men were to have prepared the ground for Skorzeny and the general. So Skorzeny had to lead the way and guide the remaining gliders in. As he approached, to his horror he saw that the green patch where they were to land was extremely steep and was littered with boulders. His glider crashed on to the meadow, and came to rest within a few yards of the hotel.

Skorzeny leapt out, rushed past open-mouthed sentries, smashed a radio-transmitter, jumped over a wall, and hurled himself into the hotel just as the bemused Italian guards tried to come out and assemble their weapons. He charged on up a flight of stairs, and found Mussolini guarded by two young Italian officers. At almost the same moment, more of his paratroops appeared at the window with their submachineguns. The young officers meekly put up their hands. Mussolini's capture had taken about four minutes and hardly a shot had been fired. The last of the gliders had not even arrived. Then Skorzeny demanded to see the garrison commander. He appeared and was given sixty seconds to surrender or be annihilated. He gave in, and at once a white sheet was waved from the window. Skorzeny then had time to explain to Mussolini that Hitler had personally sent him to carry out the rescue.

He now faced the problem of escaping with his valuable but over-weight hostage. He reckoned there would be no hope of getting out by road through the powerful Italian forces surrounding the area. One light plane had come in but it had smashed its undercarriage and was wrecked. The only hope was a Stork spotter plane, piloted by a brilliant pilot, Gerlach, who had flown Skorzeny several times. He came in and landed safely, but then another crisis arose. Gerlach refused to take off with two such huge men as Mussolini and Skorzeny in his little plane. Skorzeny explained that Hitler had given him the strictest orders never to leave Mussolini's side after the rescue. Gerlach agreed to go. Twelve paratroopers held the wings of the plane as it revved to maximum, then with bumps and crashes it finally got off. After a few more adventures, Skorzeny delivered his prize to the Imperial Hotel in Vienna where Mussolini went straight to bed, exhausted by the ordeal. Skorzeny had scarcely returned to his room, when he was telephoned first by Himmler, then by Hitler, by Göring and by Keitel. A few days later in Berlin, he was lionised by most of the top Nazi leaders, and decorated with awards for bravery.

Basking now in Hitler's personal admiration, Skorzeny was a national hero. He was promoted to major, and authorised to recruit new commando units in all the theatres of war. Many different suggestions were now put forward for this new style of warfare. One of the early plans, to seize Pétain who was wavering as the tide of war turned against Germany, had to be abandoned. Next, and more seriously, came a project to capture Tito whose partisans were tying down many German troops who were urgently needed elsewhere. Skorzeny drove into the Balkans through dangerous country controlled by trigger-happy partisans. He reported to the nearest German divisional commander, who was clearly resentful of Skorzeny's intrusion – and he a mere major. The general went ahead with his own plan for a large-scale airborne operation which failed completely, and Tito escaped. This incident was a classic example of the resentment and often antagonism felt by regular units for the Special Forces, which always seemed to get badly needed equipment as well as favourable publicity – as Wingate and the Chindits found in Burma.

After the frustration of losing the chance to capture Tito, Skorzeny spent some time assessing and developing different types of secret weapon. Frogmen, mini-submarines, and a type of double torpedo (the *Neger*) were used effectively against British ships supporting the Italian landings. Skorzeny was actively involved in planning counter-measures to the expected Allied invasion of Europe, but most of these ideas were rejected because Hitler had decreed that the Atlantic Wall was invulnerable

During July 1944, Skorzeny was in Berlin organising equipment and weapons for his different units, and was actually at a conference with senior officers, when the news arrived of the 20 July bomb plot against Hitler. Colonel von Stauffenberg, assuming that the bomb he had left in his brief-case had killed Hitler, had issued the code-word 'Valkyrie'. This caused total confusion, because supporters of the conspiracy went into action, and only later in the day was it learned authoritatively that Hitler was alive and the coup had failed. Skorzeny witnessed the chaos in the Berlin HQ, because no one could tell who was in the plot and who was not. He was still in Berlin when Himmler returned and some semblance of order was restored.

In September 1944 Skorzeny was again summoned to the Wolf's Lair, together with several top Nazi leaders and generals. Hitler outlined the very grave situation in Hungary, where the ageing dictator Admiral Horthy was wavering in his support for Germany, and was thought to be making over-tures to the Russians. This was a severe crisis for Germany, since, if Hungary gave in, thousands of Russian troops could be re-deployed elsewhere. Skorzeny was personally ordered by Hitler to go to Budapest, and if possible grab Horthy and prevent a débâcle in Hungary. Hitler gave Skorzeny wide powers, backed by a signed authority, as well as all necessary troops, weapons, gliders and his own plane.

Skorzeny left at once for Budapest, masquerading as a Dr Wolf. He stayed in a modest hotel, far removed from the German HQ. He soon built up a picture of the situation in Budapest. It appeared that Horthy was dominated by his son Nicholas, a wild playboy, but who was also involved in high-level negotiations. Skorzeny obtained details of a secret meeting in Budapest between Nicholas and some senior Yugoslav negotiators on a Sunday in October 1944. Given the rather lax Hungarian security, Skorzeny was able to infiltrate a number of his troops on the upper floor of the house where the meeting was to take place. On the Sunday morning, the civilian Dr Wolf drove up and parked his car in the square opposite the house. He noted with some concern that Hungarian soldiers were manning a machine-gun. Then two of Skorzeny's men rushed into the house and were met by a fusillade of shots. Skorzeny and his small group were badly mauled, but he signalled with a whistle and his 2i/c with a powerful group stormed into the square and routed the Hungarian guards. Skorzeny then led the way into the house. Inside, the Germans on the top floor, as soon as the firing started, had gone down, seized Nicholas Horthy, and held him at gun point. He reacted violently.

When Skorzeny arrived he forced the young Horthy to the floor, tied him up and had him bundled into the large carpet which covered the floor. Ignominiously, the prisoner was carted out, slung into the back of a truck, and taken to the German HQ. Then Skorzeny and his group waited anxiously to hear Admiral Horthy's reaction. Soon the radio programmes were interrupted for a major announcement by him. He was outraged by the incident, and stated that since Germany was losing the war, he had made peace between Hungary and Russia. For Skorzeny's group, and indeed for Germany, this was a disaster, and the reverse of what Hitler had anticipated.

Faced with this new crisis, Skorzeny had to discuss the next possible step with the senior officers present. Could they still gain the result that had been intended? The plan he then proposed was dangerous. It relied on his hope that the Hungarian troops in the city would not act immediately on what Horthy had said in his broadcast. Horthy's HQ was located in a castle on the famous Burgberg, the hill which dominates the centre of Budapest. Skorzeny planned to surreptitiously surround the Burgberg with a panzer division during the night. When this was done, he intended personally to lead an innocent looking convoy of trucks, packed with his paratroopers, and interspersed with a few tanks, towards the entrance to the castle. The regular officers opposed the scheme as far too dangerous, but Skorzeny, with his authority from Hitler, overruled them and went ahead.

The operation started at 6 o'clock on the Monday morning. Skorzeny, with a tried group of veterans from the Gran Sasso coup, led the way in a staff car followed by truck-loads of troops and the tanks. The whole issue depended on whether the Hungarian guards had been instructed, since Horthy's broadcast the previous day, to regard the Germans as their enemy. From the leading car Skorzeny waved cheerfully to the guards they passed, and they snapped smartly to attention. Then his car came to a road-block, and he had to call forward a tank to flatten it. This clearly alerted the garrison, but Skorzeny had time to reach the HQ building before there were any developments. At gun point he forced a frightened young officer to lead him to the commander's office. This officer – a major-general – saw Skorzeny's men at every window and heard that the castle had been taken. To save further bloodshed he offered to surrender, and ordered his troops not to fight. Despite this success, Skorzeny still faced a formidable difficulty. There were a large number of officers in the castle. He quickly had them assembled, and, speaking as an Austrian, and with a strong Austrian accent, appealed to the traditional alliance and loyalty between Hungary and Austria against the threat from the east. This brave speech carried the day and won the support of many officers who were opposed to Horthy's action.

There was no more firing at the Burgberg, and shortly afterwards Horthy was taken to Berlin. He was quickly replaced by a pro-German head of state who cancelled the proposed armistice with Russia. As a direct result of this, Hungarian troops continued to fight against Russia until the end of the war.

Rarely can a single attack by one man and a small picked group, have had such huge political and military repercussions. Skorzeny had created a new form of irregular warfare – not aimed at installations, or breaking through defensive lines, but, by removing crucial leaders, changing the entire political and military situation. Hitler was again delighted at the remarkable success of the operation, which he had personally chosen Skorzeny to carry out. Skorzeny was rewarded by being allowed to stay for a while in the luxury of the ruler's palace.

The successful abduction of Horthy – far more significant politically than the Mussolini coup – confirmed Hitler's faith in Skorzeny, who, after a brief period of leave in October 1944, was once again called to see the

Führer. Hitler explained his plans for a panzer offensive in the Ardennes, and the role he wanted Skorzeny to play. Already the legend of Skorzeny and his dramatic kidnapping of Mussolini and Horthy had caused great psychological damage to the enemy, and many leaders both military and civilian were feeling apprehensive. Hitler developed this theme. He ordered Skorzeny to raise special commando units of English-speaking volunteers. Dressed in captured US uniforms, driving captured jeeps, and equipped with captured weapons, these men when the Ardennes offensive began would infiltrate, and spread alarm and chaos behind the enemy lines, so that every US unit would be fearful and suspicious of all other troops.

Skorzeny returned to his old base at Friedenthal, and hastily gathered suitable volunteers. Gradually he obtained the necessary uniforms, vehicles and equipment, then, in a totally isolated camp, trained more than 3,000 men for the task ahead. Divided between sabotage and reconnaissance teams, there would be a driver, a radio-operator and an explosives expert in each jeep, all armed with machine-guns and grenades.

The main German offensive in the Ardennes started with a formidable artillery bombardment on 16 December 1944. The attack, against a weak and inexperienced US formation, was intended to break through and fan out behind the enemy's lines – just as Guderian had done in 1940. In spite of the bombardment and a mass panzer advance, the swift breakthrough did not happen. The roads were quickly clogged with vehicles, and even Skorzeny had to leave his car and walk towards the front. This hold-up put the whole of his scheme in jeopardy, though despite the delay some of his teams did get through. Some small successes were obtained in cutting telegraph cables, misdirecting enemy units, and altering signposts, after which they returned safely to base. Ironically, the greatest success in spreading alarm and confusion was achieved by some of the groups that were captured fairly close to the Meuse bridges. After the prisoners were interrogated, Allied intelligence alerted all units to the danger of this new form of attack, and to the rumour that Eisenhower was one of their targets. So a climate of hysteria, fear and uncertainty spread swiftly through Allied units all over Belgium and northern France. Some US units even arrested their own officers. Skorzeny was dubbed 'the most dangerous man in Europe', and was now believed to pose a threat to all the Allied commanders. Even the most senior generals were forced to produce their identity cards, and General Omar Bradley complained violently about time-wasting nonsense and panic. The rumour of a plot on the life of Eisenhower persuaded him to leave his HQ in Paris (which had been occupied by the Germans) – and move to a safer place in Versailles. He was held, almost a prisoner in his own HQ, during the most critical time of the Ardennes offensive.

Skorzeny's scheme to spread confusion and panic was brilliantly successful, but the expected rapid breakthrough past the Meuse bridges did not take place. Skorzeny then abandoned his plans, and his units were absorbed into Sixth SS Army. Not long afterwards he was seriously wounded in the head by shrapnel. He was taken out of the line for medical treatment and recuperation, and then was again called to see Hitler.

By this time – January 1945 – Skorzeny realised that with the Russians and the Allies advancing relentlessly into Germany's heartland, there would be no opportunities for his escapades. Because of his reputation for daring and bravery, and Hitler's total faith in him, Skorzeny became a pawn in the charade which the Nazi leaders, especially Himmler, were using to convince Hitler that a great counter-offensive was still possible. After seeing Hitler, Skorzeny was ordered by Himmler to go to the Eastern Front and establish a bridgehead over the River Oder, as the launch-pad for a two-corps offensive which would halt the Russian advance. He was able to gather together a ragbag of troops, guns and vehicles, but he soon realised that the proposed offensive was purely imaginary. Himmler – desperate to reassure Hitler – telephoned Skorzeny constantly, asking how far he had advanced and whether the bridgehead had been established.

In practice, Skorzeny was able to collect a few fighting units, and reached the small town of Schwedt on the River Oder. With his fearsome reputation for discipline, he managed to stem some of the flow of defeated and demoralised German troops fleeing before the Russian advance. Preparing to defend Schwedt, he commandeered artillery, tanks and anti-aircraft guns. Then, to his amazement, Göring came to visit him, and did send him a battalion from the Herman Göring Division. With this addition Skorzeny had about 15,000 men under command, and should have had the rank of major-general. He was more troubled, as the Russian attack drew closer, by what he considered the foolish interference of senior but remote German officers, and, even worse, odious party officials, one of whom he arrested for deserting his troops. His makeshift defences were still holding out against the Russian onslaught, when he was called back to Himmler's HQ. Himmler now berated him furiously for his failure to establish an effective bridgehead, and threatened him with court-martial. Skorzeny, towering over the wretched Himmler, lost his temper and told him the truth – that he received a lot of idiotic orders from the High Command, but no supplies, no weapons, and no reinforcements. Himmler was so completely taken aback by Skorzeny's tirade that he calmed down and invited him to stay to dinner. Afterwards Skorzeny returned to Schwedt which was still holding out against the Russians, but then, to his grief at having to leave his trusted veterans of Friedenthal, he was ordered to report to Berlin.

He left early in March and reported to Hitler's H.Q. The Führer was too ill to see him, but specific orders were given to him by General Jodl. The Americans had just, famously, captured the bridge at Remagen – giving them their first major crossing-point of the Rhine. Hitler was furious and ordered Skorzeny to organise frogmen to blow it up. His frogmen had had mixed success in the past in the murky waters of northern Europe, and Skorzeny was convinced that it would be impossible to destroy the heavily defended bridge. However, he did plan the operation for his frogmen, who did their best, but all of them were either lost or captured without having any success. Despite this failure Skorzeny was again called to see Hitler who invested him personally with the Oak Leaves to the Knight's Cross. His final order from the Führer's HQ was to go to Austria, and help to set up a unit of dedicated Nazis, who would fight to the last in an Alpine fastness.

Early in April 1945, after driving through thousands of panic-stricken and demoralised troops, he reached Vienna. He found that his mother and brother had already escaped to the west. He had a bizarre interview with von Schirach, nominally the Nazi commander of Vienna, who believed that several German divisions were coming to drive back the Russians. Skorzeny told von Schirach that there were no new divisions, indeed no fighting troops, and no defensive positions were being manned. He also radioed the same information to Hitler's HQ. As the Russian tanks drew closer, he left Vienna. Then, to his delight he met a group of about 200 of his Hunting Commando, and together they moved off into the higher Alpine region. They found no defensive positions at all, and so, with a small group of friends, he retreated into the mountains.

After the cease-fire, he heard that the Allies were actively searching for him. He sent several letters to the nearest US unit, but these were ignored, and at last, with a few colleagues, he went to Salzburg to surrender. There he was carefully guarded, but was hounded by journalists about the rumour of the plot to kill Eisenhower.

He spent about two years in a prisoner-of-war camp, and in July 1947 was brought before a war-crimes tribunal at Dachau near Munich – the former concentration-camp, which is kept exactly as it was in 1945, for future generations to see. He was acquitted of most charges, but it appeared that there might be serious difficulty over the order he gave to his men, during the Ardennes offensive, to wear American uniforms. To his amazement, his defence lawyer – an American colonel – produced as a defence witness Wing Commander Yeo Thomas (The White Rabbit), one of the most famous British secret agents. He confirmed that on certain dangerous missions he had ordered his men to wear German uniforms. This dramatic evidence from such a source caused the case against Skorzeny to collapse. When the legal case was finished, he was still held in captivity because some of the powers – notably Russia and Czechoslovakia – were demanding his extradition. With help from former SS colleagues outside, he was rescued from his prison camp. Ironically, his rescue was carried out by a small group, using forged American documents, in a stolen American car, and wearing American uniforms. For some time he hid in Düsseldorf under an assumed name, but his cover was blown and he had to flee once more.

Skorzeny's contacts with high-ranking Nazi officers was to prove useful during the next phase of his remarkable career. In several of his operations he had gained the respect of General Gehlen, who controlled much of Hitler's Intelligence service. As the war drew to a close, Gehlen gathered a small group around him, found a safe hideout in the Alps, and hid there with a vast cache of significant documents. Soon after the war ended, and as difficulties with the Russians increased, Gehlen contacted the US military authorities. Very soon he was working for various US Intelligence organisations which later merged into the CIA. Skorzeny's strong anti-Russian and anti-communist views were a considerable factor in his acceptance by the Americans as the Cold War developed.

In this shadowy phase of his life – most details of which are speculative – he certainly reached Argentina. Because of his celebrated rescue of Mussolini, he was warmly welcomed by Peron who had agreed to schemes to hide former Nazis, and to co-operate in the handling of vast sums of illicit money, gold and precious stones. Eva Peron was considered the driving-force in the handling of this treasure, and there is little doubt that Skorzeny was involved with her at that time. He also spent some time training the Argentine secret police, and was asked by Peron to plan an attack on the Falkland Islands.

Skorzeny's links with Gehlen and his organisation enabled him to return to Europe, and he established a safe base in Madrid. From there he was able to operate both for Gehlen and for the CIA. His anti-Russian and anti-Semitic views were well known, and this brought him another opportunity. During the 1950s, he and many more German ex-officers were employed by President Nasser in Egypt. At first the CIA approved of Skorzeny's appointment because their main aim was to keep Russian influence out of the Middle East. During this period Skorzeny was prominent in training Nasser's secret service, and also Palestinian agents. A delicately balanced situation enabled Skorzeny to continue to operate, but after the Suez crisis in 1956, when Nasser turned to the Russians, and then to East Germany (1965), his position was completely compromised. Throughout this time he had discreetly kept his base in Spain, and when he left Egypt he returned there, though with the approaching demise of Franco, it became more difficult to find secure hiding-places for unregenerate ex-Nazis.

Skorzeny's brilliant career, perhaps inevitably, ended in anti-climax. Like many Austrians, he had been delighted when Hitler and the Nazis took over Austria in March 1938, and the situation enabled him to rise swiftly. His fairly humdrum background gave little indication of the brilliant wartime career he was to enjoy. Then, as a result of Germany's defeat in 1945, it was perhaps inevitable that his subsequent career should prove shadowy and dubious. His later life can be considered alongside other maverick fighters, who turned to the Special Forces because they were bored or frustrated by the routine of life in a regular unit. Peacetime life had little to offer such men as Paddy Mayne, who won four DSOs in the SAS, or Mike Calvert, who was deservedly recommended for the VC for leading his brigade of Chindits behind the Japanese lines for six months. Paddy Mayne went back to being a small town solicitor in County Down, and met a questionable end in a road accident in December 1955. Calvert, court-martialled in post-war Germany for indecency, and unjustly convicted, spent most of the rest of his life in penury and fighting the ravages of alcoholism. Perhaps Skorzeny was rather fortunate?

GIAP

V o Nguyen Giap, educated at the Lycée in Hue under the stifling French colonial system, became the true maverick. He refused to accept French capitalist domination and eventually was able to render their presence in Vietnam untenable; later still he secured independence for the whole country by defeating the military might of the USA.

Born in 1912, Giap was reared in an educated family. His father, a distinguished scholar, had fought against the French intrusion into Vietnam in the 1880s. The young Giap was strongly influenced by these events, and he tended to see Roman Catholics – the main agents of French influence – as traitors to the Vietnamese cause. He realised at an early age that to achieve fundamental change the peasants must support that cause.

Vietnamese patriots often fled to Japan or to China, and were not only anti-French, but aimed to create a modern state based on scientific concepts to replace outmoded Confucianism. The French took fiercely repressive measures, especially against Vietnamese schools, but after 1910 no major revolt took place, and there was general co-operation with the French colonial authorities. During the 1920s a split developed between the constitutional reformers and the more violent revolutionary groups – notably one led by Ho Chi Minh – himself a product of the Lycée at Hue.

As a student, Giap had close contact with several revolutionary leaders, and was strongly influenced by a pamphlet, *Colonialism on Trial*, secretly circulated by Ho Chi Minh. Soon after this Giap was expelled from the Lycée, and in 1927, aged fifteen, joined the extreme wing of the revolutionary Tan Viet, which was already communist-led. The idealism of communist attitudes at the time inspired the young and intelligent Giap. Ho Chi Minh swiftly emerged as the leader, and he spent some time in exile in Russia and in Berlin, but then returned to Vietnam and gave positive leadership to the various revolutionary groups. In 1930 he created the Vietnamese Communist Party, which soon became the Indo-China Communist Party in order to include Laos and Cambodia.

In 1930 the communists led an abortive uprising, but the French crushed it brutally, and both Ho Chi Minh and Giap were arrested and imprisoned. After a short time Giap was released for good behaviour, and he appears to have given up his active political role to become a conscientious student. He attended Hanoi university, then married and became a history teacher. During the 1930s, most opposition to French colonial rule – which was seen as European capitalist exploitation of the country – rallied behind the communist groups that were receiving support from both Russia and China. By 1939 Giap had risen to a senior position in the Vietnamese communist organisation, and in 1940, because of the Japanese threat and the likely French reaction, for his own safety he was sent into exile in China. He left behind his wife, who died in a French prison, and his sister, who was guillotined by the French.

Chinese communist groups looked after Giap as he travelled through south China in the turbulent area fought over by the Japanese and the Chinese war-lords. After several weeks of clandestine travel, he was taken to see Ho Chi Minh, who recorded that Giap was attractive, rather like a girl. At this time – 1940 – the Germans occupied Paris, and the Japanese, taking advantage of French weakness, virtually occupied Vietnam. Giap went to a town near the border with China, and started to train a cadre of Vietnamese volunteers in guerrilla warfare. This was the real beginning of his military career, nurtured not by St-Cyr or Sandhurst, but by the practical advice of Mao Tse-tung, and others who had been trained in Russia, and in the harsh realities of guerrilla warfare.

Serious divisions blighted the efforts of different Vietnamese groups until May 1941, when Ho Chi Minh called a conference, which resulted in the creation of a new organisation to become known as the Vietminh. Their agents continued military training in south China, and maintained a base in Vietnam. During the next few years, while Ho was involved in the clashes between the Chinese communists and the Kuomintang under Chiang Kai-shek, Giap continued to train guerrilla groups and masterminded the flow of communist propaganda into north Vietnam.

In 1944 events in Europe once again influenced Giap's future. When the Allied forces liberated Paris, Giap and the Vietminh prepared to begin guerrilla activities, but were wisely restrained by Ho, who had just returned from China. Then in December 1944 Giap's forces, already organised on a village, district and headquarters structure, made their first attack on a French outpost. This was the birth of the Vietnamese People's Army, which Giap was to lead for the next three decades. Soon afterwards the Japanese made a strong attack on the French administration in south Vietnam, and this weakening of the French position gave Giap the opportunity to spread his influence and organise his village and district groups over a wider area. By the end of the war with Japan, Giap controlled several thousand troops, and was Ho's main military commander in Vietnam.

Ho realised that there would be only a brief period between the Japanese withdrawal in August 1945, and the appearance of the British forces of SEAC, Chiang Kai-shek's Chinese, and then the French colonialists once more. The sudden and unexpected end to the war after Hiroshima – 7 August 1945 – gave the Vietminh an opportunity. Ho and Giap worked urgently to establish control in the vacuum left by the Japanese withdrawal. Giap led a powerful military group and took over Hanoi. After the ejection of the Japanese puppet regime, it was agreed that Ho should head a government in the newly formed republic. Soon after this, the French returned and Ho appointed Giap to negotiate with them. By September 1945 Ho had established his government in Hanoi, and Giap was a senior minister, while in the south the Vietminh, the only organisation credited with effective opposition to the Japanese, gained considerable support.

Ho then had the difficult task of handling the situation where British occupation forces moved into the south of the country, Chiang's Chinese moved into North Vietnam and stripped it bare, and the French returned with increasingly aggressive demands. Because of the demands of other representative Vietnamese groups, and because of his intransigence, Giap was temporarily removed from Ho's cabinet, but he continued his propaganda work and cadre training for the Vietminh.

As French power increased, Giap was sent to Paris in 1946 to negotiate with the French government, but he soon returned, convinced that there would be war between the Vietminh and the French. By this time the Vietminh, largely because of Giap's work and training, was powerful enough to dominate most other organisations in Vietnam, and to prepare for war with the French. Both sides hurried to procure weapons, and the first military clash came at Haiphong in November 1946, when the French deployed a cruiser and an aircraft carrier to bombard a Vietminh position. Several thousand Vietminh were killed. Fierce fighting continued throughout December and January, but Ho was still attempting to negotiate with the French. To assist with the negotiations, and to gain wider support from the Vietnamese people, Ho again removed Giap, the hard-line communist, from his government.

The French rapidly extended their military presence in Vietnam, but they were not strong enough effectively to hold the entire country. Thus began, under Giap's leadership, a guerrilla war in which the Vietminh had substantial advantages. Because of his efficient village and district organisation, Giap was almost always able to concentrate sufficient force to overwhelm the small and generally isolated French garrisons. The Vietminh blew up roads and bridges, and destroyed small French detachments, and then easily disappeared into the jungle where the road-bound French forces rarely ventured.

In October 1947 the French launched a determined attack in the rugged jungle-covered mountains in an area north-west of Hanoi. They employed nine battalions in a two-pronged attack, and dropped more than 1,000 paratroops on a village which they suspected of being Ho's HQ. They achieved initial surprise, and both Ho and Giap had to hide in a ditch only yards from the attacking paratroops. Giap now had to fight his first major battle. The French were moving in two pincer movements to link up with the strong paratroop force. Giap tried to halt the northern pincer by blowing up roads and bridges, but after three days of hard fighting the French, supported by artillery and air strikes, reached the besieged paratroops. The French had achieved some success, but they finally withdrew having achieved only limited military advantage, and having failed to capture either Ho or Giap. The French launched another attack in December 1947, but again the Vietminh were able to avoid a pitched battle and disappear into the jungle until the French withdrew. Giap quickly learned the lessons of these campaigns. He dispersed his forces more widely, and sent his companies into many different areas of the country to carry on guerrilla activities and – equally important – to fire the local people with enthusiasm for the Vietminh cause. Meanwhile in China, by 1948 Mao Tse-tung and the communists were clearly winning the civil war against Chiang Kai-shek, and the French commanders in Vietnam began to realise that the Vietminh would soon be receiving an excellent supply of weapons from China, while they themselves were getting dwindling support from the government in Paris.

During a lull in the fighting in 1948, Giap had some leisure to think out his strategy. He had absorbed many military ideas from Mao Tse-tung, and he adapted these to his own situation. Mao had taught that victory would not come quickly, and Giap developed this thesis. He gave a higher priority to political activity, and to gaining the support of the people, than to military issues. In this he was strongly influenced by the ideas of the great Chinese strategist Sun Tzu, who, as John Keegan says, 'encouraged the integration of Chinese military and political theory'. The French were always hurrying to win quick battles, while Giap avoided battle and realised that with the support of the people whom the French alienated, he would win in the end.

His troops had to take an oath to respect, help and defend the people, and army units were deliberately employed to help with farming and with measures to defend the villages. At the same time Giap used his own experience of guerrilla warfare to train all his troops in sound tactics. In 1950 he published his seminal work, *The War of Liberation*, and this helped to consolidate his position in the military hierarchy. He continued actively to build up his military power base, and by 1951 he had more than 100 regular battalions and about 40 regional units. He did not yet organise divisions, because the Vietminh lacked the tanks and artillery that would have justified this level of organisation. Under Giap's policy, all units had a political officer who could overrule the military commander.

On the wider scene Giap faced formidable problems. Communication with units in the south was difficult, and many of the southern people were suspicious of the north and its ideology. The French, in addition to their 100,000 regulars, used almost as many Vietnamese troops as the total of the Vietminh. Giap realised that the war would be decided in the north, and his whole position was strengthened by Mao's victory over Chiang Kai-shek in 1949. Thereafter, substantial military supplies began to reach the Vietminh, though because of the totally inadequate roads and hostile terrain, most had to be carried by porters. With the increasing support from China – including heavier weapons and tanks – Giap was at last in a position to organise some of his units into divisions. This soon enabled him to attack and overcome French battalion-strength units, and effectively to disrupt the main French supply routes.

The main French garrisons were located along Route 4, which lay to the north of Hanoi and fairly close to the Chinese border. Giap planned his attacks wisely, taking advantage of the wet season, and deploying his forces economically. The first large-scale attack in May 1950 was only a partial success, but the Vietminh withdrew having learned valuable lessons. Giap next planned to threaten several French bases simultaneously and eventually to force the French troops into open country where the Vietminh guerrilla groups could easily destroy them.

In September 1950 Giap was ready to attack the main French garrisons strung out along Route 4. He captured a stronghold in the middle of the line, and ambushed and destroyed French troops from adjacent garrisons who were coming up in support. By the end of October 1950 most of the garrisons along Route 4 had been eliminated. Under increasing Vietminh pressure, the garrison at Lang Son, the most important town on Route 4, and the closest to Hanoi, was hurriedly abandoned. This was a remarkable victory for Giap at very little cost. The French lost more than 6,000 troops, but, more significantly, a huge arsenal of tanks, artillery, trucks, small arms and a thousand tons of ammunition fell to the Vietminh. Soon afterwards the last isolated garrison, at the northern of the Red River valley, was ignominiously abandoned.

After the military successes of 1950, Ho Chi Minh and Giap had to consider their future strategy. Despite their achievements, the French retained a strong grip on the most populated areas: the Red River valley in the north, and the southern area around Saigon. The Vietminh's overall aim of gaining political control and independence for the entire country, meant that these powerful French bases would have to be attacked. This would mean that the advantages of operating in the misty highlands along the northern border where supplies and help from communist China were readily available, would be lost. The French would have the advantage of fighting a defensive campaign from two secure bases, both easily supplied by sea. Giap's military task was made more difficult by the arrival in Vietnam of one of the most able French commanders, General De Lattre de Tassigny, who had established his reputation as an attacking leader during the final rout of the Germans from France in 1945.

Giap's determination to attack the French in the Red River valley has been widely criticised. By making a frontal attack he appeared to reject the advice of his Chinese supporters – supplied by Mao Tse-tung – and also the traditions of Sun Tzu, whose precepts he appeared to follow. Sun Tzu advocated deception, and warned above all against frontal attacks on powerful strongholds. It might have been wiser for Giap to have held off and considered the wider issues, but understandably, as a commander in the field, he wanted to keep up the momentum of his successful campaign. Consequently, after only a few weeks' delay, he attacked the French outpost at Vinh Yen in the Red River valley, about thirty miles north-west of Hanoi. He chose this point because a jungle-covered mountain spur made a hidden approach much easier, though even with this advantage it was not possible to conceal the approach of 20,000 men from the French, with their unchallenged air superiority.

Giap began the offensive in January 1951 with a powerful attack on a small French garrison, and again ambushed another French detachment hurrying to the rescue. This clash alerted the French, and De Lattre de Tassigny took personal charge of the battle. He was able to fly in reinforcements from Saigon, and he used close-support bombers to wipe out Vietminh units as they moved into the attack. After prolonged fighting during which he lost more than 6,000 killed, and as many wounded, Giap had to admit defeat. He had learned a costly lesson.

He now decided to probe in a different area – the delta of the Red River, close to Haiphong, the main French supply port. He chose as his target a small town in a mining district north of Haiphong. Much of this part of the country features deep sea inlets, and the French defences included naval guns to reinforce their already dominant artillery and air power. Giap had chosen a target where he hoped the enemy's naval power would be irrelevant, but De Lattre de Tassigny's ships and gun boats were instrumental in inflicting another heavy defeat on Giap's forces. By the end of March 1951 Giap had lost more than 2,000 men killed, and he had to withdraw and reconsider the situation.

Such defeats could well have led to the dismissal of a military commander, but Giap's experience and achievements, and his close alliance with Ho Chi Minh, made his position secure. Despite his defeats, he decided to attack again. On the south side of the Red River delta was a large area of limestone rock, with scant road access, and pocketed with numerous large caves. Here Giap reckoned his troops would be safe from naval bombardment, and he reckoned that if he launched his attack when the rainy season started, the weather and the caves would give protection against air attack. He had hoped too that he would gain support for his troops from the local people, but the predominantly Roman Catholic villages of the delta had established anti-communist militias who fought against the Vietminh. At the same time, the French, reacting to Giap's advance, used landing-craft and small boats to defeat the Vietminh units. Here the French were able to grasp the initiative, and by the end of June 1951 Giap had sustained further heavy casualties, his supply system had been disrupted, and his troops were dispirited by their constant defeats. In view of the events of 1951, it is remarkable that in later years Giap had the reputation as the commander who never lost a battle.

While these serious military defeats – which had resulted in 20,000 casualties – had caused Giap grave problems, his deliberate policy of linking military training with political indoctrination, safeguarded his cause. His precepts for the People's Army: 'Be polite'; 'Be fair'; 'Cause no damage'; 'Do not bully'; 'Do not abuse women', continued to bring him support and to build-up a moral ascendancy.

During the remainder of 1951 Giap had to regroup and rebuild his shattered forces. The next initiative came from the French, though they were not strong enough to launch a major offensive. General De Lattre de Tassigny had departed – he died of cancer soon afterwards – and his successor decided to make a substantial paratroop drop and seize a town on the southern edge of the main French defensive position. This was a triangular area protected by the 'De Lattre Line', based on the delta coast, and stretching up the Red River to Hanoi and beyond. The French launched their operation in November 1951. Giap now showed that he had learned valuable lessons. The Vietminh troops refused to give battle, but merely observed the French lines of supply and communication along the inadequate roads and up the rivers. Then Giap started to make sudden sharp attacks on the minor garrisons along the route, and on road and river crossings. This restored the military initiative to him, and effectively occupied an increasing number of French troops. This new policy achieved success with very little loss, and early in 1952 the French were forced to withdraw the paratroops.

During 1952 Giap had to decide where next to harass the French. The south of Vietnam – including Saigon and the Mekong delta – was the most heavily populated and developed part of the country, but the people did not support the communist Vietminh, and an uprising in 1950 had failed. The neighbouring country of Laos, which had closer links with North Vietnam, looked a better option. In October 1952 Giap decided to advance towards Laos with three divisions from his base in the north-west, close to the Chinese border. The French reacted strongly to this move, and flew in a whole division to their base at Na Sam. The Vietminh made good progress, hampered only by their lengthening supply lines. The French commander realised this, and made a sudden foray against one of Giap's main supply bases. The French captured this and took over a large supply of Russian *matériel*, but they lacked the forces to hold the base. For his part, Giap saw that the French would soon have to withdraw, and he deployed several brigades in ambush at a steep gorge several miles long – a good example of a senior commander studying the terrain in which his troops would fight. Heavy casualties were inflicted on the French. Giap continued to attack Na Sam, but failed to capture it, and sustained unacceptably high casualties.

During the Korean War, 1950–3, the increasing involvement of the USA encouraged the French to look to Washington for military assistance. US technical support also helped the French to undertake one of their more successful initiatives. They knew that the north and west of Vietnam, and northern Laos were inhabited by rugged hill people who resented the domination of the Vietminh. The French therefore created new units – based roughly on Wingate's Chindits, who during the Burma campaign operated behind the Japanese lines and were supplied by air. These groups were used to threaten and disrupt Giap's supply routes. They operated successfully, and during the crucial campaign for Dien Bien Phu they tied down many Vietminh battalions. Despite the irritation of these guerrilla attacks, in April 1953 Giap made an incursion into northern Laos, but when the rainy season started in May his supply problems increased and he withdrew to his main bases in the north of the province of Tonkin.

In 1953 the French were involved in negotiations with Laos whereby, while retaining Laos within the French union, a measure of political independence would be ceded and French defence commitments would be limited. The new French commander in Vietnam, General Navarre, appears to have been unhappy about his government's policy, and – perhaps deliberately – misunderstood their intentions. In November 1953, he went ahead with his own plan to drop six battalions of the élite French paras into the small but strategically important village of Dien Bien Phu, situated on the border with Laos. Navarre bears a grave responsibility for the catastrophe which followed, because his plan was strongly opposed by his own military advisers, and particularly his air adviser, who did not believe that he could supply such a large garrison at Dien Bien Phu during the rainy season. Thus, in a state of military and political confusion, Dien Bien Phu was occupied. Although it was an insignificant settlement, it had always been strategically important because it controlled the main trade route from China to Laos and Cambodia. Giap later commented shrewdly that the taking of Dien Bien Phu illustrated the contradiction between the occupation of territory and the concentration of force. For the French, another factor obtruded. Navarre, sitting in Saigon, was almost completely at loggerheads with Cogny, the French commander on the spot, who had to deal with the problems both at Dien Bien Phu and in the Red River valley. In December 1953 Navarre was confident that with his air force, artillery and tanks he could hold Dien Bien Phu and destroy the Vietminh. He planned

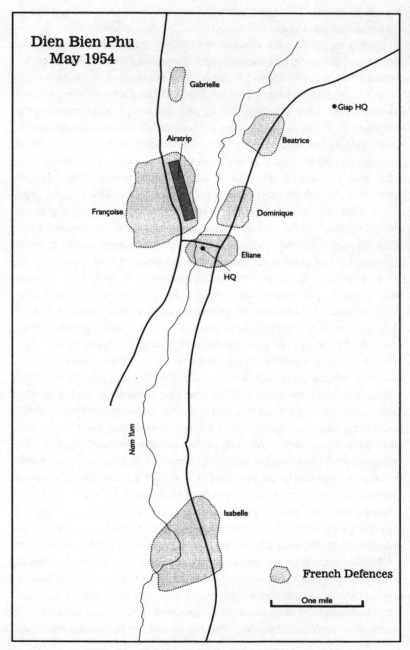

Dien Bien Phu
May 1954

Gabrielle

● Giap HQ

Airstrip

Beatrice

Françoise

Dominique

Eliane

HQ

Nam Yum

Isabelle

French Defences

One mile

to fly in thousands of tons of concrete, barbed wire and other defensive stores, and make Dien Bien Phu impregnable. He did not have time to achieve this.

During this period, Giap ordered the Vietminh to harass every French unit in the Red River delta and force them to disperse their fighting formations. He was also able, with the aid of his communist allies in Laos, the Pathet Lao, to do the same thing there. This was the situation when Navarre flew his paras in to Dien Bien Phu. Giap's assessment – in contrast to the muddle and confusion on the French side – was clear-cut. He knew that in the wake of the Korean armistice, the great powers were demanding an end to the hostilities in Vietnam. He decided that the only way to achieve a dramatic victory over the French – a victory significant enough to influence the future political outcome for Vietnam – would be to defeat them at Dien Bien Phu, even at heavy cost to his own forces.

The French started to reinforce Dien Bien Phu with men and *matériel*, but everything had to be flown in, and from the start it was impossible to provide enough. Within the garrison, men were forced to dig underground defences and to patrol against the Vietminh, but neither was done adequately. Giap realised that he had to win a victory by May 1954, when the decisions of the major powers might inhibit further action. He therefore made his decision: 'We decided to wipe out at all costs the whole enemy force at Dien Bien Phu.'

In late November 1953 he ordered his forces to move. Five divisions, drawn from all over North Vietnam, advanced towards their target. Giap was able to muster more than thirty battalions of infantry and six regiments of artillery against the French garrison of six infantry battalions and one artillery regiment. In the siege of Imphal by the Japanese in 1944, the British had proved that a large garrison could hold out successfully when supplied by air, and supported by overwhelming air superiority, but Dien Bien Phu was a very different case. Isolated on the remote border of Laos and North Vietnam, with no possibility of reinforcement by land, the French garrison, with an inadequate air supply, began to realise as early as December 1953 that they were in dire peril. The French commander Cogny, when ordered to prepare a withdrawal plan, pointed out that there was no prospect of withdrawal through territory entirely dominated by the Vietminh.

Within the garrison, the French made a series of fatal blunders. Because of their disdainful attitude to the Vietminh artillery, they failed to protect or even camouflage their guns. The defended area lay in a flat valley, and Giap's forces held all the surrounding hills. Even before the battle started, Vietminh observers were able to pinpoint every French gun emplacement, every unit HQ – revealed by their radio aerials – and to range their heavy guns on these targets. The French – dilatory and careless in their entire approach – made no provision for the effects of the heavy monsoon rains, expected at the end of April. They suffered accordingly. The French contempt for the Vietminh fire-power meant that when the battle started, their supply aircraft were constantly damaged or destroyed by Giap's anti-aircraft guns, and his heavy artillery was easily able to plaster the main runway. By the end of the siege, the supply of food and ammunition was minimal.

By January 1954, Giap, in a brilliant feat of organisation, had assembled more than 50,000 combat troops, another 50,000 support troops, together with many thousands of porters to carry ammunition, food and supplies more than 500 miles from their northern bases. He was generously supplied with heavy guns and ammunition taken from Chiang Kai-shek during the Chinese civil war, and from the Americans in the Korean War. Even with these advantages, Giap decided not to make a sudden attack but to select targets and overwhelm them one at a time.

There are several interesting parallels between Dien Bien Phu and the Chindit débâcle at 'Broadway' in 1944, when 111 Brigade under John Masters was destroyed by the Japanese. Both disasters were caused by the commanders making woefully wrong decisions at the start. Secondly, and indicative of a less than professional approach, the French commander identified each sector with a woman's name – said to be those of his mistresses – while Masters called his sectors after the fielding positions for a cricket team. Few of their unfortunate men appreciated this foolishness.

Giap's decision not to make an immediate assault, which might have failed because of the lack of experience of his troops in attacking strongly defended positions, was not popular with his men. They were to be subjected to a long and arduous campaign, but he overcame their opposition by patient explanation. Having decided on the strategy, Giap now concentrated on the tactics. He protected his vital heavy guns from French air attack by digging very deep emplacements and carefully camouflaging them. Next, miles of trenches and tunnels were dug so that attacking infantry could approach under cover to within a few yards of the French perimeter. He further illustrated his care for his troops by ensuring as far as possible that they were well fed with hot food, and had dry sleeping accommodation.

After weeks of careful preparation, Giap's forces attacked on 13 March 1954. On successive days, the two most northerly bastions – 'Beatrice' and 'Gabrielle' – were overwhelmed by divisional attacks on battalion positions. Giap had copied the technique used by the Chinese in Korea, of attacks by wave after wave of infantry despite horrendous losses, and the capture of 'Beatrice' and 'Gabrielle' cost him dear. The French, too, had sustained grievous losses of dead and wounded. After the battle, Giap offered to hand over more than eighty of the French wounded, which might seem to have been a humane gesture, but it presented the hard-pressed French with a cruel dilemma. Following the initial assault, there was a two-weeks' lull while the Vietminh brought forward reinforcements, and constructed new gun emplacements in the surrounding hills from where they could directly dominate the airstrip and the main fortifications of Dien Bien Phu.

Giap admitted that after the heavy losses in the first attacks, urgent work had to be done by the political officers to restore the morale of many disgruntled soldiers, but his tactical advantages were increased all the time. Given his total dominance of the airstrip, the defenders could only obtain supplies by parachute. The Vietminh guns kept aircraft at a high level, and frequently Giap's troops received an unexpected bonus of French supplies. On 30 March 1954 he renewed the attack, and overran two more positions – 'Dominique' and 'Eliane' – close to the airstrip. This threatened the entire French supply system, and as the battle continued, the defenders were short of ammunition, food and even drinking-water.

Throughout April Giap kept up the relentless assault. He had sufficient forces to probe one sector, and as the French rushed reinforcements to the danger point, to assault another, and then a third. Conditions inside the beleaguered garrison became horrific as the attacks continued and as the monsoon rains increased. The wounded with torn limbs lay untended, the dead bodies piled up, and over all lay the stench of gangrene, putrefaction and death.

On 1 May the Vietminh, in the final phase of the battle, captured the defensive position at 'Isabelle', a few miles south of the main defences. When this fell, the French realised that there was little hope, but they fought on for a few more days. On 7 May Giap's forward troops, within a few hundred yards of the command post, swept aside some feeble opposition, and then noticed white flags being raised. The battle was over. The Vietminh had captured nearly 2,000 officers and, in all, 10,000 men, and had won one of the most significant victories of the post-war era. For the

French it was a total catastrophe – militarily, politically and psychologically – and largely caused by Navarre's ludicrous decision to make a stand at Dien Bien Phu. On 8 May the great powers began to discuss Indo-China at Geneva.

Dien Bien Phu did not end the war. For a few more months French units, trying to reach the sanctuary of Hanoi or Haiphong, were ambushed and slaughtered. Of the thousands of prisoners taken, very few escaped or reappeared, the majority dying on the long marches away from Dien Bien Phu. During the war the French had lost nearly 100,000 killed, and 150,000 wounded.

The Geneva Conference, itself the victim of growing Cold War enmity, eventually secured agreement. Vietnam was divided at the 17th Parallel – intended as a temporary division; the French agreed to withdraw from Vietnam; Laos and Cambodia were to be independent; for three years refugees could move freely between north and south; and free elections were to be held in both North and South Vietnam. The Americans became increasingly concerned at the dangerous vacuum left by the French, and led the West's paranoia about communist expansion in South East Asia. Now the domino theory began to take effect. In 1955, in the South Vietnam elections the inadequate leader Diem came to power, and the predominantly Roman Catholic people voted to remain separate from the atheistic power to the north. Although Diem failed to inspire or organise the people of the south, the majority of the refugees moved from north to south. The French, facing further problems in Algeria, decided to cut their losses in Vietnam. American concern burgeoned rapidly, and in 1955 the South East Asia Treaty Organisation (SEATO) was established to guarantee the security of South Vietnam, Laos and Cambodia.

Giap, the true victor of Dien Bien Phu, had enjoyed the great communist victory celebration in Hanoi in October 1954. Thousands of troops paraded, carrying banners of Marx, Lenin, Mao Tse-tung and Ho Chi Minh before tens of thousands of exultant spectators proclaiming the triumph of communism. Their joy was to be short-lived, for the country was soon to suffer from that most disastrous of all communist obsessions – land reform. In 1944 Stalin had admitted that in Russia agricultural reform and the collective farm policy had cost the lives of five million people. In China it had been even worse. Despite such precedents, Ho Chi Minh instigated an aggressive policy of land reform, directed primarily against landlords. Anyone who owned more than the miserable holding of the poorest peasant was liable to be denounced, and to lose all his possessions. This policy of denunciation ruined society and caused the deaths of more than 100,000 people. Eventually, Ho realised that the whole country was in a state of revolt, and decided to change the policy. It fell to Giap, who because of his military responsibilities had been distanced from the political centre, to make an official apology to the people on behalf of the government. He announced changes to the policy, and admitted that many decent and honest people had been denounced and killed.

During the late 1950s, Giap had undertaken to re-organise the entire military apparatus and develop a policy which could find a middle way between the now conflicting influences of Russia and China. Russia argued for peaceful co-existence; China urged more aggressive action. At this time Giap favoured the Russian view. During periods of leisure he wrote his famous work, *People's War People's Army*, which was published in 1960. This text-book of guerrilla warfare, with blue-prints for subversion and the overthrow of bourgeois governments, also contained his own detailed description of the campaign for Dien Bien Phu.

In South Vietnam, Diem had imposed a harsh and virtually fascist regime, and in 1959 there was an outcry about his use of concentration camps for his opponents. These included both South Vietnamese people, as well as many of the cadres whom Giap had deliberately left behind when the division along the 17th Parallel, and the demilitarised zone, had been established. Then in 1963, under increasing pressure from the left-wing National Liberation Front, and the virtual civil war between the Front and Diem's army, an uprising took place and Diem was killed. Giap hoped that the Viet Cong would be able to establish control discreetly, in a way which would not activate American intervention. That was not to be. The other hope of the Viet Cong, that they might be able to gain control in local rural areas before any response from outside could materialise, was also dashed.

In the confused years after the Geneva Settlement, while Giap was re-organising the army, he was also busy planning and preparing for action in South Vietnam. Through the cadres which had remained in the south after the settlement, although some had been eliminated by Diem, many were able to build up Viet Cong cells and train them in their political and military role. These groups permeated nearly the whole of society in South Vietnam. Their training and their attitude ensured that they won fairly easy victories over the badly led units under Diem's corrupt leadership, and they went on to build up their political and military power throughout the country. Their military strength was to depend on adequate supplies, and in this field Giap showed his outstanding grasp of detail and organising ability. By the early 1960s he had already set up the supply system known as the Ho Chi Minh Trail. Tens of thousands of porters carried supplies from the border with communist China, through North Vietnam, and by jungle trails down through Laos and Cambodia to distribution points in South Vietnam. What had started as a jungle trail developed into a super highway.

More publicly, on the world stage, John F. Kennedy was elected President in 1960. He inherited Eisenhower's belief in the domino theory, and he treated the world to rousing rhetoric about the defence of freedom, though this message could easily be misunderstood in South Vietnam. Soon after his election, Kennedy, keen to show he that was as strong as the Republicans against the communist threat, had greatly increased the number of military 'advisers' in South Vietnam. Then in 1963 he took the momentous step of deploying a part of the US 7th Air Division to South Vietnam. Lyndon Johnson – elevated to the presidency after the assassination of Kennedy in November 1963 – took the next steps. Early in 1964, he agreed to step up military pressure on North Vietnam. Then in August 1964, there was a confusing incident in the Gulf of Tonkin, when some US warships blazed away for a couple of hours at suspected, but non-existent enemy torpedo-boats. Johnson took the decision that this incident justified a serious military response. On 5 August 1964, without declaring war, US aircraft attacked the main oil depot in North Vietnam, close to the 17th Parallel. These were the steps by which America was drawn into the Vietnam débâcle, in which they would be defeated by Giap, who was already preparing for victory in his style of warfare.

Johnson, fearful of provoking Russia and China, let the action in Vietnam build up piecemeal and within strict limits, but without any overall plan. In fact, Russia – keen to develop its nuclear arsenal – was happy to see America embroiled in Vietnam, and China was preoccupied with the Cultural Revolution, but both supplied Giap with *matériel* on a massive scale. Military action in Vietnam slowly escalated during 1965, and by the end of the year 100,000 US troops were involved. Giap had directed nearly as many troops to the south, but still pursued the policy of guerrilla attacks rather than battles with major US units. While Johnson blundered forward – having been warned that even with half a million men he might not win – Giap was planning and preparing on a gigantic scale. The whole of society was conscripted and organised for a prolonged war. More than two million people were drafted into military and support groups. Thousands went to Russia and to China for training in every aspect of war from jet pilots to explosive experts. Giap created the People's Liberation Armed Forces, and co-ordinated all their activities.

At the end of 1965 Ho Chi Minh outlined his strategy, which Giap would carry out. Their first priority was to build up the strength of the north; equally important was political education and indoctrination, so that the people would give total support, confident that ultimately they would win. Increasing military support was sent to the south, but action was still restricted to guerrilla attacks. At the same time, all over North and South Vietnam Giap organised the creation of a sub-structure of party cells and military units in every town and village. They laboured constantly, digging slit-trenches and tunnels, hiding supplies of weapons, and building up stores of grenades and bottle bombs. He continued the policy which had worked so well against the French that political issues must override military, and at this time he disagreed with the Viet Cong commander in the south, who wanted to challenge the Americans to large-scale battles. Giap argued that the war could last twenty years, but in the end the Americans, provided that they did not win a decisive victory, would give up. As the Americans stepped up their attacks with bombing, defoliants and napalm, Giap reckoned that, by totally alienating the people, the enemy were bound ultimately to lose. He rejoiced when, after every American attack, thousands of people eagerly turned out to repair the damage.

From 1965, although there was still no declaration of war, Johnson built up vast military ground forces. Starting with four divisions in 1965, at the climax of the war there were more than ten in Vietnam. Expenditure increased from one billion dollars to thirty billion dollars a year, but even so there appeared to be no overall strategy. To defeat the Viet Cong, large numbers of attack helicopters were used, but the Viet Cong rarely responded to this challenge, and would melt away into the jungle, to fight another day. The fleets of helicopters were used increasingly to rescue survivors of units ambushed or destroyed by the Viet Cong, who used Russian weapons and explosives. As Peter Macdonald wrote in *Giap, the Victor in Vietnam*, 'Russia was fighting to the last drop of Vietnamese blood.'

Closely linked to the US military build-up, was Johnson's determination to achieve victory by strategic saturation bombing, using the air force and navy to supplement artillery bombardments. The operation, called 'Rolling Thunder', which started in South Vietnam in 1965, dropped a truly amazing

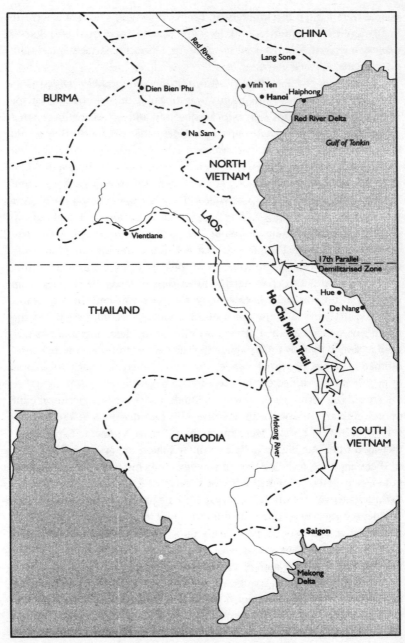

weight of bombs, and when it failed to achieve the submission of the enemy, was extended to North Vietnam as well. The bomb tonnage dropped on Vietnam equalled 25 per cent of the tonnage dropped by US bombers during the whole of the Second World War; one town was bombed almost hourly for three years. Under this onslaught, the Vietnamese people merely dug deeper and deeper tunnels, and when the raids stopped, would come out to tend their crops and animals or give their children a brief blink of sunshine. Johnson even considered using nuclear weapons, but realised that in the Cold War context world opinion would not tolerate it.

In January 1967, when the saturation bombing and the campaigns on the ground had failed to bring expected victory, two offensives, 'Cedar Falls' and 'Junction City', were launched against strong Viet Cong positions in what was known as the Iron Triangle, an area lying about twenty miles north of Saigon. These operations involved more than 30,000 US troops supported by massive aerial bombardment. A number of Viet Cong positions were overrun, casualties inflicted and supply bases captured, but this appeared to have little effect on the continued activity of Giap's fighting forces. During 1967, when further campaigns again failed to achieve victory, more and more of the American people began to oppose the war and demand that peace overtures be made, but Johnson was determined to fight on.

The Ho Chi Minh Trail played a key role in all the battles of these campaigns. It started as a jungle path, but was developed into a great highway along which trucks and tankers by day and night supplied Viet Cong units spread all over South Vietnam. The US commanders realised its significance and it was bombed continually; one section was bombed every two minutes. At the height of the 1968 campaigns and during the Tet Offensive, two million tons of bombs were dropped on the Trail, but still supplies got through to Giap's units in both the south and the north. These supplies enabled him to mount his two main campaigns of 1968: the attack on Khe Sanh and the Tet Offensive.

At the beginning of 1968 the American commander, General Westmoreland, had moved several divisions northwards to Khe Sanh, which lay close to the 17th Parallel, and just north of the city of Hue. He hoped to bring Giap's forces to battle and annihilate them by the superior fire-power of his arsenal. By this time military actions were taking place against a background of international diplomacy, and public opinion in America was becoming increasingly volatile. Giap, who always stressed the importance of keeping the initiative, had also made plans for carefully co-ordinated action. In January 1968 he launched an attack on the strong US position at Khe Sanh. American and world media showed great interest in this battle, and valid comparisons were made with Dien Bien Phu. The serious fighting and heavy casualties reported every day on television screens across the world helped to increase the American people's opposition to the war. More significantly, the battle at Khe Sanh helped to distract the attention of the American and South Vietnamese forces from Giap's next main stroke – the Tet Offensive.

It was planned to begin on the first day of the Vietnamese New Year, 30 January 1968. This was a traditional period for leave and holidays, and when the offensive started many South Vietnamese and US units had a substantial percentage of their troops away on leave. Giap's plan called for a well-trained force of more than 80,000, operating in small units and carefully controlled, to attack towns and cities all over South Vietnam with the hope of bringing about a widespread uprising against the US forces and the ineffective and corrupt government of South Vietnam. In these country-wide actions, the US and South Vietnam forces rallied swiftly, and in most areas were able to defeat the Viet Cong attackers. In the actual fighting, the various Viet Cong groups were not well co-ordinated, and the majority were rounded up and destroyed. The Americans sustained more than 2,000 casualties, but the Viet Cong suffered ten times as many. The Tet Offensive was Giap's greatest military defeat, and it completely failed to bring the hoped-for national uprising. Giap took a philosophical view. In his own description of the offensive, he claimed that it succeeded because the ferocious struggles – notably in the city of Hue – were relayed to television screens all over the world. This more than anything changed world opinion, and began to convince the American people of the absurdity and futility of the war in Vietnam. Constant scenes of bloody fighting and horrendous casualties contradicted the optimistic view of Westmoreland that the war was going well.

Westmoreland was encouraged by the failure of Tet and continued to build up his forces at Khe Sanh with the intention of mounting a large-scale offensive against the Viet Cong working along the Ho Chi Minh Trail in Laos. Westmoreland had problems in Khe Sanh. Like Dien Bien Phu, it was situated in remote rain-swept hills, and had to be supplied by air because the roads were controlled by the Viet Cong. His difficulties were exacerbated by the rivalry between the Marines and The Green Berets, but he felt that he was in a winning position.

Having increased his forces to four divisions – more than 20,000 men – Giap personally took command of a siege of Khe Sanh in January 1968. On the 20th a fierce battle took place at a strongpoint called Hill 861, which was captured and recaptured. As the fighting continued, the Vietnamese divisions made a rocket attack on the main US supply base, and this blew up so much ammunition and petrol that witnesses thought that an atomic bomb had exploded. The rapid escalation of the fighting around Khe Sanh, which was held by the Marines, caused Westmoreland to take more direct control. He had some seven strongly defended bases which were expecting an all-out infantry assault. Instead they received daily bombardments from Giap's well-concealed artillery which despite sensors and sophisticated technology, the Americans could rarely pinpoint. Giap's artillery kept up the pounding and the defenders were in deep trouble. Fleets of helicopters brought in supplies and took out the wounded, but inside the garrison serious shortages of food, ammunition, medical supplies and even water, created conditions similar to those at Dien Bien Phu. Prolonged storms alternating with thick fog made regular supply impossible. Then in February a US post was overrun in an attack by tanks crewed by women – which further lowered US morale.

The Americans responded to the increased pressure of Giap's divisions by ever-increasing aerial bombing. Fleets of B52s were brought in from all over South East Asia and the Pacific. High explosives, defoliants and napalm cascaded down on the surrounding jungle, but still the attacks and bombardments continued against the Marine defenders.

Early in March 1968, when the defenders were close to despair, Giap suddenly withdrew his forces. A US rescue column came in and was so shocked by the conditions they found that the whole of the Khe Sanh complex was bulldozed. After the battle, Giap commented that Khe Sanh was not very important, but it did occupy American forces which could have been used more effectively elsewhere. Giap himself was severely criticised for accepting appalling casualties as he had done at Dien Bien Phu.

The long and bloody struggle for Khe Sanh was disastrous for the Americans, but also for Giap and the People's Liberation Army. Even for the stoical Vietnamese, there had been too many casualties, and too much suffering and anguish. At the highest level there was serious disagreement over the conduct of the war. Giap continued to argue for the continuation of low-level guerrilla activity to keep up the pressure while negotiations took place. He now had to transfer his attention from the tactics at Khe Sanh to the wider strategic and political scene. This illustrates his true brilliance.

He argued constantly that in the end America would be unable to sustain the war effort and would pull out, and he was heartened by the ever increasing anti-war demonstrations across the USA. Johnson had been obsessed with winning a victory at Khe Sanh, but the growing opposition to the war forced him to start negotiations, and these began in Paris in 1968. The Tet Offensive and the Khe Sanh battles probably cost Johnson the 1968 election, when he was beaten by Nixon, who then had to take on the Vietnam responsibility. After Nixon became President in 1969, the political scene changed rapidly. In June 1969 he announced that he would withdraw troops from Vietnam, but this did not solve his problems. In November 1969, a quarter of a million people protested in Washington against the war. Deep social unrest spread across the country, and troops clashed violently with students, many of whom tried to dodge the draft to Vietnam. At this point Giap knew he had to win, as the cost of the war in blood and treasure had become unacceptable to the majority of the American people.

The long-drawn-out peace negotiations in Vietnam and the political discussions in Washington had a catastrophic effect on the US troops. The anti-war hysteria spread from home to the front line. In many areas a situation of near mutinous anarchy prevailed. The percentage of US troops suffering from the effects of heroin, marijuana and other drug abuse, and from psychological breakdown, far outweighed battle casualties. The complete failure of fleets of B52s dropping thousands of tons of bombs to achieve a victory exacerbated the feelings of hopelessness among the US military in Vietnam. Similarly, the attempts to root out Viet Cong supporters from the civilian population, which resulted in the death of virtually everyone who was interrogated, also failed. The American decision to hand over the defence of South Vietnam to the Vietnamese army was equally doomed. Their senior officers were corrupt and incompetent, the troops were hated by the people whom they terrorised, and many officers openly sold US military equipment on the black market. In one year 100,000 men deserted to join Giap's forces. Such a situation merely reinforced the contemptuous attitude of the Americans towards the Vietnamese people – itself one of the causes of their failure.

In 1972, in order to influence the peace negotiations, Giap planned what he hoped would be a final massive offensive, using twenty divisions in three assaults: one from the north over the demilitarised zone; one towards

Hue; and one towards Saigon. The attacks, which started in April 1972, made considerable progress, and caused deep consternation, but in each case the use of B52s on a gigantic scale against Giap's leading troops blunted their progress, and by May the advances had petered out.

Giap kept up the pressure of guerrilla attacks on US bases, while Nixon and Kissinger shuttled round the world trying to reach a settlement. Vietnam featured increasingly on the main world agenda, as China and Russia disagreed and Nixon, on his historic visit to China in 1972, tried to drive a wedge between them. At last, in January 1973, agreement was reached, with four main provisions:

A ceasefire
All US troops to be withdrawn
All prisoners to be exchanged
No more troops to be sent to South Vietnam by either side.

This simple-sounding agreement was the most humiliating defeat for a great nation which had spent more than 300 billion dollars, had dropped ten million tons of bombs, and had lost 50,000 dead and 300,000 wounded. In fairness it must be stated that the People's Liberation Army also received billions of dollars worth of aid from Russia and China who used Vietnam to undermine their ultimate enemy. Giap, remarkable for combining both political and military leadership, and waging total war by controlling military, political, psychological and ideological factors, did not intend to end the struggle with the ceasefire. Nor did he intend to observe the restriction on sending troops to South Vietnam.

With the US withdrawal, there was little likelihood of American opinion allowing a resumption of the struggle, and after the ceasefire Giap started to prepare the next stage of his strategy to re-unite and control the whole of Vietnam. In October 1973 he persuaded his government to support the military conquest of South Vietnam, and he handed over direct control of the armies to his long-time colleague Tien Dung, though he remained Commander-in-Chief. In the south, after the US forces left, conditions rapidly deteriorated. Graft, corruption and embezzlement raged unchecked, and morale plummeted. By the beginning of 1975 Tien Dung was ready to finalise Giap's plans. In March an advance from the north led to the swift capture of Hue and Da Nang after a military assault and uprisings from inside. As the northern armies advanced, they obliterated soldiers and civilians alike in the captured territory, and created a massive refugee problem. Further south, Tien Dung was poised with twenty divisions ready to attack Saigon – so much for not sending troops to South Vietnam. After a brief but ruthless campaign against the demoralised South Vietnam army, during which artillery and rockets pounded Saigon, on 29 April 1975 the People's Liberation Army captured the city. Huge numbers of American and French 'specialists' had stayed behind in Saigon. Now the television screens of the world were to be reminded of the worst aspects of the previous defeats – of the Tet Offensive and the bloody struggles around Khe Sanh. The fall of Saigon was the final phase of the abject and ignominious defeat of the USA by Giap and the People's Liberation Army. The whole world was to witness the frantic scenes as desperate people tried to board the helicopters from the roof of the American embassy. Shortly afterwards Giap entered Saigon to savour his victory.

Having achieved his goal of re-uniting his country – his overriding aim since 1945 – he continued the ideological struggle, and in 1978 master-minded the invasion of Cambodia and the establishment of the Republic of Kampuchea. With this, and with Saigon renamed Ho Chi Minh City, his task was fulfilled.

Few commanders have been so revered by their erstwhile enemies, and General Westmoreland paid generous tributes to the man who had beaten him. Giap excelled in every aspect of war – especially in his ability to see the whole spectrum and to ensure that political issues took priority over mili-tary ones. He created, inspired and led the People's Liberation Army – he was its Commander-in-Chief for thirty years. He had brilliant organising ability, and he himself stressed the fact that logistics are the key to every victory. His fierce energy, total ruthlessness, positive leadership, ability to plan, and to delegate wisely, gave him a grasp which few commanders have ever enjoyed. He could assess the highest levels of strategy – for example in gauging the anti-war feeling in America, or the Sino–Soviet split – and at the same time work out the tactics for digging tunnels so that infantry could approach an enemy unseen – as they did at Dien Bien Phu. Most of his victories in Vietnam depended on the unending volume of supplies flowing down the Ho Chi Minh Trail on trucks, bicycles, packhorses, mules and tens of thousands of porters. This – above all – was his achievement. But, while Giap served gladly and loyally under Ho Chi Minh, the great victories over the French and the Americans were his.

SELECT BIBLIOGRAPHY

The following books should be available in libraries for those readers who wish to follow up any of the topics covered by this book.

Alexander the Great

Hammond, N. G. L., *Alexander the Great*, London, 1994

Lane Fox, R., *Alexander the Great*, Penguin, 1986

Shaka Zulu

Laband, J., *The Rise and Fall of the Zulu Nation*, London, 1997

Ritter, E., *Shaka Zulu*, London, 1955

Taylor, S., *Shaka's Children*, London, 1994

Stonewall Jackson

McPherson, J., *Battle Cry of Freedom*, London, 1988

Parrish, W., *The American Civil War*, London, 1970

Selby, J., *Stonewall Jackson*, London, 1966

Garibaldi

Hibbert, C., *Garibaldi*, London, 1965

Mack Smith, *Garibaldi*, London, 1970

Lawrence of Arabia

James, L., *The Golden Warrior*, London, 1995

Mack, J., *The Prince of Our Disorder*, London, 1990

Wilson, J., *T. E. Lawrence*, London, 1989

Von Lettow-Vorbeck and Smuts

Armstrong, H., *Grey Steel*, London, 1937

Brett-Young, Francis, *Marching on Tanga*, London, 1926

Clifford, H., *The Gold Coast Regiment in East Africa*, London, 1920

Von Lettow-Vorbeck, *Reminiscences of East Africa*, London, 1920

Guderian

Guderian, H., *Achtung Panzer!*, London, 1992

— *Panzer Leader*, London, 1952

Macksey, K., *Guderian*, London, 1975

Patton

D'Este, C., *A Genius for War*, London, 1995

Farago, L., *Patton*, New York, 1963

Forty, G., *The Armies of George S. Patton*, London, 1996

Patton, G., *War as I Knew It*, Boston, 1947

Stilwell

Rooney, D., *Stilwell*, London, 1971

Stilwell, J., *The Stilwell Papers*,
London, 1950

Tuchman, B., *Sand Against the Wind*,
London, 1972

Wingate

Rooney, D., *Burma Victory*, London,
1992

— *Wingate and the Chindits*,
London, 1994

Sykes, C., *Orde Wingate*, London,
1959

Skorzeny

Foley, C., *Commando Extraordinary*,
London, 1987

Whiting, C., *Skorzeny*, London,
1998

Giap

Colvin, J., *Volcano Under the Snow*,
London, 1996

O'Neill, *General Giap*, London, 1969

Macdonald, P., *Giap*, London, 1993

INDEX